HIGHER

BUSINESS MANAGEMENT

SECOND EDITION

Peter Hagan

The Publishers would like to thank the following for permission to reproduce copyright material:

Photo credits

Section opener image reproduced on pages 1, 59, 99, 127 and 173 © Rawpixel – Fotolia.com

p.5 (left) © Vasily Smirnov – Fotolia.com (middle) © eyetronic – Fotolia.com (right) © Monkey Business – Fotolia.com; **p.8** (top) © Virgin Atlantic (bottom) © Dixon's Carphone; **p.10** For more information about SUBWAY® brand, visit www.subway.com; **p.14** © Sebastian Gauert – Fotolia.com; **p.15** © Google; **p.19** The BT Logo is a registered trade mark of British Telecommunications public limited company; **p.24** © pkfawcett – iStockphoto; **p.29** © jfergusonphotos – Fotolia.com; **p.31** © Yuri Arcurs – Fotolia.com; **p.32** (top) © Joe Gough – Fotolia.com; (bottom) © deanm1974 – Fotolia.com; **p.33** © xy – Fotolia.com; **p.45** © kikkerdirk – Fotolia.com; **p.47** © Virgin Atlantic; **p.50** © artstudio_pro – Fotolia.com; **p.56** © pressmaster – Fotolia.com; **p.67** © Marzky Ragsac Jr. – Fotolia.com; **p.70** (top left) © Twitter (top right) © Facebook (bottom right) © Phanie/Alamy; **p.79** © Anna Frajtova – Fotolia.com; **p.85** © JasonBatterham – iStock via Thinkstock/Getty Images; **p.90** © Sergey Nivens – Fotolia.com; **p.91** © opolja – Fotolia.com; **p.92** © zhu difeng – Fotolia.com; **p.96** © violetkaipa – Fotolia.com; **p.101** © endostock – Fotolia.com; **p.102** © Pavel Losevsky – Fotolia.com; **p.103** © Imagestate Media (John Foxx)/Industrial World V3050; **p.104** © Photographee.eu – Fotolia.com; **p.105** © Ferenc Szelepcsenyi – Fotolia.com; **p.108** © AKP Photos/Alamy; **p.109** © artstudio_pro – Fotolia.com; **p.110** © picsfive – Fotolia.com; **p.113** (left) © Monkey Business – Fotolia.com (right) © destina – Fotolia.com; **p.116** © BSI Group; **p.122** © Fairtrade Foundation; **p.123** © zavgsg – Fotolia.com; **p.130** © Brian Jackson – Fotolia.com; **p.133** © Andrey Popov – Fotolia.com; **p.136** © nyul – Fotolia.com; **p.137** © shock – Fotolia.com; **p.144** © Bettmann/Getty Images; **p.145** PHOTOGRAPH BY BERNARD CHARLON/L'EXPRESS, CAMERA PRESS LONDON; **p.146** © bst2012 – Fotolia.com; **p.150** © Monkey Business – Fotolia.com; **p.153** © Douglas Carr/Alamy; **p.156** © REX; **p.162** © yosef19 – Fotolia.com; **p.175** © Brian Jackson – Fotolia.com; **p.177** © BrianAJackson – iStock via Thinkstock/Getty Images; **p.182** © fazon – Fotolia.com; **p.184** © Dancing Fish – Fotolia.com; **p.188** © Tran-Photography – Fotolia.com

Acknowledgements

p.197 consolidated cash-flow statement © Marks and Spencer Group Plc; p.198 group cash-flow statement © Tesco plc

Course assessment specification tables on pages 2–3, 60–61, 100, 128–129 and 174 reproduced by permission Copyright © Scottish Qualifications Authority.

Every effort has been made to trace all copyright holders, but if any have been inadvertently overlooked the Publishers will be pleased to make the necessary arrangements at the first opportunity.

Although every effort has been made to ensure that website addresses are correct at time of going to press, Hodder Gibson cannot be held responsible for the content of any website mentioned in this book. It is sometimes possible to find a relocated web page by typing in the address of the home page for a website in the URL window of your browser.

Hachette UK's policy is to use papers that are natural, renewable and recyclable products and made from wood grown in well-managed forests and other controlled sources. The logging and manufacturing processes are expected to conform to the environmental regulations of the country of origin.

Orders: please contact Bookpoint Ltd, 130 Park Drive, Milton Park, Abingdon, Oxon OX14 4SE.
Telephone: (44) 01235 827827. Fax: (44) 01235 400454. Lines are open 9.00–5.00, Monday to Saturday, with a 24-hour message answering service. Visit our website at www.hoddereducation.co.uk. Hodder Gibson can also be contacted directly at hoddergibson@hodder.co.uk

© Peter Hagan 2018

First published in 2015 © Peter Hagan
This second edition published in 2018 by
Hodder Gibson, an imprint of Hodder Education,
An Hachette UK Company
211 St Vincent Street
Glasgow G2 5QY

Impression number	5	4	3	2	1
Year	2022	2021	2020	2019	2018

All rights reserved. Apart from any use permitted under UK copyright law, no part of this publication may be reproduced or transmitted in any form or by any means, electronic or mechanical, including photocopying and recording, or held within any information storage and retrieval system, without permission in writing from the publisher or under licence from the Copyright Licensing Agency Limited. Further details of such licences (for reprographic reproduction) may be obtained from the Copyright Licensing Agency Limited, www.cla.co.uk

Cover photo © Image'in/Stock.adobe.com
Illustrations by Barking Dog Art Design and Illustration (p. 210) and Integra Software Services Pvt. Ltd.
Typeset in Candara Regular 11/14 by Integra Software Services Pvt. Ltd., Pondicherry, India
Printed in Italy

A catalogue record for this title is available from the British Library

ISBN: 978 1 5104 5774 4

Contents

Introduction	v
Preparing for course assessment	vi

Section 1 Understanding Business — 1

1.1 Role of business in society	3
1.2 Types of organisation	7
1.3 Objectives	13
1.4 Methods of growth	16
1.5 External factors	22
1.6 Internal factors	30
1.7 Stakeholders	34
1.8 Structures	37
1.9 Decision making	51
Section Assessment	**57**

Section 2 Management of Marketing — 59

2.1 Customers	62
2.2 Market research	66
2.3 Marketing mix	73
2.4 Product	74
2.5 Price	79
2.6 Place	82
2.7 Promotion	88
2.8 People	90
2.9 Process	91
2.10 Physical evidence	92
2.11 Technology	95
Section Assessment	**97**

Section 3 Management of Operations — 99

3.1 Inventory management	101
3.2 Methods of production	109
3.3 Quality	113

3.4 Ethical and environmental issues	120
3.5 Technology	123
Section Assessment	**125**

Section 4 Management of People — 127

4.1 Workforce planning	129
4.2 Training and development	137
4.3 Motivation and leadership	143
4.4 Employee relations	150
4.5 Legislation	162
4.6 Technology	168
Section Assessment	**170**

Section 5 Management of Finance — 173

5.1 Sources of finance	175
5.2 Cash budgeting	184
5.3 Financial statements	190
5.4 Ratios	199
5.5 Technology	209
Section Assessment	**212**

Index — 215

Introduction

Welcome to the second edition of *Higher Business Management*. This book is designed to give comprehensive course coverage of the revised SQA course in Higher Business Management, which runs for the first time in the Academic Session 2018–19. It is the most up-to-date and definitive source for the revised course and, unlike other companion books, there is full coverage of the course content as well as a section dedicated to the coursework assignment, with handy tips. The format of the extended external examination is also covered, so that you are fully prepared and ready to face that all-important final question paper and achieve the best result through a combination of your examination and coursework performance.

The book has been written in simple everyday language wherever possible, while still ensuring good coverage of business terminology appropriate to the level of the course. It is intended for use by students and teachers alike.

Each section in this book has the same structure, which follows the layout of the course as prescribed by the SQA. There are five main sections which each contain topics broken down into manageable chunks of learning. As a minimum, each section of the book contains the following information:

- Introduction
- Topics covered in the section
- Tasks (some of these could be linked to a chosen assignment topic)
    - All tasks can be adapted. For example, some research tasks could be undertaken as project work out of class time. Most tasks can be done individually or as part of group work, etc.
- An end-of-section assessment.

I have drawn on my many years of experience as a teacher delivering this course and also as a senior examiner working with SQA. I have also taken on board feedback from many teachers who have used the previous edition of this book as their main teaching resource over a sustained period of time, achieving excellent results with many students.

I would like to express my thanks to everyone involved in the production of this book, in particular Claire Spinks and the other editorial staff from Hodder Gibson.

I hope that you find this book a useful companion to a new and exciting course of study and positive achievement.

Peter Hagan

December 2018

Preparing for course assessment

Higher Business Management – question paper

The question paper component of Higher Business Management is worth **90 marks** and is sat as part of the main national examination diet. The time allocation is 2 hours and 45 minutes. The question paper is compulsory, meaning that you *must* answer all questions. There are two sections to the question paper and questions can be based on any area of the course.

Section 1 is based on a case study and is worth **30 marks**. It consists of a multi-part question, with each part attracting a mark from a range of 1–8. You should expect the majority of questions in Section 1 to relate to the case study content and the business that features in the case study. Section 1 is **interpretative**, meaning that the questions will demand that you interpret information provided in the case study. The case study will also feature some appendices. The number of appendices can vary from year to year and the information contained in them will be different too, depending on the business explored in the case study. It is important that you spend 10–15 minutes reading the case study and appendices before attempting any questions. This is part of good examination technique.

There are likely to be around eight questions in Section 1 and they will cover a wide range of the topics in the course. This is not to say that there will be questions touching on every topic area of the course, but the coverage of the questions in Section 1 is broad based compared with Section 2 of the question paper.

Section 2 tests the depth of your course knowledge. It is worth **60 marks** in total; this is split into four questions carrying a total of **15 marks** each. These are also multi-part questions, with each part attracting a mark from a range of 1–8.

> You may wish to tackle Section 2 before reading the case study and answering the questions in Section 1. As long as you number your answers appropriately, this will make no difference to the examiner marking your work.

As a reminder, the broad topic areas of the course are:

- Understanding Business
- Marketing
- Operations
- People
- Finance
- Technology – remember that this is a cross-cutting theme throughout every topic area and is unlikely to be tested as a stand-alone topic.

Important information on how marks are awarded and responding to command words

In Higher Business Management, the examination is a test of your knowledge and understanding of the course, but it is also a test of your written communication abilities. This is because the method of assessment used for the final examination is a question paper. It is essential that you are able to clearly and concisely communicate your answers to the examiner to attract the best possible marks.

The SQA uses *command* words in all of its assessments and your teacher should have prepared you throughout the year to be able to answer the types of questions that you will face in the final examination. You should view the use of command words as something positive – you should not be afraid of them! Command words make the questions being asked much clearer since each command word has a specific meaning. You will always be credited for correct knowledge in Higher Business Management, but to gain full marks, you must also answer in response to the specific command word in the question.

Marking is always positive. This means that when your examination paper is being marked, you start with zero marks and marks are awarded for everything that you answer correctly. No marks are deducted for things that you do wrong.

In order to attract the best possible marks, you need to answer the question that is asked. This means that you must be able to understand, or comprehend, what is being asked. Read all questions carefully and pay attention to the command word and the number of marks for each question. Only then should you start to formulate an answer in your head before writing it down.

It is good practice to write in sentences and paragraphs. It is acceptable to use bullet points, but if they are too brief or are simply used as a list then they will be unlikely to attract many marks. A brief bulleted list will not fully address the command word and so will not be able to gain full marks. Bullets are a good way to gain some marks if you are running out of time, but only use them as a last resort – you want to get as many marks as possible!

The following gives an overview of the general marking principles that are applied to Higher Business Management. You can refer to the specific marking instructions on the SQA website, which are published a few months after the previous examination has been sat, for further guidance on how these principles have been applied by the examiners.

Marks will be awarded for:

Describe...

You must make a number of relevant factual points, which may be characteristics and/or features, as appropriate to the question asked. These points may relate to a concept, process or situation.

You may provide a number of straightforward points or a smaller number of developed points, or a combination of these.

Up to the total mark allocation for this question:

- **1 mark** can be given for each relevant factual point.
- **1 mark** can be given for any further development of a relevant point, including exemplification when appropriate.

Explain…

You must make a number of accurate, relevant points that relate cause and effect and/or make the relationships clear. These points may apply to a concept, process or situation.

You may provide a number of straightforward points of explanation or a smaller number of developed points, or a combination of these.

Up to the total mark allocation for this question:

- **1 mark** can be given for each relevant point of explanation.
- **1 mark** can be given for a further development of a relevant point, including exemplification when appropriate.

Compare…

You must demonstrate knowledge and understanding of the similarities and/or differences between things, methods or choices, for example. The relevant comparison points could include theoretical concepts.

Up to the total mark allocation for this question:

- **1 mark** can be given for each accurate point of comparison.

Discuss…

You must make a number of points that communicate issues, ideas or information about a given topic or context that will make a case for and/or against. It is not always necessary to give both sides of the debate in your response to gain full marks.

Up to the total mark allocation for this question:

- **1 mark** can be given for each accurate point of knowledge that is clearly relevant.

You can find the General Principles for Marking included as part of the Marking Instructions for Higher Business Management. These can be downloaded from the SQA website (www.sqa.org.uk) using the Past Papers and Marking Instructions service.

Distinguish…

You must identify and convey the differences between two factors. No marks will be given for similarities, only differences.

Up to the total mark allocation for this question:

- **1 mark** can be awarded for each valid distinction.

Justify...

Here you must provide reasons for a particular course of action. Essentially, because the verb 'justify' (in this context) means to give good reason for, all you need to do here is highlight the advantages.

Up to the total mark allocation for this question:

- **1 mark** can be awarded for each valid justification

Higher Business Management – assignment

The assignment component for Higher Business Management is worth **30 marks**, which represents 25% of the overall course award. It is your opportunity to gain some marks for a piece of work over which you have some control. The examination paper you will face is *unseen* and it is therefore difficult to predict which topics and areas of the course will be assessed. By comparison, the assignment allows you some degree of flexibility and personal choice.

If you follow the instructions provided by the SQA and the guidance given by your teacher and choose a business which is of interest to you, there is no reason why you should not be able to attain a high mark.

The following information is to give you some extra assistance and is based on the information supplied by the SQA.

The assignment covers the following areas:

- Selecting an appropriate business and topic.
- Collecting information/evidence relating to the context of the assignment from a range of sources.
- Applying relevant business concepts and theories to the context of the assignment.
- Analysing and evaluating the business data/information.
- Solving problems by applying relatively complex business ideas and concepts relevant to the context of the assignment.
- Communicating valid, justified conclusions and/or recommendations.
- Producing a business report relating to the context of the assignment.

Conditions for the completion of the assignment

Time

The assignment is designed to be completed over a notional period of 8 hours. This includes time for research and producing the final business report. You can complete the research and write-up simultaneously. The report can be completed using only secondary research; however, if you carry out field research you may need more than 8 hours. The report should preferably start once most of the course content has been delivered in class, to allow you to choose your topic from a wide range of course content.

You must carry out the assignment on an individual basis, gathering your own research and producing your own report independently.

Volume

The business report should be no longer than 2000 words (excluding appendices). If the word count exceeds the maximum by more than ten per cent then a penalty will be applied. There should be no more than four pages of appendices with your report.

Sections of the assignment

The SQA has provided guidelines for appropriate headings and layout for the assignment in the form of **sections** which should be completed, and each section has a maximum number of marks that can be awarded. Examiners will be looking for your assignment to correspond to this layout in order to award marks which are in line with the marking instructions. General marking principles for the assignment are available on the Higher Business Management section of the SQA website.

The following maximum marks are available for each of the sections:

1. Introduction – **2 marks**
2. Research – **4 marks**
3. Analysis and interpretation – **13 marks**
4. Conclusion and recommendations – **10 marks**
5. Structure (collating and reporting) – **1 mark**

In addition to the information contained in the general marking principles, here are some extra tips and pointers that will help you maximise the number of marks you can attain from the assignment.

Introduction

The introduction section should clearly state the aim of your report and be concise. The following points are important to ensure that you are awarded the **2 marks** available:

- You should include any suitable piece(s) of background information that describes what the company does. If it is not clear what the company is about/ what it does, the available mark cannot be awarded.
- The purpose of the report needs to be clear to achieve the mark. If any analytical point made later on does not relate to this then marks cannot be awarded for it. If you use a broad purpose, this will create a better opportunity for attracting marks.

No marks are awarded under the appendices headings for information which should appear in the Introduction section.

Research

This section has a maximum of **4 marks** available. It should be possible to achieve the maximum marks if you follow the instructions as well as these tips. Do not list research findings in this section. This section is about assessing the suitability of the source and why it was used. Marks will only be awarded for this and not for any findings themselves.

You should reinforce the reasons for and against the suitability of each source and explain why each source is suitable. Each explained point that is applied to the source will be credited. It is also good practice to give the purpose of using each source so the examiner can understand why it is relevant and/or helpful in producing your report. Do not just give textbook definitions of why you used a source, e.g. 'the information is up to date'. You need to explain why this source helped and why it has value for the topic of your report.

And it's worth repeating: research findings should be in the appendices – *not* under this heading!

Analysis and interpretation

This section has a maximum of **13 marks** available. It is likely that this section will provide the biggest differentiation between stronger and weaker candidates. Bear in mind the following when completing this section:

- Every mark *must* relate to the purpose stated.
- Facts and findings are not credited but are required for analysis to be drawn.
- If the source of the fact or finding, upon which the analytical point is made, is not clear then credit cannot be given. Referencing is important here, for example:
    - 'From my questionnaire (appendix 2) …'
    - 'From my observation …'
    - 'The website (www.nike.co.uk/news) stated …'
    - 'Trip Advisor (see screenshot) claimed …'
    - 'This tells me that …'
- No marks are awarded for recommendations in this section.

Conclusion and recommendations

This section carries a maximum of **10 marks**. Conclusions appear to be one of the most difficult areas for candidates. Do not simply repeat a list of your findings; your conclusion should provide a summary of your main points.

It is easier to get marks from **justified** recommendations, so always try to give a reason or justification for any recommendation you make.

It is important that you are able to write concise, conclusive statements in order to attract the marks. You should avoid writing anything in the conclusion that is not based on evidence you have already included in your assignment. This is unlikely to attract any marks.

You should begin any conclusive statement in one of the following ways:

- 'From the following evidence … it is clear that …'
- 'Overall it appears … which suggests that …'

Structure

This section has a maximum of **1 mark** available. This is an easy mark to pick up if you follow the following tips:

- Use the given headings. Information under the wrong headings will not be awarded a mark.
- There are no marks for appendices or any information included in them.
- Stick to the word limit – part of the skill of the assignment is being able to produce a complete and cohesive report to the specification given, and this includes the length. You may find that excessive length is penalised!
- If you include a display, this can be a graphic, logo, table and/or chart.
- Since this is a business report, it should be typed – minimum 1.5 line spacing, minimum 11 point font and sensible margins should be set within the document.

Section 1

Understanding Business

Once you complete this section you will be able to:

- ✓ analyse the features, objectives and internal structures of large organisations

- ✓ analyse the environment in which large organisations operate

The Understanding Business section of this book looks at how businesses are set up and run in today's economy. A business is any organisation set up to achieve objectives, so while we will focus mostly on profit-making businesses in this book we will also look at the government sector and the third/charity sector.

We will look at how they are run, how they work to achieve their objectives, and what determines their success.

In particular we will look at management's role in achieving success, and how that can vary from one organisation to another. This is important to remember when it comes to the exam.

Questions will often focus on one business or business type, so you must answer the question in relation to the business specified in the question. General points that get marks in some questions will not achieve marks in others. For example, a question on objectives for a charity will not get marks for objectives that relate to commercial business.

SECTION 1 UNDERSTANDING BUSINESS

Topic 1.1 Role of business in society	You should be aware of how business activity:
	
	• adds value
	• helps satisfy the needs of the customer in a changing environment.
	
	You should be able to classify and describe the following:
	
	• the sectors of industry and business activity in them:
	  • primary sector
	  • secondary sector
	  • tertiary sector
	  • quaternary sector
	• the sectors of the economy
	• organisations in the public, private and third sectors.

Topic 1.2 Types of organisation	You should be able to describe the similarities and differences between structures in the private, public and third sectors: • private limited companies • public limited companies • franchises • multinational organisations • public sector organisations • third sector organisations.

Topic 1.3 Objectives	• You should know the aims/objectives of the organisations.
	• You should be able to explain any similarities or differences in these aims/objectives.
	• You should understand the need to set objectives.
	• You should understand why organisations have more than one objective.
	• You should know what they do to achieve the objectives.
	• You should understand why these objectives may change as circumstances change.
	• Main objectives include:
	  • Corporate social responsibility
	  • Growth
	  • Satisficing
	  • Managerial objectives.

Topic 1.4 Methods of growth	• You should know the methods of growth available to an organisation.
	• You should be able to describe the methods of growth.
	• You should be able to give reasons for using each method and give any disadvantages to the method.
	• Methods of growth include:
	  • organic
	  • horizontal
	  • forward vertical
	  • backward vertical
	  • lateral
	  • conglomerate
	  • diversification.
	• Ways to achieve growth include:
	  • mergers
	  • acquisitions
	  • takeovers
	  • franchising
	  • becoming a multinational
	  • product development
	  • advertising
	  • increasing staffing.
	• Ways of funding growth include:
	  • retained profits
	  • divestment.

Topic 1.4 Methods of growth	<ul><li>de-integration</li><li>asset stripping</li><li>demerger</li><li>buy-in</li><li>buy-out</li><li>outsourcing.</li></ul>
Topic 1.5 External factors	<ul><li>You should know the impact of external factors.</li><li>You should be able to offer solutions as to how the organisation might lessen their effect.</li><li>Factors include:<ul><li>political</li><li>economic</li><li>social</li><li>technical</li><li>environmental</li><li>ethical</li><li>competitive.</li></ul></li></ul>
Topic 1.6 Internal factors	<ul><li>You should know the impact of internal factors.</li><li>You should understand the ways the organisation might be able to overcome them:<ul><li>staffing</li><li>finance</li><li>technology</li><li>corporate culture.</li></ul></li></ul>
Topic 1.7 Stakeholders	You should know the differing objectives of groups of stakeholders in terms of:<ul><li>stakeholder conflict and resolution</li><li>stakeholder interdependence.</li></ul>
Topic 1.8 Structures	<ul><li>You should know the business structures available to an organisation:<ul><li>tall and flat management structures</li><li>centralised and decentralised management structures</li><li>matrix management structure</li><li>entrepreneurial management structure</li><li>staff groupings such as function, location, product, customer and technology.</li></ul></li><li>You should also be able to describe the benefits and disadvantages of each structure.</li></ul>
Topic 1.9 Decision making	In decision making you should know:<ul><li>strategic, tactical and operational decisions</li><li>centralised and decentralised decision making</li><li>the role of a manager in making decisions</li><li>SWOT analysis as a decision-making tool</li><li>factors that affect quality decisions.</li></ul>

1.1 Role of business in society

Business's role is to create wealth for society by adding value. Adding value means changing or adding something to a resource that increases the price that can be charged to the customer. This allows the business to make a profit and employ people, and provides better choice and quality to the customer. A business's aims can be summarised as:

- provides employment
- provides choice
- is a source of innovation and ideas
- creates competition needed for low prices and efficiency
- develops infrastructure
- increases individuals' personal wealth
- supports worthy causes, e.g. charities.

Sectors of industry

Businesses can be grouped together into different types in what we call the chain of production. This is where natural resources are turned into goods and then finally sold to the customer.

Primary industries

The primary industries are involved in exploiting natural resources from the land, sea and air.

Secondary industries

Secondary industries include all the manufacturing industries and construction, so building houses, bridges, hospitals and even your school.

Tertiary industries

These industries do things for us and will include bus travel, restaurants and holiday companies.

Quaternary industries

These are referred to as the knowledge-based part of the economy. They are a subset of the tertiary industries and include technology, education, consultation and research and development.

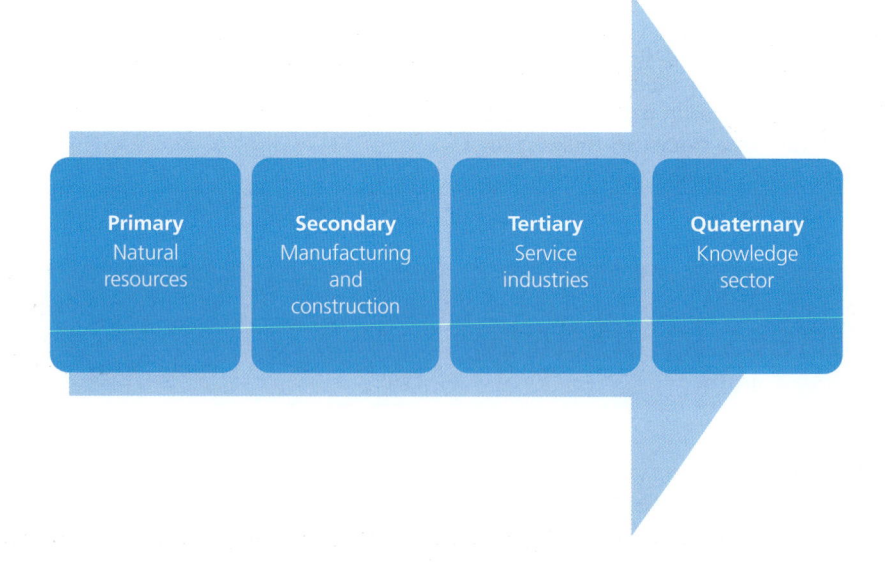

Primary	Secondary	Tertiary	Quaternary
Natural resources	Manufacturing and construction	Service industries	Knowledge sector

Changes in sectors

The introduction of automation and mechanisation, together with the lower cost of labour abroad, has led to a decrease in employment in the primary and secondary sectors in the UK. At the same time, the increasing importance of retail, financial services and leisure activities has created growth in the tertiary sector. There has also been growth in the quaternary sector with technology and medical sciences becoming increasingly successful and important for our economy.

Research task

Identify a business in each of the four sectors of industry and then explain why they belong to those sectors.

Sectors of the economy

There are three sectors of the economy.

1. The first includes businesses set up by private individuals whose main aim is to make a profit.
2. The second includes businesses set up by the government, normally to provide services that are thought to be of benefit to society, like health and education.
3. The third sector includes businesses or organisations that are set up to benefit individuals in society or members of that organisation.

Private sector

This sector is made up of profit-making businesses. In this sector private groups/shareholders invest their own money, or borrow money, to set up and run businesses. They can be multinationals, public limited companies or private limited companies.

Public sector

The public sector is made up of organisations set up by the government to provide services, either locally (council) or nationally (Holyrood or Westminster). Examples would include the NHS, police, fire brigade and education.

SECTION 1 UNDERSTANDING BUSINESS

Local councils provide a wide range of services such as street lighting, environmental services and, of course, education. National government provides services across the country including police and fire services and defence.

Overall, this sector is controlled by central/local government. It provides services that cannot be or are too expensive to be provided by the private sector.

Third sector

The third sector is made up of charities, voluntary groups, clubs and associations. It exists to provide a service or services that the private and the public sector will not do or would not do well. Their main aim is not profit making. Their activities can generate surpluses, which are then used to help their cause.

Charities and voluntary groups are set up and run for the benefit of specific groups of people who need additional support or help from society. There are many local and national charities that raise money from donations or government grants to help good causes.

Private	Public	Third
• Controlled by board of directors • Owned by shareholders • Limited liability • Financed by shares	• Government owned • Financed by taxes • Controlled by government-appointed managers	• Controlled by trustees • Financed through donations • Not owned but trustees can be liable

Research task

Identify a business in each of the three sectors of the economy and then explain why they belong to those sectors.

Report

Prepare a report on the difference between the sectors of the economy and the sectors of industry.

Revision questions

1. Describe the primary and secondary sectors of industry.
2. Describe the changes in the sectors of industry over the past 50 years.
3. Describe the sectors of the economy.
4. Describe the role of the quaternary sector of industry.

1.2 Types of organisation

Public sector organisations

There are a large number of different government organisations and agencies. The main features are listed below:

- owned by the government/taxpaying public
- run by a board of trustees/committee/elected officials
- financed by government through taxation, national insurance, VAT and income tax
- controlled overall by central/local government
- provide services that government consider to be basic needs but which cannot be/are too expensive to be provided by the private sector.

Government organisations

Local councils provide a wide range of services including education, housing and social services. They are also responsible for street lighting and refuse collection.

The public vote in council elections to elect their local councillor. When elected, councillors vote in their meetings to decide things like how the budget will be allocated and council policy. Councillors represent the geographical area for which they were elected, and will be keen to be re-elected in the future.

Directors are appointed to actually run the various departments of the council and are accountable to the elected officials. Their main role is to ensure their department stays within the budget allocated, and they ensure that the council's policy is followed. They must also ensure they meet the requirements of national government policy and act within the law.

The NHS is an example of a government organisation. In Scotland, fourteen individual Health Boards cover different areas of the country. A Chief Executive is appointed to oversee the running of each of the Health Boards. In addition, there are a number of other boards for national services such as NHS 24 and the Scottish Ambulance Service. Again, they are responsible for ensuring that government policies are implemented and that each board stays within the budget set by the government.

Scottish Enterprise

- This agency provides grants and funding options.
- It also provides management training.
- It gives support for international trading.
- It helps develop innovation.

- It was created to help new businesses set up and to provide help and assistance to existing businesses to survive and grow.
- It provides training for start-up businesses.
- Business managers give advice on financial planning and preparing a business plan.
- It can give advice on the type of business organisation to choose.
- It can offer advice on location.
- It may give advice on the local market/competitors.
- It is often able to provide useful local contacts.

Research task

Search for your local government agency and make a note of the kind of help and assistance it provides.

Private sector organisations

Limited companies

There are two types of limited company, public (plc) and private (Ltd).

- Both are owned by their shareholders, and both are controlled by a board of directors.
- The main difference between them is that plcs can sell their shares to anyone on the stock market, whereas private limited companies can only sell shares to invited individuals with the agreement of the existing shareholders.
- A private limited company requires a minimum of one shareholder to register, whereas a plc requires a minimum of two. In addition, both are required by law to produce a memorandum and articles of association, which are documents detailing the running and formal procedures established within the firm.
- Both benefit from limited liability, which means the shareholders are not personally responsible for the debts of the business.
- Because the cost of becoming a private limited company is now relatively cheap (currently £15), and because profit is taxed as corporation tax as opposed to income tax (which can be much higher*), most small businesses now operate as private limited companies.
- Other businesses also prefer to do business with limited companies as it is seen as a formal structure.

*At the time of writing, corporation tax in Scotland is 20 per cent up to the first £300,000 of profit. Income tax is 41 per cent for profits over £43,430 plus 12 per cent for National Insurance.

1.2 TYPES OF ORGANISATION

A private limited company has more control over the business, as bigger businesses cannot buy its shares on the stock market and take over the business.

To become a limited company with Companies House a business must:

- state the company name and address
- give details of Directors (at least one), and Company Secretary
- give details of Share Capital
- provide number and class of shares, including amount paid
- send a payment of £15
- register for corporation tax.

Larger businesses also need to trademark their name.

This can all be done online, but most businesses would use professionals such as accountants or lawyers as the rules and regulations on operating as a limited company can be quite complicated.

Benefits of a private limited company (Ltd)
- Limited liability
- Allows for economies of scale
- Control is not lost to outsiders
- Experience and skill gained from shareholders
- Less risk of liquidation
- Large amounts of finance can be raised from selling shares publicly.

Disadvantages of a private limited company (Ltd)
- Profits shared among more people (shareholders)
- Dividends are paid to shareholders at the end of the financial year only if a profit is made
- Shares can't be sold to the public on the stock market, which limits finance available
- Must abide by the Companies Act
- Must produce annual accounts, which can be viewed by competitors and investors

Research task

Visit **www.companieshouse.co.uk** and prepare a presentation on the information you find about setting up a limited company.

Public limited companies

Public limited companies (plc) have an added benefit of being able to raise more capital by issuing shares and debentures for sale on the stock market without needing to borrow money.

They should also find it much easier to do business with other companies and gain finance from banks and other investors due to the formal nature of the business.

Plcs have to publish their annual report and accounts, and issue them to shareholders, which means it is easier for competitors to obtain information about their plans and performance.

> Public limited companies (plc) are in the private sector.
> They are called 'public' because members of the public can buy shares on the stock market.
> The public sector is the government sector.

Features of a public limited company (plc)
- Shares sold on the stock market
- Normally large businesses
- Publish annual report
- Can lose control of the business
- Benefits similar to Ltd

Report
Prepare a report on the benefits and disadvantages of becoming a plc.

Franchising

Franchises are business arrangements where one firm pays for the right to run under the trading name of another.

The person or firm who owns and runs the business is called the franchisee.

The firm that owns the trading name is called the franchisor.

The franchisee buys the right to trade as the franchising business, but has to run the business in a way agreed with the franchisor.

Franchise
- **Franchisor** – owner of the overall business
- **Franchisee** – the business which pays to operate the franchise

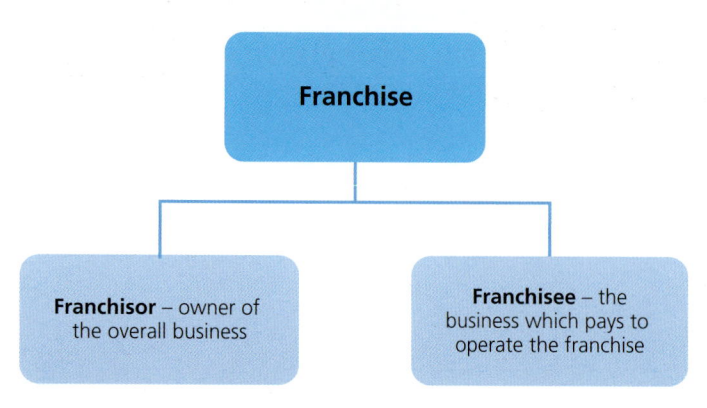

Advantages for franchisor
- Expand quickly and cheaply
- Receive a share of profits and sales
- Protection from competition
- Can become a recognised brand
- Have control over franchisee
- Franchisee may help innovation

1.2 TYPES OF ORGANISATION

Advantages for franchisee
- Starts with established name, increasing the chance of success
- Attracts new customers quickly, reducing the risk of failure
- Given training from franchisor
- Innovation from other franchisees
- Help and support from franchisor

Disadvantages for franchisee
- Has to run the business as directed by franchisor
- Part of profits/sales are paid to franchisor

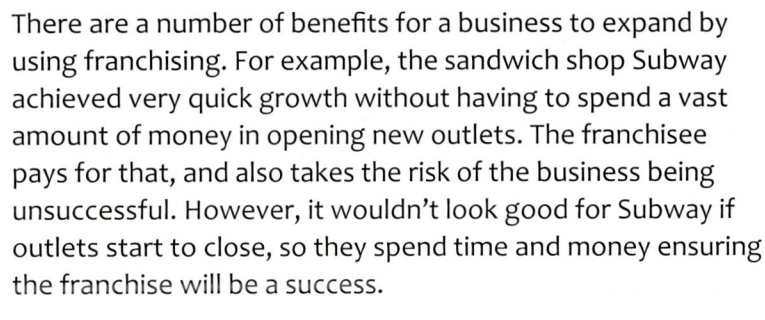

There are a number of benefits for a business to expand by using franchising. For example, the sandwich shop Subway achieved very quick growth without having to spend a vast amount of money in opening new outlets. The franchisee pays for that, and also takes the risk of the business being unsuccessful. However, it wouldn't look good for Subway if outlets start to close, so they spend time and money ensuring the franchise will be a success.

They train their prospective franchisees to ensure they know how to run the business successfully; make sure market research shows that the franchise will be successful; and monitor the performance of the franchisee.

There is also the benefit that the franchisee, as an entrepreneur, will be highly motivated to make the business successful, much more so than an employee.

However, if the franchise is badly run it will reflect badly on the whole organisation and affect the reputation of the business.

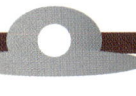

Report
Prepare a presentation on the benefits and disadvantages of becoming a franchise for the franchisee.

Research task
Carry out a search for franchise opportunities in the UK.

Multinationals

Multinational companies are businesses that trade internationally with operations in more than one country. Most large, well-known businesses will be multinational. Their products will be available in many different countries.

If you are asked to describe the features, benefits or disadvantages of a multinational company in an exam question, you should make sure that your answers are in sentences. If you are asked to explain then you will need to include additional detail.

Example

Question
Explain the advantages of operating as a multinational.

Answer
They can take advantage of local wage rates, which will reduce the costs to the business.

Multinational features	Multinational benefits	Multinational disadvantages
• Operations in several countries • Has distinct home base country • Global brand • Can dominate markets across many countries • Budgets can be larger than some countries • Can greatly influence local economies	• Much larger market – more customers • Economies of scale will be available – bulk buying and centralised administration • Profits/sales will be greater – shareholders/owners happier • Reputation will be enhanced – loyal customers • Can take advantage of local tax rates – reducing business costs • Can take advantage of lower wage rates	• Cultural variations have to be overcome for products/marketing – e.g. McDonald's can't sell beef burgers in India • Transportation can become expensive – moving inventory/people between countries • Difficult to control – harder to manage in many countries • Language barriers will exist – need to adapt marketing for each country • Political stability can be a problem in some countries – can lose part of the business • Legislation in some countries may make trading difficult

Third sector organisations

The main aim of these organisations is not to make a profit.

- Clubs are run for the benefit of their members, for example, a golf club.
- Charities are run to help groups or individuals in society, for example, Oxfam.
- Social enterprises are set up to achieve specific objectives, for example, *The Big Issue*.

Social enterprises:

- reinvest some profit/surplus into a social aim
- do not operate in the public sector as no profit/surplus to reinvest but can be in the private or third sector
- Asset locks prevent owners selling the business to make profits rather than benefit the cause
- Community Interest Company (CIC) is one registered with Companies House, with special features to ensure they benefit the community.

Clubs are set up to meet the needs of groups of individuals. They exist to provide a service to people with common interests.

Charities must meet one of four criteria to achieve charitable status. They must do one of the following:

- relieve poverty
- advance education
- advance religion
- carry out activities beneficial to the community.

Charities receive money from donations, from shop sales, from government grants and from fees for services. They do not have to pay some forms of tax.

Both charities and clubs can have some commercial activities to help raise funds.

Revision questions

1. Compare the ownership and control of private and public sector organisations.
2. Explain the benefits of franchising for an organisation.
3. Discuss the benefits of becoming a multinational organisation.
4. Describe the benefits and disadvantages of becoming a public limited company.
5. Discuss the benefits of becoming a private limited company.
6. Describe how organisations such as Scottish Enterprise could provide assistance to a new business.

1.3 Objectives

All organisations have objectives. These strategic objectives give the organisation goals or targets to work towards. For public sector organisations, they could be to provide best service or stay within budget. For third sector organisations, they could be to raise awareness or increase donations. Objectives will change over time as the business responds to changes in its environment. For example, in times of austerity, public-sector organisations may decide to keep their prices low in order to maintain or maximise sales, or they may reduce the quality of the product to maintain their profitability.

Different organisations will have different objectives but the most common ones are corporate social responsibility and profit maximisation.

Report
Prepare a report showing how corporate social responsibility could conflict with profit maximisation.

Corporate social responsibility

In order to have a positive public image and gain customer trust, many businesses look to improve the working conditions of their employees and their treatment of the environment.

Policies could include:

- Paying staff living wage instead of minimum wage
- Ethical marketing
- Recycling to reduce waste
- Ensuring suppliers have the same standards
- Minimising packaging for customers
- Ensuring processes do not pollute

Profit maximisation

This means making as much profit as possible. It can be achieved through charging high prices and keeping costs as low as possible. However, competition and the need for growth and development may make this difficult. There are a number of important factors to be kept in mind.

- Higher profits will attract more investment
- Seen as a sign of success for the business
- High prices may attract negative publicity
- Lowering costs could affect quality
- High profits may attract higher pay claims
- High profits may attract competition

Satisficing

This means ensuring the stakeholders of the business are happy with the way it operates. For example:

Shareholders	Happy with the profits of the business
Managers	Avoiding unnecessary risk
Employees	Content with their pay and conditions
Banks	Satisfied with the financial position of the business
Suppliers	Willing to maintain supplying the business
Customers	Pleased with the service provided
Government	Satisfied the business is meeting all legal requirements
Community	Happy with the way the business operates

Managerial objectives

Managers within an organisation make the decisions that determine the success and direction of the business.

Profit maximisation is a key objective as every business hopes to be successful by making as much profit as possible, and to purchase more resources/give dividends to shareholders, etc.

Social/ethical responsibility is desirable as the business wants to present a positive image to the community and gain more customers.

Managers may want the business to grow or to maximise sales in order to increase their own salary, benefits, importance, etc. This can conflict with the objectives of the organisation.

- Profit maximisation
- Working within budget
- Social/ethical responsibility
- Sales/revenue maximisation
- Growth/expansion
- Survival

Mission statements

The mission statement (company philosophy) summarises the strategic aims of the business. It can be released to the press to help market the business and its products, and issued to all employees and other stakeholders.

- It will show that the business has plans for the future, and how those plans will affect the stakeholders.
- The mission statement may contain information on how the business will treat shareholders, the environment and, importantly, consumers.
- It can be motivating for employees as it provides direction.
- It will reassure shareholders and customers, which will lead to greater business success.
- It provides the opportunity to improve the reputation of the business.
- It can attract high-quality candidates in the recruitment process.

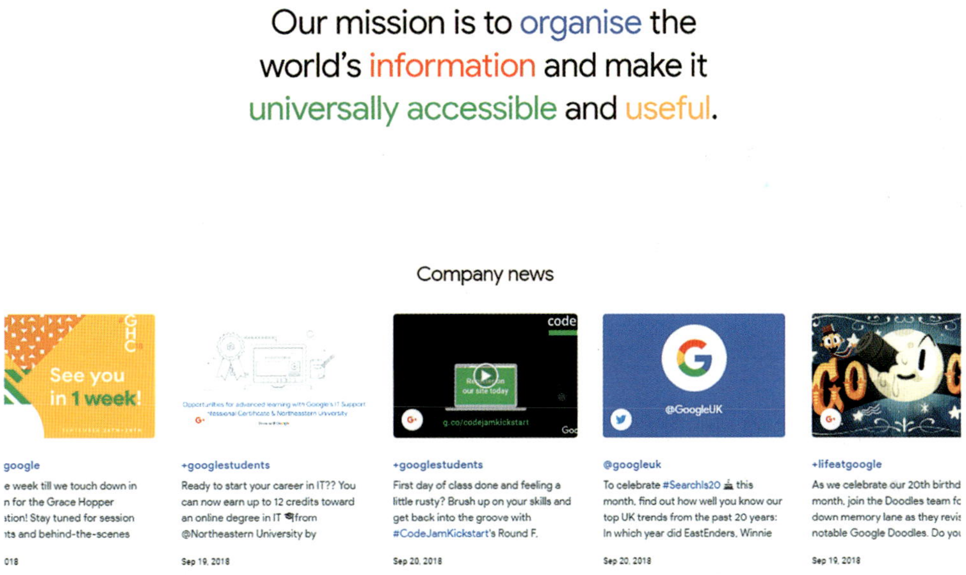

Our mission is to organise the world's information and make it universally accessible and useful.

Google's company mission statement

Revision questions

1. Describe how objectives may conflict within an organisation.
2. Explain the reasons for an organisation adopting a policy of corporate social responsibility.
3. Describe managerial objectives within a large organisation.
4. Describe the strategic objectives of a public sector organisation.
5. Describe the benefits of producing a mission statement for the business.

1.4 Methods of growth

Growth

If the business grows, it has greater control of its market. Being able to compete better with other firms, it can reach more customers, is more able to resist takeovers and has a better chance of survival.

Organic/internal growth

Most businesses will expect to grow over time. There are a number of ways internal growth can be achieved, including opening new outlets, increasing sales, increasing profits, operating in more markets/countries and introducing new products.

> **Report**
> Prepare a report describing methods of internal growth.

Benefits of internal growth
- Can be less risky than taking over another business
- Can be financed through internal sources
- Can build on existing strengths such as brands and good customer relations

Disadvantages of internal growth
- A slower method of growth
- Limited by the size of existing market

External growth

This can be achieved by buying/taking over another business, or by merging with another business.

There are a number of methods of external growth you should be aware of:

Vertical integration

Backward vertical integration is when a business takes over a supplier.

- This allows the business to control its source of goods/materials.
- It adds the supplier's profit to its own.
- It can ensure the quality and quantity of supplies.
- It can control supplies to competitors.

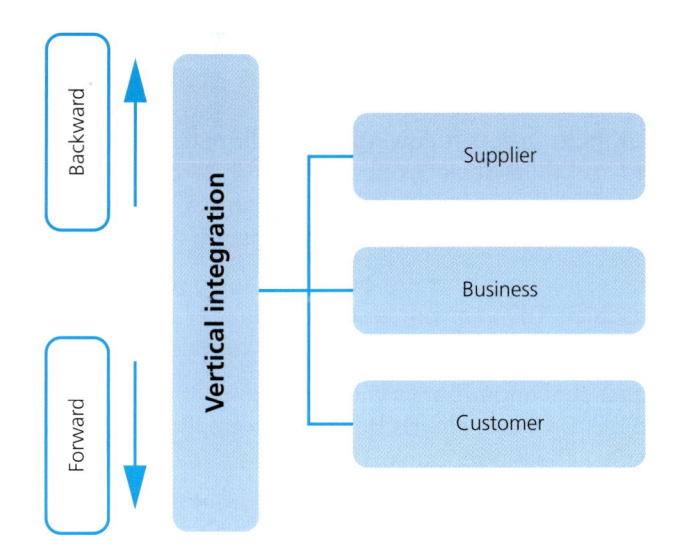

1.4 METHODS OF GROWTH

Forward vertical integration is when the business takes over its customer.

- This guarantees an outlet for its goods.
- It can control the marketing mix for its products.
- It adds the profit of the customer to its own.

Horizontal integration

This is when two businesses at the same stage in the production process join together. They can be seen as competitors. An example would be two mobile phone operators joining together.

Horizontal integration can involve one business completely taking over another, or it may be a joining of the two businesses to create a new business.

Report
Prepare a report comparing forward and backward vertical integration.

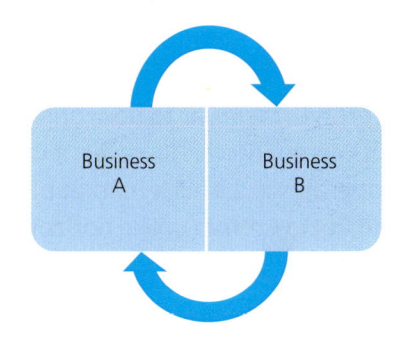

Benefits of horizontal integration
- It removes a competitor from the market.
- The business may be able to dominate the market.
- It can enjoy greater economies of scale through merging functional areas.

Takeover

Benefits of a takeover
- Larger, more financially secure
- Gets the profits of the other business
- Increases its customer base
- Greater market presence

Disadvantages of a takeover
- Requires allocation of financial and HR resources
- Risk of harming the main business
- Takes time to merge the two business systems

Case study: Merger

Two additional big names look set to disappear from UK high streets following the confirmation of the £1.7bn takeover of Virgin Money by the Clydesdale and Yorkshire Bank Group (CYBG). Under the deal, the combined group will create the UK's sixth-largest bank, with around six million customers, and total lending power of £70 bn. The merger is likely to result in the loss of more than 1500 jobs.

Despite CYBG driving the move, the 70 Clydesdale Bank branches and 97 Yorkshire Bank outlets will be rebranded as Virgin Money, marking the end of Clydesdale's 180-year presence on the high street since its launch in Glasgow in 1838. It's sister brand, Yorkshire Bank, was established in 1859 in Halifax.

CYBG has stated that the merging of the UK's two largest challenger banks will create the "first true national competitor to the large incumbent banks" (HSBC, Barclays, Lloyds Banking Group, Royal Bank of Scotland and Santander), being twice as big as the nearest challenger bank, TSB.

The group says it is committed to moving all its retail customers over to Virgin Money over the next three years. There is a possibility that the Clydesdale and Yorkshire brands may be retained for the group's small- and medium-sized business banking division, while the Virgin brand is tested out on the retail customers. It is estimated that the rebranding will cost £60 m.

Adapted from https://www.theguardian.com/business/2018/jun/18/virgin-money-bought-clydesdale-bank-cybg

Lateral

Lateral growth is similar to horizontal growth, where the business merges or takes over one of its competitors. However, it can also be where a business is taking over a firm which operates in a similar market but is **not** in direct competition, for example, Coca Cola and Costa Coffee (unlike horizontal integration where competitors combine).

Diversification

This where a business moves into a new market either by itself, or by taking over or merging with a business already in the new market.

By doing so:

- it reduces the risk of business failure
- it increases its profit stream
- customers in the new market can be attracted to the existing products
- it can be seen as a more successful business.

> **Report**
> Prepare a report describing the benefits and disadvantages of taking over another business.

Case study: Diversification

BT and EE

BT have added to their list of product services as their sales revenue declines. Going from simply providing residential phone lines, they currently also offer broadband and TV including BT Sport. Now they want to add mobile services. Taking on Sky with the launch of BT Sport was very successful in recruiting many new customers and they see mobile as the next step.

Ironically, they sold off O2 many years ago as they did not see it as part of their core business, but as technology changes along with customer demands, they see mobile as essential to continue to grow the business. They have now taken over EE and acquired their 31 million customers and the largest 4G customer base in Europe.

Research task

Carry out a search to show how BT has diversified away from just providing landlines, and then give reasons why it might have done so.

Conglomerate

A conglomerate is a business that is a parent firm to a range of different businesses in many different markets that it has bought over simply to increase its profitability. Unilever is an example of a conglomerate, making a wide range of different products from ice cream to deodorants. Conglomerate integration is entering into a new target market via an external growth method, for example, an acquisition or joint venture with another firm.

- The parent firm may not be involved in producing goods or services itself.
- Each of the businesses will be seen as a separate division of the parent firm.
- It will be easy to identify how each division is performing.
- Underperforming businesses may be sold off to increase profitability and raise cash for investment.

De-merger/divestment

Organisations can sell off unwanted subsidiary businesses or divisions in order to:

- raise capital for new projects
- increase the efficiency of their operations
- remove underperforming parts of the business
- remove themselves from negative publicity.

The money raised can be used to fund growth in the areas where they feel they will have more success.

Case study: Divestment

Edrington, the Glasgow-based distiller, has put the Glenturret malt distillery in Crieff, and the Cutty Sark whisky brand up for sale. It declared its intention to focus investment on its single malts, including The Macallan and Highland Park and its blended whisky, Famous Grouse.

The sale was announced along with Edrington's financial results for the year to 31 March. Despite holding on to its leading position in the UK market, the company suffered a drop of around 4% in sales last year.

Edrington, like William Grant & Sons, is one of the big Scottish-based whisky distillers, with its profits going to the Robertson charitable trust, originally set up in the 1960s by three sisters who had inherited the company.

Adapted from https://www.bbc.co.uk/news/uk-scotland-44582314

De-integration

While integration is the addition of suppliers, customers or rivals, de-integration involves selling off one of the businesses previously taken over.

It may be that the business decides to focus on its customers, and so sells off suppliers previously purchased in order to focus on areas where it has greatest expertise and brand value, allowing it to grow where it is most profitable.

Buy-in

This is where an outside management company buys the business as it believes it can manage it more successfully. It is commonly seen in cases where the existing business is struggling to achieve success in the market.

Buyout

This involves an interested party buying or taking over control of the firm. This may be the existing management, where they think that the owners' vision for the business will not lead to any great success.

It could also refer to an employee buyout, where the employees get together to fund buying the existing business.

Asset stripping

When a business is seen to be unsuccessful in trading but has a large number of assets, it may become prey to asset stripping. This happens when the value of its shares is lower than the value of its assets.

The business is bought over by an outside firm and each of the assets of the business is sold off to fund the purchase and increase the wealth of the buyers.

Outsourcing

This is where part of the operations of the organisation is passed or 'outsourced' to a specialist who may well be able to do the job better than the organisation itself.

Advantages of outsourcing

- Specialists can be used to do the work.
- It reduces staff and other costs in the area that has been outsourced.
- Outsourced companies will have specialist equipment.
- The specialist firm may carry out the task to a higher standard.
- The service can be provided cheaper as the unit cost for the specialist supplier may be lower.
- The service needs to be paid for only when it is required.
- Organisations can concentrate on core activities.

Disadvantages of outsourcing

- The service can be more expensive as the specialist supplier will add their own profit to the price charged.
- Organisations can lose control over outsourced work.
- Sensitive information may need to be passed to the specialist supplier.
- Communication needs to be very clear or mistakes can arise.
- Bad publicity may arise if staff are made redundant as a result.
- If the specialist supplier fails to deliver then the business will be seen in a bad light.

Case study: Outsourcing

Marks and Spencer has announced it will outsource over half its IT division. In a bid to save £30 m a year, the company plans to transfer around 250 roles from its current 430-strong IT team to Indian tech giant Tata Consultancy.

Although all staff involved would now be employed directly by Tata, M&S assured that they would continue to be based at its offices in Stockley Park in west London. A spokeswoman for the retailer confirmed, 'We're not moving additional services offshore as a result of these changes'.

Spearheaded by chief executive, Steve Rowe, the move forms part of the high-street chain's five-year, cost-cutting plan to attempt to reverse its declining fortunes. Mr Rowe stated the changes to its technology team would save £30 m a year by 2021/22, claiming: 'Our business will be faster, simpler and more focused on achieving a seamless customer experience'.

Adapted from https://www.bbc.co.uk/news/business-42629522

Report
Prepare a report describing the advantages and disadvantages of outsourcing.

Methods of funding growth

This will be dealt with in more detail under Management of Finance; however, there are different ways that can be used depending on the method of growth. For example, if a business takes over another this could be done through a new share issue or offering shares in the business to the shareholders of the business being taken over. Divesting some parts of the business in order to raise funds for growth (both internal and external) is common.

Revision questions

1. Describe methods of external growth available to an organisation.
2. Discuss the use of outsourcing for an organisation.
3. Describe the problems a business might face after a takeover.
4. Describe methods of internal growth available to an organisation.
5. Discuss the use of forward vertical integration.

1.5 External factors

External factors are those things that affect the success of the business, but that it cannot directly control. These are normally described as the PESTEC factors. They will often have a direct impact on the business, for example:

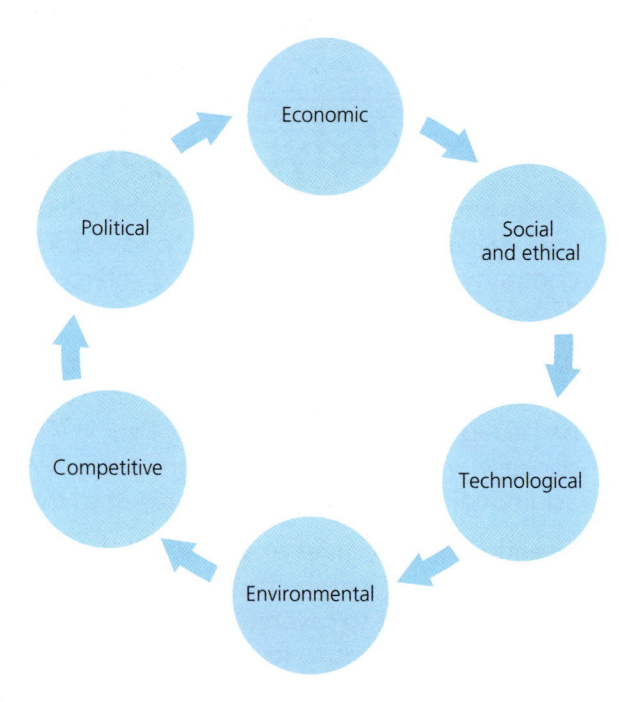

Political	An increase in the minimum wage will mean the business is paying more for its labour force, so may have a smaller profit, or it may have to increase its prices.
Economic	A recession may force an organisation to downsize/pay off staff.
Social and Ethical	A change in tastes and fashions may mean demand for the business's products falls or increases, which will affect its profitability.
Technological	Improvements in communications technology may mean customers demand a better service from the business, so it may need to upgrade its technology, adding to the costs of the business.
Environmental	Organisations should now attempt to reduce their carbon footprint and try to recycle more. Consumer expectations on the sourcing of raw materials, animal welfare and fair pay and conditions of all workers in the supply chain mean businesses must ensure that their activities are seen as ethical to governments and consumers.
Competitive	Competitors may introduce an improved product which reduces sales for the business, meaning it has to develop new products quickly or lose sales.

Political factors

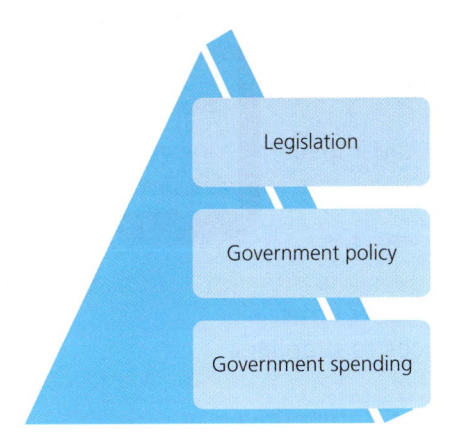

- Legislation
- Government policy
- Government spending

The Houses of Parliament

The government can have many influences on the business economy as a whole and on individual businesses, depending on the industry they are involved with, or the area they are situated in.

Below are just some of the areas where the government can impact on the success of a business.

Legislation	- Employment law - Equality Act - Environmental law - Competition law - Data protection - Financial services - Health and safety at work - Trade descriptions - Product safety and labelling - Minimum wage
Government policy	- Immigration - Recycling - National Insurance contributions - Economic - Competition - Planning permission
Government spending	- Grants and allowances - Investment – infrastructure, e.g. transport, broadband - Regional support - Environmental, e.g. flood defences - Taxation, e.g. business tax relief

Competition policy

The Competition and Markets Authority is responsible for implementing government competition policy. The main areas it is involved in are:

- consumer protection
- mergers

It aims to prevent market domination through mergers and acquisitions in order to maintain customer choice and fair market prices. Market domination is also seen as a barrier to new businesses coming to the market to offer better/cheaper services.

There are a number of ways that competition policy can impact on a business.

> **Report**
> Prepare a report on how government policy can impact on a business.

- Cannot collude with other organisations to fix prices, for example, a cartel.
- Cannot fix the bid for tendering on projects with other firms.
- Cannot use market power to pay unfairly low prices to suppliers.
- Prevents monopolies occurring.
- Blocks mergers and takeovers that are deemed anti-competitive.
- Enforces the selling of divisions/branches/premises, for example, divestment.
- May be forced to change prices.
- May be fined for anti-competitive behaviour.

Economic factors

- Inflation
- Employment
- Exchange rates
- Boom/recession
- International trade
- Interest rates

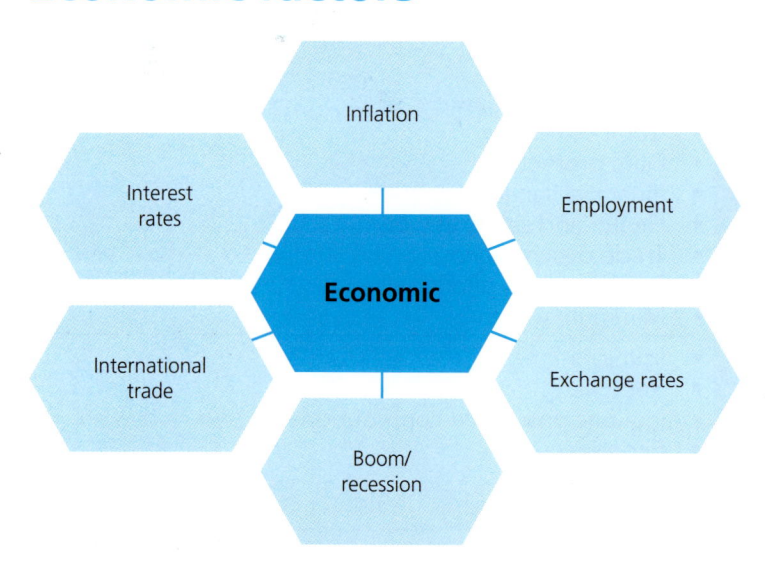

There is a range of economic factors that will impact on a business. Some of them relate to the action the government takes.

Inflation	Rising prices not only affect consumers but will also impact on the business itself. For example, an increase in the price of materials will mean higher production costs for the business. It may have to increase prices to the consumer which could lead to a drop in sales, or it may have to accept lower profits.
Employment	When unemployment is high, the business will find it easier to recruit new workers and pay them less; however, it will usually mean lower demand for its products. The opposite is also true.
Exchange rates	If the business is involved in international trade, this will affect how expensive its product is to foreign consumers. The higher the value of the £, the more expensive the product is to overseas customers. If it is buying supplies from abroad, the higher the value of the £, the less expensive the supplies are to buy.
Boom/recession	During boom periods demand for products is high, unemployment is low, and prices tend to rise quicker. The opposite is true during a recession.
International trade	The UK will officially continue membership of the EU up to and including March 2019. It remains to be seen how trade will be affected after this point, following Brexit. The EU has free movement of goods from one country to another, making it easy to trade internationally within the EU. Outside the EU there are a number of trade agreements between governments, but changes in these can make it difficult to carry on trading profitably.
Interest rates	Rising interest rates increase costs to both consumers and business. For example, an increase for consumers would mean an increase in monthly mortgage or loan payments which could lead to less spending on other goods, leading to a reduction in demand. For business it will increase finance costs which could mean lower profits.

Economic policy

The government will always try to create growth within the economy. They will introduce measures to increase the number of people employed and develop international trade. Inflation and interest rates are the responsibility of the Bank of England, which acts independently of the government.

The impact of these on the business could be:

Fiscal policy

- Increase in income tax can reduce sales as customers may have less to spend.
- Increase in VAT means the selling price may have to be increased.
- Increase in corporation tax will reduce the profit for the year.

Monetary policy

- Increase in interest rates increases the costs of borrowing finance.
- Lowering of interest rates means firms may invest more into growth.

Research task

Carry out a search to find out how the exchange rate between the euro and sterling has changed in the last year. Explain how the changes will affect UK business.

Social and ethical factors

Social factors

Business has to be aware of, and respond to, changes in what consumers buy, when they buy it, and what they consider to be quality/value. If a business doesn't change with its customers, it risks losing sales to competitors.

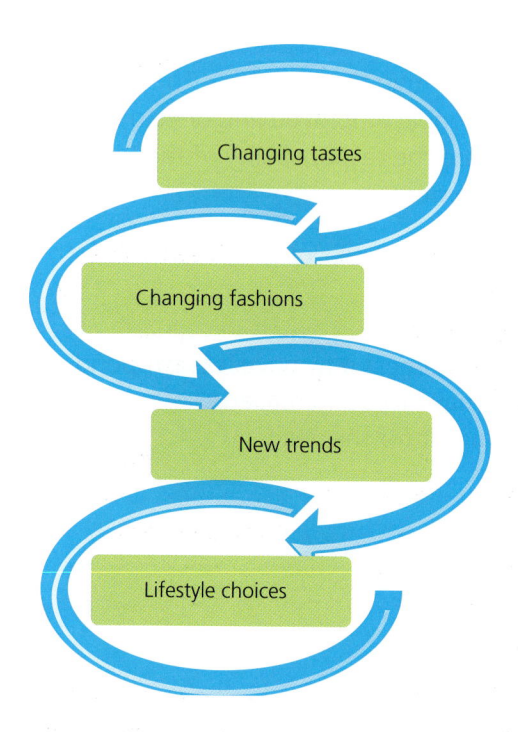

- Changing tastes
- Changing fashions
- New trends
- Lifestyle choices

For example, the big supermarket retailers like Tesco, Asda and Sainsbury's have all lost business to smaller chains like Aldi and Lidl, which can supply similar products at lower prices. This has happened at the same time as consumers have begun to move away from the large monthly/weekly shop (that can now be done online and delivered to your home) to regular, smaller shopping trips. Consumers are now seeking much better value for their money.

- In clothing, many brands have a limited life cycle as fashions change.
- Consumers are more considerate about 'free from' foods, food miles and organic produce.
- Supporting local business has become popular.

Ethical factors

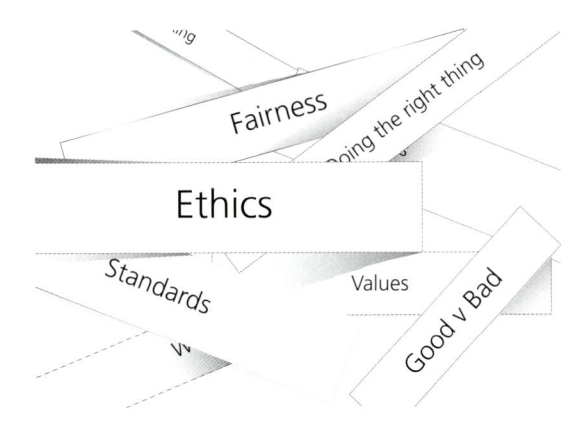

Business ethics is seen as increasingly important in society. The way society views ethical issues changes over time, forcing businesses to adapt and change their ways of operating in order to meet society's current view.

This could involve:

- rejecting the use of child labour in the supply chain
- supporting local businesses
- paying suppliers on time
- not putting undue pressure on suppliers
- not using its market strength to disadvantage consumers
- taking account of concerns over issues such as recycling and packaging
- focusing on reducing food miles
- ensuring suppliers' treatment and health and safety of employees is of a high standard.

Technological factors

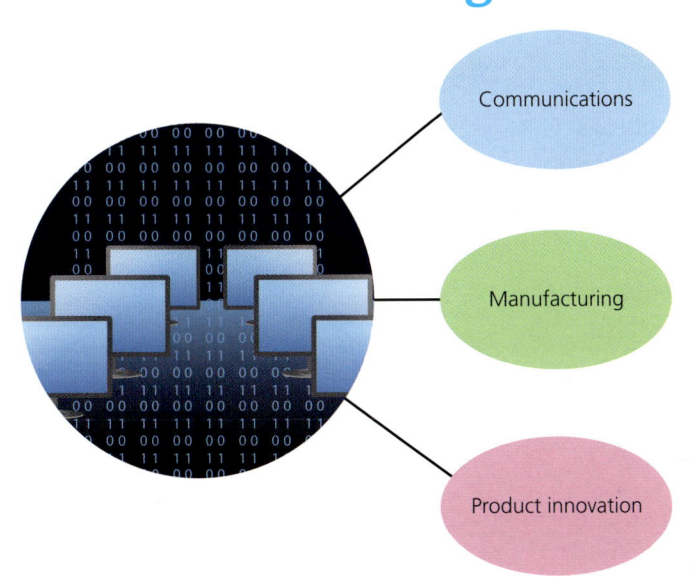

Investing in new technology can give a business a competitive edge over its rivals, so it is important for the success of the business to keep up to date and, if possible, to try to steal a lead on the competition.

Increased use of social media, smartphones and e-commerce among consumers has changed their expectations of what a business should offer. Some businesses have now moved their complaints/customer service sections to Twitter to meet this need.

Using technology like this does come with some risks as it can be expensive, but the rewards can be significant.

Benefits of new technology
- Increased efficiency – fewer workers/more output
- Increased flexibility – can adapt to changes more easily
- Better communication – increase in the volume and speed of information handling
- Increased customer satisfaction – greater convenience
- Enhanced reputation – seen as modern and up to date
- Competitive edge – until rivals catch up
- Reduced staffing costs – due to automation
- Creation of home workers – through use of broadband
- Access to new markets and customers with online selling

Disadvantages of new technology
- Cost of hardware and equipment
- Cost of replacing and upgrading obsolete systems
- Installation costs
- New furniture to house equipment
- Staff training costs
- Losses in efficiency during training
- Loss of electronic information – data protection
- Computer viruses
- Commercial espionage and hacking
- Health and safety issues
- General Data Protection Regulation

Environmental factors

Every year in the UK snow, flooding and high winds bring disruption not only to people living in affected areas, but also to the businesses that operate in those areas.

Transport becomes more difficult so goods can't be delivered, customers can't get to the shops and workers can't get to work, leading to delays and closures. For a business the loss of sales and profits can have a severe impact.

A lack of or reduction in the availability of natural resources can lead to an increase in prices for raw materials. A reduction in supply will reduce production and subsequently lead to an increase in price for consumers.

Long periods of hot weather may lead to greater demand for summer products such as clothing and food, but may also cause droughts which may lead to some manufacturers being forced to close temporarily.

Report
Prepare a report to show the benefits and disadvantages of introducing new technology to a business.

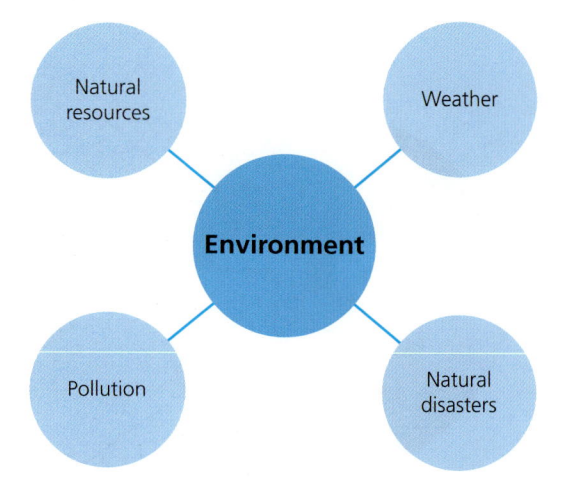

Report
Prepare a report describing how the weather can affect businesses.

Environment: Natural resources, Weather, Pollution, Natural disasters

1.5 EXTERNAL FACTORS

29

Natural disasters around the world will affect the supply chain for many businesses in this country, again leading to a loss of production, sales and profits.

Pollution levels affect businesses where they are seen as contributing to its cause. They may have to take action to avoid bad publicity and loss of reputation, otherwise they risk losing sales and custom. Greater use of biofuels, recycling and taking greater consideration of their carbon footprint will be required.

Competitive factors

Most businesses operate in a competitive market. They have control over their marketing strategy and can alter it in order to gain some competitive advantage.

- They can alter their price to attract new customers.
- They can bring out new or improved versions of their product.
- They can launch a new marketing campaign to attract customers from their competitors.
- New competitors could enter the market.
- They could introduce better customer support or after-sales service.
- They could improve their stores to attract new customers.
- They could improve their range of services to customers.

All of these may reduce the sales and profits of competitors, as well as harm their reputation. It is important for a business to keep up to date with changes in the market or the success of the business will be reduced.v

Report
Prepare a report on what Samsung could do if Apple introduced a new mobile phone.

Case study: External factors

You wouldn't think that a shortage of CO_2 would have a negative effect on so many of our favourite brands, but that is what has just happened. CO_2 is used to provide the gas for all our favourite fizzy drinks, whether in a can or bottle, or from a pump at the restaurant. It also provides the fizz for many of the nation's favourite beers. Some manufacturers have had to cease production until they can source alternative supplies.

Meat producers also use CO_2 for their sealed packs of fresh food as it helps to prevent them spoiling, and members of the British poultry trade are seriously worried. The Food and Drink Federation said it would affect much of the 'farm to fork' supply chain. Both are calling on the government to intervene.

The problem arose because CO_2 is produced as a by-product in fertiliser factories, and most of them are closed for summer maintenance as fertiliser is not in huge demand in the summer months.

Revision questions

1 Describe how government policy may impact on an organisation.
2 Describe other external factors that can impact on an organisation.
3 Describe how external factors can affect an organisation's objectives.
4 Discuss ways in which an organisation can avoid negative impact of social factors.
5 Discuss the advantages and disadvantages of introducing new technology to a business.

1.6 Internal factors

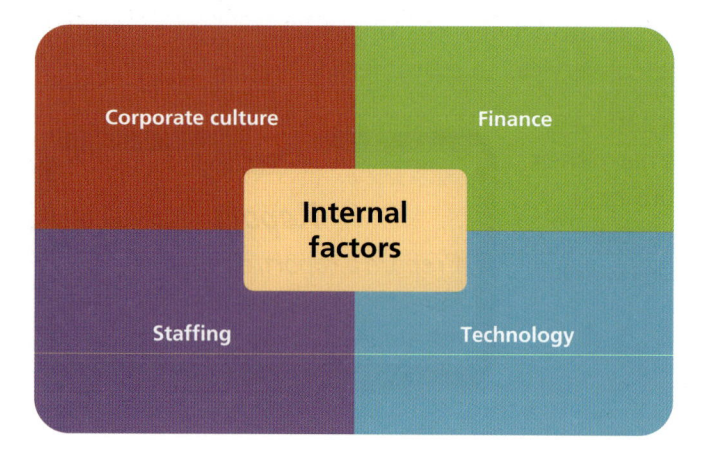

Corporate culture | Finance
Staffing | Technology
(Internal factors)

Corporate culture

This is normally a difficult topic for students to grasp. Any social group forms their own ways of talking and behaving. Your class or group of friends will have their own acceptable way; if you don't believe me then ask someone who had to change schools, or move house.

It's not easy to fit right in, or to pick a group that you are comfortable with. It's the same when you change jobs. You look for the best way to act or behave so you become accepted into a group you feel comfortable with.

A business will try to use this social need of individuals to belong and be part of the team. The textbook definition of a business's culture is:

'The values, beliefs and norms relating to the organisation that are shared by all staff.'

This is creating an idea that the business and its employees are all part of one social group, giving a sense of belonging and identity. It will affect the thinking and decision making of the management and employees.

Benefits of corporate culture
- Employees feel part of the organisation.
- It is motivational to staff.
- It improves employee relationships.
- It increases employee loyalty.
- It gives customers a sense of quality/efficiency.
- It may attract new workers.
- It improves the business image.

Disadvantages of corporate culture
- It may stifle creative thinking.
- Some essential staff might find it difficult to fit in.
- Time and effort are required to maintain the culture and for new staff to adapt to the culture.
- Change may be more difficult to implement.

To create a corporate culture a business could:

- introduce standardised working practices and systems
- have uniforms for staff
- organise staff training on culture
- keep layout and design of all offices/outlets the same
- create a mission statement which sets out the business goals and ideals.

The corporate culture will impact on the decision making of the business as managers have to take it into account when setting out future aims for the business.

The policies may restrict managers from doing what they feel is necessary if it conflicts with the corporate culture of the organisation.

Report
Prepare a report describing how a business could create a corporate culture.

Availability of finance

The amount of money a business has available to spend will have to be split between competing demands. It is important to make sure that there is enough available to pay the costs of running the business, and if there is anything left over, decisions on what to do with it will come down to what will benefit the business the most.

We will look at the conflicting demands of different stakeholders later in the book, but there will also be conflict between departments or managers who will see the need to spend money in their particular area.

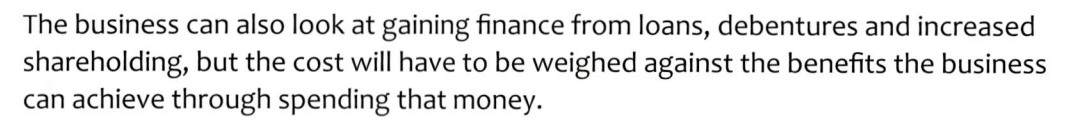

The business can also look at gaining finance from loans, debentures and increased shareholding, but the cost will have to be weighed against the benefits the business can achieve through spending that money.

Things to consider:

- Finance may be restricted which might mean the organisation cannot afford to implement decisions.
- The business may not be in a position to raise finance externally, e.g. loans.
- Lack of finance can affect the organisation because if there is no money to expand or buy new resources, it will limit the success of the business.

Staffing

The quality and quantity of employees that are available will have to be considered when making decisions that change what the business is currently doing. This includes all the employees and the managers.

Are the current employees capable of taking on new tasks? Are the managers capable of picking the right options for change? If the answer is no, then the business will be restricted in what it can achieve without bringing in new employees. However, the new employees that it needs may not be available, or the business may not be able to afford them.

Things to consider:

- Staff may be resistant to change, meaning decision making is difficult.
- Managers may not have the appropriate skills or initiative to make the best decisions.
- Managers may be unable to cope with complex decisions.
- The quality of information available to managers may be insufficient to allow them to make good decisions.
- The level of risk managers are willing/expected to take.
- The number of staff available.
- Staff skills to implement change – are they adequate?
- Employees can affect the organisation if they are not motivated. Their work could be poor, they may be more likely to take time off or they may take less care in the job they are doing.

Technology

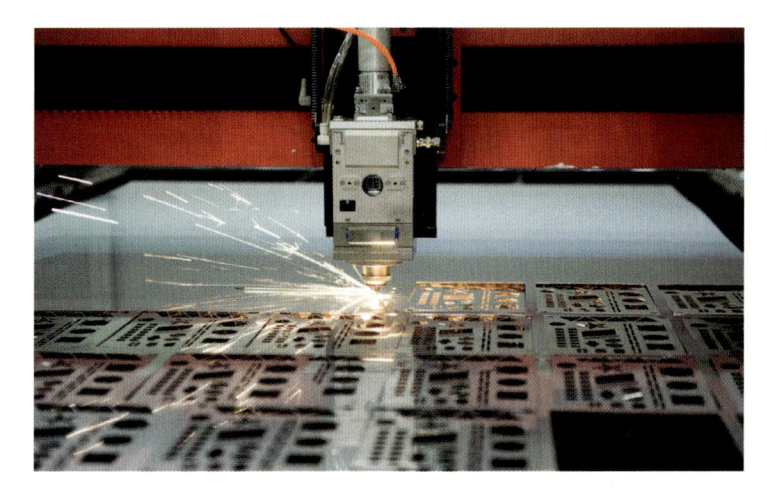

Most businesses will see technology as a way of increasing profitability and the success of the organisation. The availability of that technology, whether or not it is affordable, and whether staff are available to operate it will restrict what can be achieved.

It may be that the technology will conflict with the organisation's corporate culture. For example, if the business sees one-to-one contact with the customer as essential, then introducing web support may reduce the personal interaction with the customer.

Things to consider:

- Decisions may be constrained by the business's lack of technology and may mean that new technology needs to be purchased or decisions shelved.
- The technology currently available may not be sufficient for what the managers want to achieve.

Revision questions

1 Discuss the importance of corporate culture for an organisation.
2 Describe internal factors that can impact on an organisation's objectives.

1.7 Stakeholders

Stakeholders have an interest in or an influence on the business. To simply ignore them would lead to the failure of the business and make it unable to achieve any objectives.

It is part of the manager's job to try to ensure that all stakeholders are satisfied with the way the business operates. The problem is that their expectations can often conflict and the manager has to balance their competing needs.

It should be remembered that each stakeholder will also have an interest or 'stake' in the success of the business, and it is to their advantage that they try to avoid conflict wherever possible.

The stakeholders you need to be aware of include:

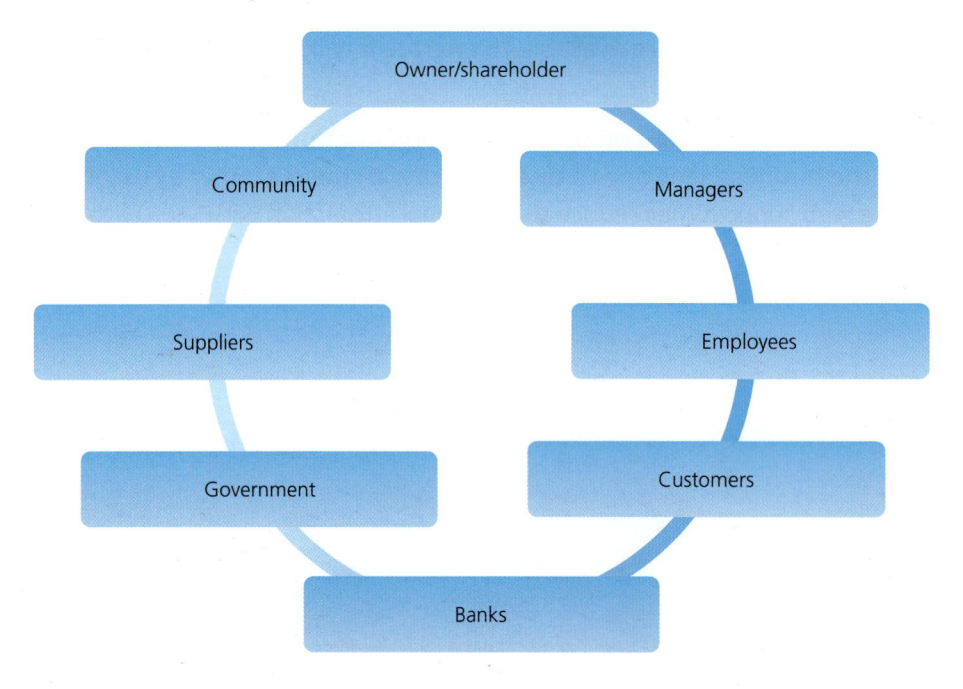

- Owner/shareholder
- Managers
- Employees
- Customers
- Banks
- Government
- Suppliers
- Community

1.7 STAKEHOLDERS

Their influence is as follows:

Owner/shareholder	can purchase more shares or sell them; can vote at the AGM
Managers	make decisions on future plans of the organisation
Employees	can affect the quality of a product or service by working hard or not; can take industrial action
Customers	buy the product or service, or not, if they are unhappy
Banks	can provide or not provide finance
Government	can alter legislation which affects the business
Suppliers	can alter the price of supplies; can fail to deliver
Community	can petition the organisation to make a change to its environmental policies

Report
Prepare a report showing how stakeholders could affect a business's success.

Stakeholders' conflict of interest

At Higher level we are more interested in the conflict of interest that can arise between the stakeholders and their interdependence or how they have to rely on each other to be successful.

Conflict

Stakeholder	Interest	Stakeholder	Interest
Shareholders	higher profits	Employees	higher wages
Shareholders	reduced costs	Employees	no redundancies
Shareholders	higher dividends	Managers	new investment
Managers	flexible working	Employees	retained conditions of employment
Managers	reduced costs	Suppliers	price increase
Managers	maintenance of cash flow	Suppliers	prompt payment
Government	reduced pollution	Managers	reduced costs
Government	increased employment	Managers	factory closure
Government	increased exports	Managers	low risk investment
Banks	higher interest rates	Managers	lower borrowing costs
Customer	reduced prices	Managers	higher profits
Customer	high quality	Managers	reduced costs

In each case it is difficult for both groups of stakeholders to achieve their goal. For example, higher profits for shareholders may mean no pay rise for the employees. Employees want a high wage for the work they do, but the business owner might want to keep wage costs at a minimum. Customers want value for money and lower prices while the owner might want to charge as high a price as possible to gain more profit.

> **Report**
> Prepare a report to show how stakeholder conflict might be avoided.

Interdependence of stakeholders

As we have seen, each stakeholder also has an interest in the success of the business. They will all have to be satisfied that they are getting a 'good deal' from the business continuing to operate.

If one stakeholder feels unhappy enough to take action then it can lead to the failure of the business, so agreement is necessary.

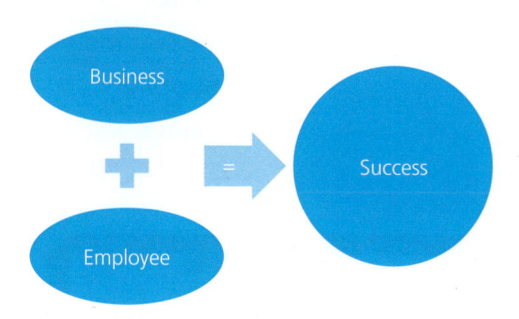

Examples of stakeholder interdependence include:

- Employees need the business to provide jobs/business needs employees to do the work.
- Customers need the business to provide goods and services/business needs customers to make sales.
- Suppliers need business to keep making purchases/business needs suppliers to keep supplying.
- Government needs business to provide jobs and pay tax/business needs the government to ensure it can continue trading.

Revision questions

1. Describe possible conflicts of interest between management and shareholders.
2. Discuss the role of stakeholders in the business achieving its objectives.
3. Discuss the interdependence of a business and its suppliers.

1.8 Structures

Flat structure

In a flat structure there are fewer levels of management and a short chain of command. Managers tend to have a wider span of control – they are directly responsible for more employees.

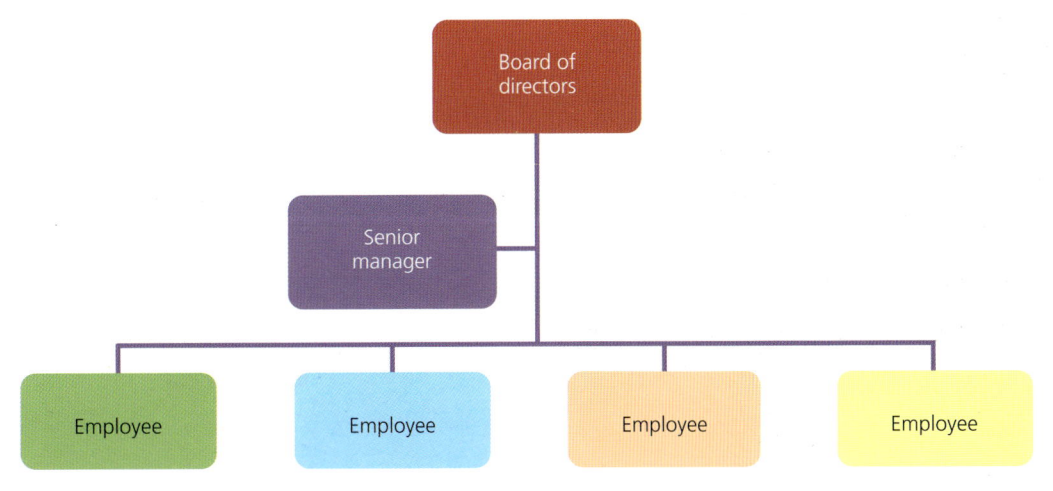

Flat structure

Advantages of a flat structure
- It is much quicker for information to flow up and down the organisation.
- Gathering information and consulting staff takes less time, and so some decisions can be made more quickly.
- The business is more able to respond quickly to changes in the market.
- Customers' needs are quickly identified and dealt with.

Disadvantages of a flat structure
- The removal of management or supervision levels means that there is less control throughout the organisation.
- Mistakes are easier to make and harder to identify.

SECTION 1 UNDERSTANDING BUSINESS

Hierarchical (tall) structure

In this structure there are many layers of management within the business. There is a long chain of command from the top to the bottom. Each manager has a narrow span of control. Information and decisions have to go through each level. This type of structure is useful where there has to be tight control over operations, such as the military and hospitals, where mistakes could lead to loss of life.

Research task

Carry out research to find out whether your school/college has a tall or flat structure.

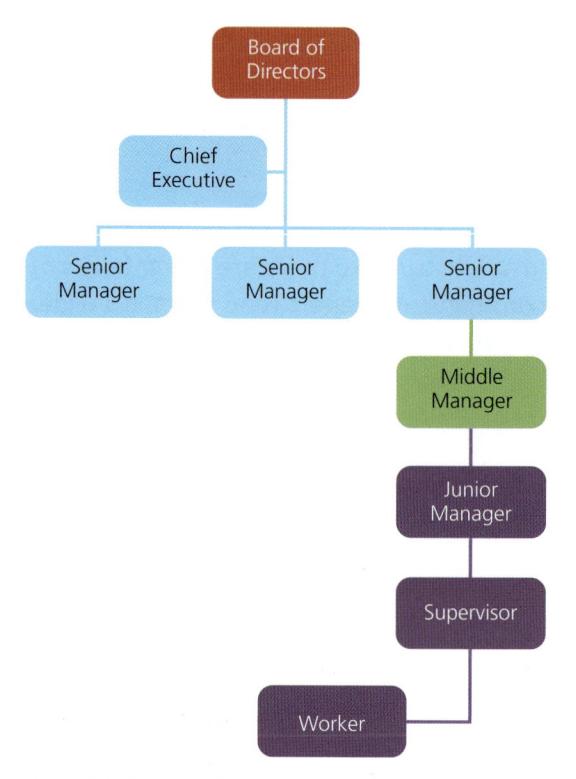

Hierarchical structure

Advantages of hierarchical structure

- There is a great deal of control and supervision.
- There are clearly defined roles, and also clearly defined procedures for carrying out those roles.
- Each member of staff will have someone who will supervise their work.
- Staff will become expert in the performance of their roles.

Disadvantages of hierarchical structure

- Decisions that require information from the various levels can take a long time to be made.
- Communication can be slow.
- Because of this, staff can often find it difficult to respond to the customer's request speedily.
- Inability to change quickly also makes the business vulnerable to changes in the market in which it operates.

Entrepreneurial structure

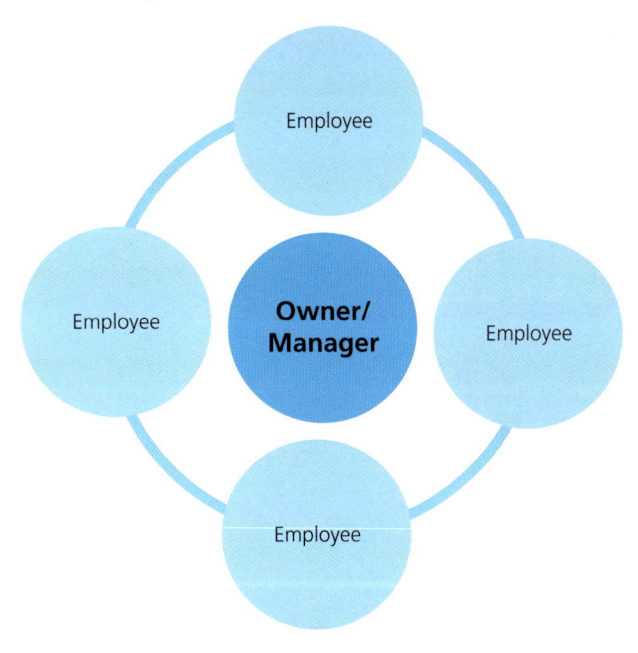

Entrepreneurial structure

In an entrepreneurial structure there are only one or two main decision makers. This structure is normally used in small businesses but also in newspaper editing and money markets. The business relies wholly on the expertise of the decision maker.

Advantages of an entrepreneurial structure
- Decisions are made quickly.
- Decisions are made for the benefit of the organisation.
- Decision makers are very experienced.
- Staff know who they are accountable to.

Disadvantages of an entrepreneurial structure
- If the decision maker is unavailable, then the decisions can't be made.
- The stresses involved mean that the decision makers can only work effectively for a short period of time.
- It places a very heavy workload on these few individuals.
- It does not allow for initiative from staff.
- Staff can become demotivated as they are not included in the decision making.
- It is difficult to use in a large business.

Matrix structure

Matrix structure

Matrix structures are used when the business is involved in a number of large projects, such as a construction firm that may build bridges, new schools, hospitals, etc., or where the business has a few large customers, such as suppliers to the oil industry. Both types of business have reasonably long-term contracts with their customers to produce goods or services.

Teams are formed with staff from all, or most, of the functional departments. Each member of the team will have their own specialist skills, and will be responsible for their own particular expertise.

The teams can be created and disbanded as required.

Advantages of a matrix structure
- Teams of different specialists provide a range of skills that can increase innovation.
- There will be an opportunity to become involved in areas out of their normal expertise.
- The matrix structure allows for the possibility for individuals to have more freedom to use their talents effectively.
- Complex problems can be solved effectively.
- There is no need to fund the structure permanently.
- Employees can learn new skills and gain experience from working in diverse teams.
- Employees can be motivated and empowered.
- Relationships between peers can develop from different functional areas.

Disadvantages of a matrix structure
- The main drawback of the matrix structure is that employees will, in effect, have two managers to report to, their functional manager and the matrix.
- There can be confusion and conflict between the functional department and the project.
- Matrix structures can be costly to set up and manage.

Centralised structure

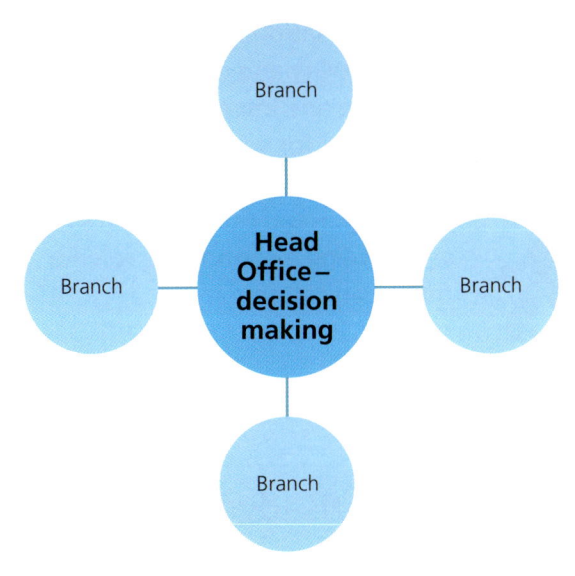

Centralised structure

Like an entrepreneurial structure, a centralised structure relies heavily on a number of key individuals who make most of the decisions within the organisation. There may be more of them, but complete control of the organisation is held by these key members.

Normally, they will be the senior managers or directors of the business, but they could also be the owners.

Hierarchical structures are often highly centralised in terms of decision making, and they share many of the same advantages.

Advantages of a centralised structure

- A standard method of operation is developed across the whole business.
- Economies of scale can be achieved through centralised purchasing.
- All decisions are made for the benefit of the whole organisation.
- It is easier to promote a corporate culture/image.
- Decisions are made by experienced senior managers.
- Leadership should be strong.
- All control of the organisation is held by key members of the organisation.

Disadvantages of a centralised structure

- There is a heavy reliance on key decision makers.
- It stifles the creativity of the staff.
- It is difficult for decision makers to relate to local conditions or markets because they are removed from the day-to-day operations of the business.
- Staff may become demotivated through lack of decision-making powers.
- It does not allow for staff to be easily prepared for promotion.

Decentralised structure

Decentralisation gives responsibility and decision making to middle and lower managers. This allows for some decisions to be taken locally, delegating authority. Head office is seen more as providing a supporting role for the organisation.

Decentralised structure

Advantages of a decentralised structure

- Decision making can be quicker as there is no need to refer matters up the chain of command.
- It allows the organisation to be more responsive to changes in the market or environment in which it operates.
- The people making the decisions are much closer to their customers and have a far better knowledge of their customers' needs.
- Delegation and empowerment of staff allow them to develop their professional skills and give them greater opportunities to display their own abilities.
- Being trusted to make decisions can make the staff feel more wanted and appreciated, which in turn increases their motivation.
- Staff can be prepared for promotion.
- It allows senior managers to focus on key decisions.

Disadvantages of a decentralised structure

- Some overall control of the business will be lost.
- Inexperienced managers can make decisions that harm the whole business.
- Greater supervision may be required.
- Lower and middle managers may need additional training.
- Higher salaries may have to be paid.

Report
Prepare a report to compare centralised and decentralised structures.

De-layering

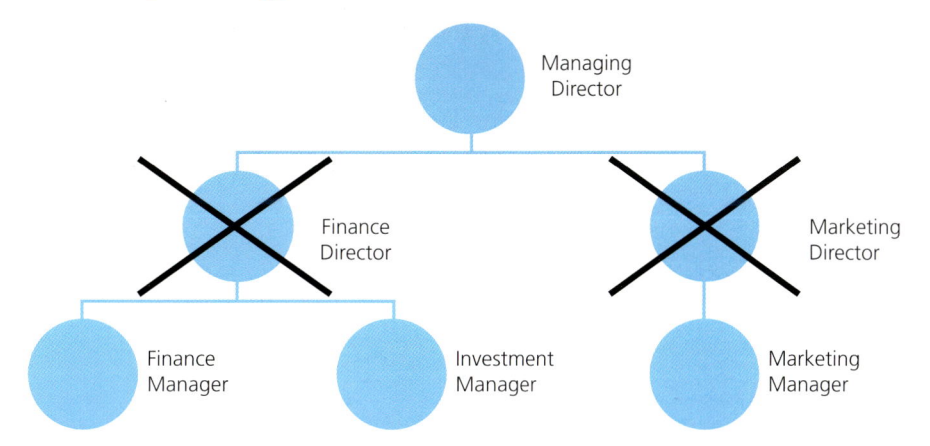

```
                    Managing
                    Director
         ┌─────────────┴─────────────┐
      Finance                     Marketing
      Director (X)                Director (X)
     ┌────┴────┐                      │
  Finance   Investment            Marketing
  Manager   Manager               Manager
```

De-layering is the removal of levels of management or supervision from the organisation. Changing from a tall structure to a flat structure would involve the removal of layers of management from the hierarchy.

As we have already seen, additional levels of management slow down the communication process and consequently the business's ability to respond to changes in the market.

One of the main problems with changing the structure is the resistance to change among the staff employed by the organisation. Any change has to be managed properly. This would include planning within a realistic timescale; keeping staff informed and updated about the changes, including reasons for the change; and monitoring the impact of changes as they take place, with adjustments as necessary.

> ! It is important to remember only managers/supervisors lose their jobs with de-layering.

The consequences of de-layering

- Each manager has a wider span of control.
- It can lead to better communication.
- Decision making can be quicker, allowing the organisation to respond better to changes in the markets.
- It empowers staff as they will have increased responsibility.
- It may improve productivity.
- Employees are more motivated as they are empowered to make decisions.
- It allows greater opportunity for delegation.
- It reduces the cost of salaries for the organisation.
- It prepares staff for promotion as they have more decision-making powers; however, it also reduces the opportunities for promotion.

Span of control

The span of control is the number of people any manager or supervisor has working directly for him or her.

In the example below we can see the production line supervisor has a span of control of three. There are three production assistants who report directly to the production line supervisor.

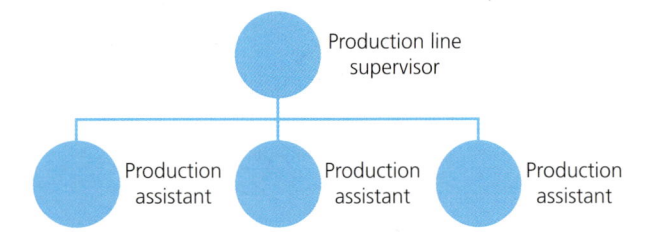

```
                Production line
                  supervisor
        ┌──────────────┼──────────────┐
   Production      Production      Production
   assistant       assistant       assistant
```

The size of the span of control is important because the bigger the span, the less supervision or control can take place. Flat organisations tend to have a wide span of control for managers. Highly centralised organisations tend to have small spans of control.

Where the tasks that are being worked upon are very important or require a great deal of technical understanding, then the span would be quite small.

The individual manager or supervisor will have their own level of interpersonal and leadership skills. Where these are high, the span of control can be high, as staff will be highly motivated to work without supervision. Where the level of skill of the manager is low, then the span of control should be low.

The span of control is also dependent on the skills and abilities of staff. Where staff are skilled and highly motivated they need less supervision, so the span of control can be high. Where there is a lack of skilled motivated workers then supervision will need to be a lot higher, so the span of control will be lower.

Advantages of a wide span of control

- It allows for delegation to staff as they should be reasonably skilled.
- It can be motivational to managers as can be seen as having greater power.
- Staff are empowered to make their own decisions and to carry out their own tasks without interference by managers.
- Fewer managers are required and wages are saved.
- There are fewer levels of communication for decisions to pass through.
- Quality of staff will be improved.

Disadvantages of a wide span of control

- Managers' time to deal with staff problems will be at a premium.
- It can place managers under stress.
- It can mean workers rarely have time to meet with their line manager to discuss ideas.
- Subordinates may resent having to make all the decisions.
- Managers will have less time for planning.
- It can result in poor decisions.

Downsizing

Downsizing involves reducing the operating costs of the organisation by looking for what it does not need to spend money on. This could include:

- reducing the scale of operations to meet actual market demand
- removing excess capacity within the organisation
- consolidating complementary operations under one function
- reducing the resources of the organisation following increases in productivity
- focusing only on core operations.

Advantages of downsizing
- Reduces the costs for the organisation, making it more efficient and competitive.
- The remaining staff will feel that their importance has been recognised.
- The remaining staff may also find that they have far greater power than before.
- Increases shareholders' confidence.

Disadvantages of downsizing
- Redundancy costs.
- Loss of knowledgeable and experienced staff.
- Staff uncertainty about the security of their jobs.
- Possible bad publicity.

Factors affecting structure

Which structure is best for any business will depend on a number of different factors as shown in the table below.

Size	As a business grows, it becomes harder to control all the staff within the organisation. A more formal structure is needed for large businesses.
Technology	The introduction of new technology can change the structure of a business. It will be easier to communicate over larger distances.
Product	Having a small number of large customers means a flat structure or a matrix structure.
Market	If the market is small and local then the organisation will be small, with an entrepreneurial structure.
Staff knowledge and skills	If staff are highly skilled, a less formal structure can exist.
Finance available	Additional managers cost money.

Groupings

Businesses have to decide how they should be organised. There is no single way that suits all businesses as every business is different, and so is the way they are organised.

There are some basic ways in which they group their activities. Most businesses will use one, or more likely a mix, of these groupings. This mix is called a hybrid structure.

Functional grouping

The organisation is split into departments which represent the main functional areas of the business. These would typically be:

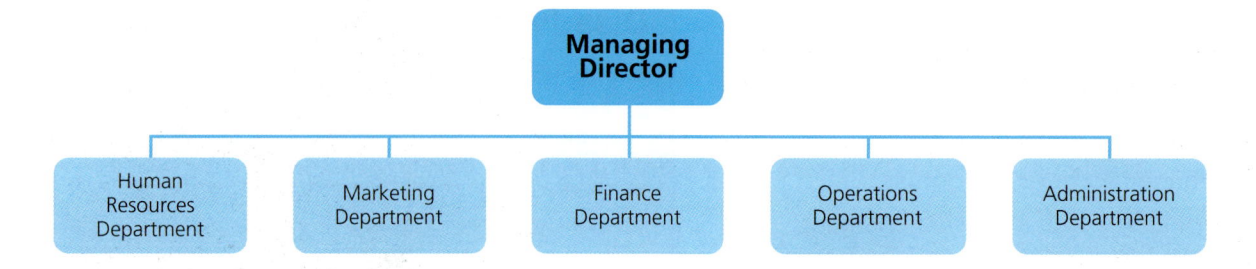

```
                    Managing Director
        ┌───────┬───────┬───────┬───────┐
     Human    Marketing Finance Operations Administration
   Resources  Department Department Department Department
   Department
```

Advantages of functional grouping

- The resources of the organisation or the business will be better used.
- Staff will become experts in their own field.
- Allows for specialisation in each functional area.
- Career paths are created within the departments.
- Communication and co-operation within the department are excellent.
- Teamworking improves – staff can seek support from colleagues if required.
- Decision making is better.
- There is a clear structure to the organisation.
- Clear lines of authority exist.
- Staff know who to turn to if they need specific expertise.

Disadvantages of functional grouping

- Staff loyalty is to the department rather than the organisation.
- Communication barriers between departments can exist.
- Some decisions take a long time to be made.
- Response to the changes in the business environment is slow.
- Some problems cannot be solved by a single department.

Product/service grouping

Here the organisation's activities are grouped around the different products or services that it provides.

Each product or service requires specialist knowledge and expertise so it makes sense to gather all staff with this knowledge and skill in one grouping, or division.

The divisions will be able to make most of their own decisions, with the organisation decentralised.

They will all have their own functional staff, and these may well be formed into smaller departments.

Example

Virgin organises its business group around the broad areas shown below:

- Travel (air, holidays, trains, galactic, limobike and limousines)
- Lifestyle (active, books, games, wines, balloon flights, drinks, spa)
- Media and mobile (mobile, media, Virgin 1, connect)
- Music (megastore, radio international, festivals)
- Money (banking, savings, insurance).

Advantages of product/service grouping

- Each division will be a self-contained unit.
- Each member of staff in that division will have knowledge about that specific product. Expertise is developed within each specialised division.
- It is easier to see which areas or products of the organisation are doing well and which are having problems.
- This grouping allows for a quicker response to external changes such as changes in customer requirements.

Disadvantages of product/service grouping

- Because each division requires its own support staff (administration, finance, human resources, etc.) there is bound to be duplication of resources, tasks and personnel.
- Divisions may find themselves competing against each other.
- It is difficult to share research and development or equipment across divisions.

Customer grouping

Where the individual needs of different customers are important, then businesses will organise in such a way that they have close contact with their customers.

Many service industries such as insurance and other financial services find that each customer has their own set of needs.

Barclays bank groups its business around three main types of customer as shown below.

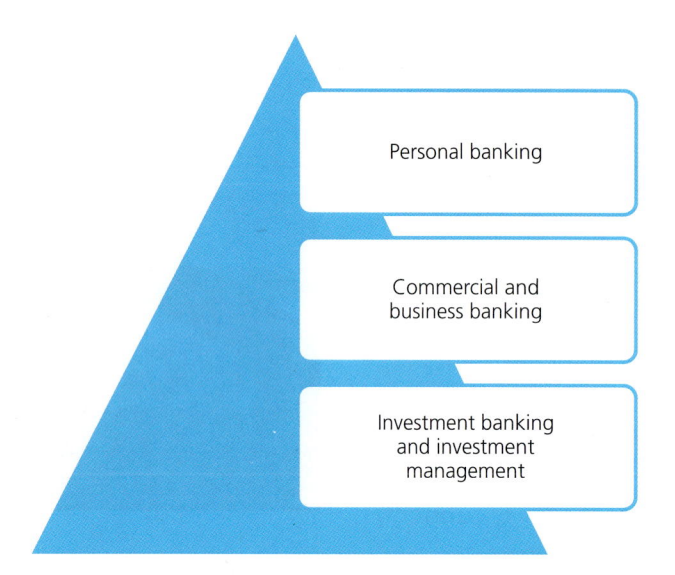

- Personal banking
- Commercial and business banking
- Investment banking and investment management

Advantages of customer grouping
- Because the customer's needs are identified as a priority, customer loyalty can be built up.
- It allows for services to be tailored to each group of customers or a specific customer.
- The customer gets the feeling of receiving a personal service even when dealing with large firms.
- The organisation can respond much faster to the customer's needs.

Disadvantages of customer grouping
- Administration of such a grouping can be time-consuming as individual customer needs take time and effort to meet.
- There can be large staffing costs with this type of grouping.
- The feeling of personal service can be lost if staff change positions.
- There will be duplication of personnel and resources.
- Competition between groups can exist.

Report
Prepare a report to show the advantages and disadvantages of using a customer grouping.

Place/territory/geographic grouping

Businesses whose customers are spread over a wide area of a country, or over many countries, often find it better to organise themselves around the place where their products are delivered. The other main reason for organising this way is the location of raw materials.

This type of organisation allows the business to appoint regional managers who can then better control the activities in their area, and take account of different market conditions in different areas in the country.

Unilever groups its business into three areas:

- Americas
- Asia Africa
- Europe.

Advantages of place grouping
- Local offices with local knowledge can cater for local clients' needs.
- Local offices can overcome problems caused by different countries having language and cultural differences.
- Because the local office is responsible for that area, it can be held accountable for success/failure in that area.
- Customer loyalty can be built up through a local, personal service.
- The local office is more responsive to changes in customer needs.

Disadvantages of place grouping
- Administration can be time-consuming.
- If staff members change, continuity of personal contact is lost.
- There will be duplication of personnel and resources.
- It is expensive with regard to administration and staffing costs.

Research task

Carry out a search to find out how McDonald's groups its business.

Technology grouping

Here activities are grouped around the technological requirements of the product, mostly in its manufacture or in the process of delivery to the customer.

In the manufacturing industry there are often distinct processes or stages that a product has to pass through on its way to completion.

Each of these stages requires different technical input, and it may make sense for the manufacturer to organise its business around each of these technical processes.

There is no need for staff to be involved in learning other processes, and so the work that they do can be kept as simple as possible, making it easier to train new staff and adapt to changes.

Advantages of technology grouping
- The degree of specialisation in the production process can be increased.
- Suitable for large organisations with different production processes.
- Problems with the technology can be easily identified.
- It can reduce wastage and costs.

Disadvantages of technology grouping
- There is a high degree of specialised training of the staff required.
- Duplication of resources occurs.
- These industries tend to be very capital intensive, which is expensive.
- It is only an option for very large organisations that have different products with similar production processes.

Revision questions

1. Discuss the benefits and disadvantages of a flat structure for a multinational organisation.
2. Discuss the use of matrix structures in a business.
3. Compare the features of hierarchical and flat structures.
4. Describe the use of customer grouping within an organisation.
5. Compare the use of geographical grouping with product grouping.

1.9 Decision making

Types of decisions

There are three main types of decisions in business:

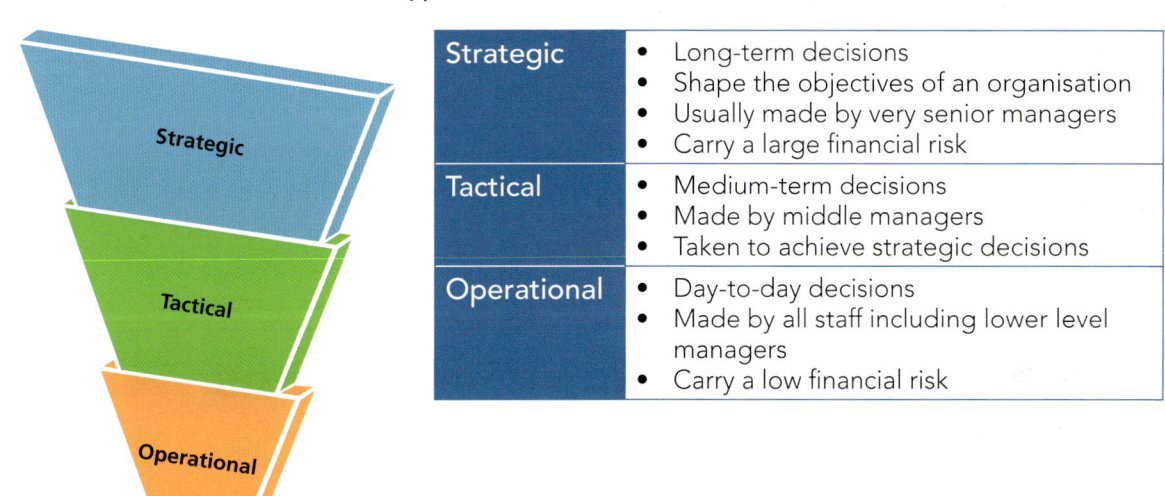

Strategic	• Long-term decisions • Shape the objectives of an organisation • Usually made by very senior managers • Carry a large financial risk
Tactical	• Medium-term decisions • Made by middle managers • Taken to achieve strategic decisions
Operational	• Day-to-day decisions • Made by all staff including lower level managers • Carry a low financial risk

Strategic decisions

These don't go into great detail about how the objectives will be achieved. They involve a large number of variables about the future of the organisation and as such they are non-routine decisions. Major policy statements represent strategic decisions.

Examples of strategic decisions
- What products the firm will produce in the future.
- To increase market share by ten per cent within five years.
- To maximise sales.
- To have 100 per cent customer satisfaction.

Tactical decisions

These are generally medium-term decisions about how the strategic decisions are going to be achieved, but are likely to have long-term consequences for the organisation. They are often made by middle managers within the organisation in finance, operations, human resources and marketing.

They are based on achieving the goals or the aims of the organisation.

They go into detail about what resources will be needed and how these will be used to achieve the aims. They will be subject to change as political, economic, social, competitive and technology factors change.

Examples of tactical decisions

- To increase the number of staff employed.
- To rename the business.
- To issue more shares on the stock market to fund a new factory.
- To merge with a competitor.
- To increase the selling price.
- To reduce costs.

Operational decisions

These are the day-to-day routine decisions that can be made by all levels of management, but mostly by lower level managers and supervisors. They are made in response to relatively minor but sometimes important problems that arise each day or week, so are routine and repetitive.

Examples of operational decisions

- Arranging work rotas.
- Dealing with customer complaints.
- Ordering materials from suppliers.

Quality decisions

There are a number of steps managers should take to ensure that the decision taken is the correct one for the organisation as shown below.

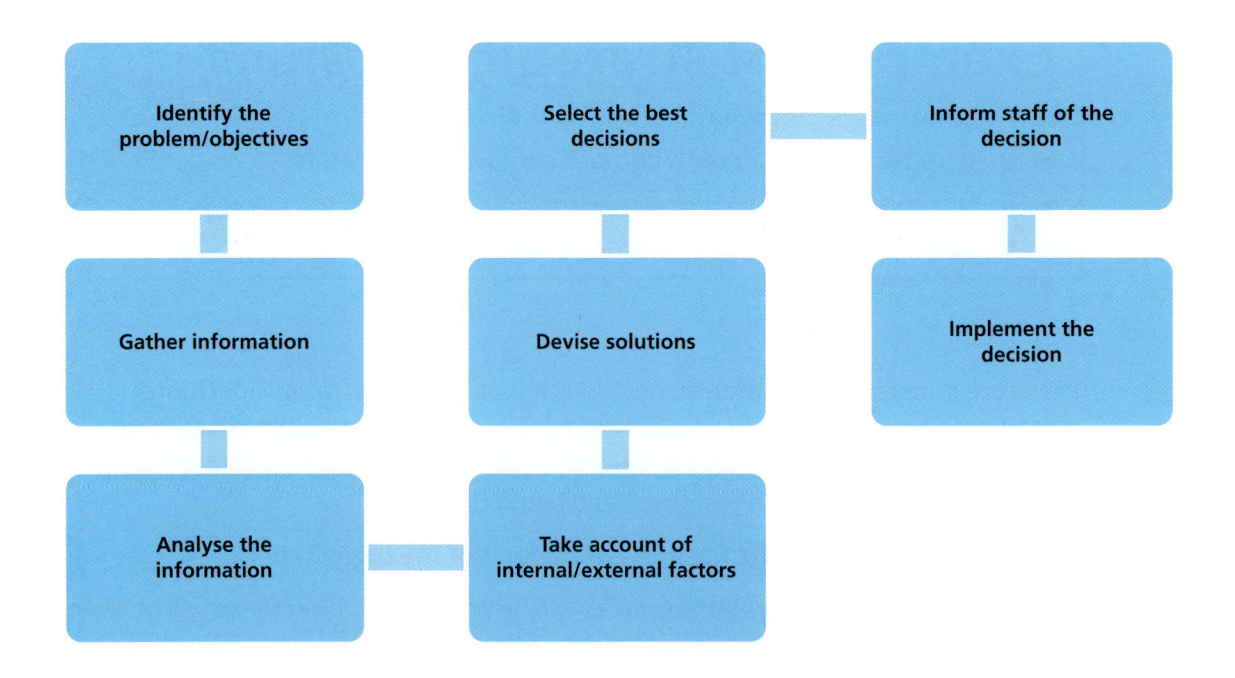

- Identify the problem/objectives
- Gather information
- Analyse the information
- Take account of internal/external factors
- Devise solutions
- Select the best decisions
- Inform staff of the decision
- Implement the decision

Quality decisions are made by experienced managers who are willing to make decisions when necessary, including taking risks where justified. They can only base their decisions around the finance, staffing and technology they have available.

There are a number of advantages and disadvantages in using this process as shown below.

Advantages of quality decisions
- Helps to ensure the organisation's objectives are met.
- Motivates staff, as seen as successful.
- Leads to better reputation with consumers.
- Helps to retain and attract investment.

To achieve quality decisions, a business must consider:
- the need to take account of all internal and external factors
- the quality of information available from functional areas.

Disadvantages of quality decisions
- It can be difficult to choose from many alternative solutions.
- Creativity and initiative can be stifled, meaning creative opportunities may be lost.
- It is time-consuming to follow the process and this may cause delays in decision making.
- The business may be too slow to respond to any changes in the market.

Technology and decision making

Continued developments in computer hardware and software have allowed them to become increasingly sophisticated. This will allow the decision-making process to be completed more quickly and efficiently, as the information available can then be analysed more quickly and efficiently.

Records held on databases can be accessed, sorted and processed into a structure that helps decision making. Spreadsheets can run 'what if' analyses to compare the outcomes of different courses of action. Management decision-making software can also help identify the best solution from a number of alternatives. The internet can provide huge amounts of up-to-date information on any number of topics, including market information such as trends and competitors' products.

All this means that decisions can be made more accurately than before, and with increased speed. The only major drawback, apart from the costs involved, is information overload, with many managers finding that there is too much information being received, and time will have to be spent selecting the information that is relevant.

SWOT analysis

Strengths	Weaknesses
Opportunities	Threats

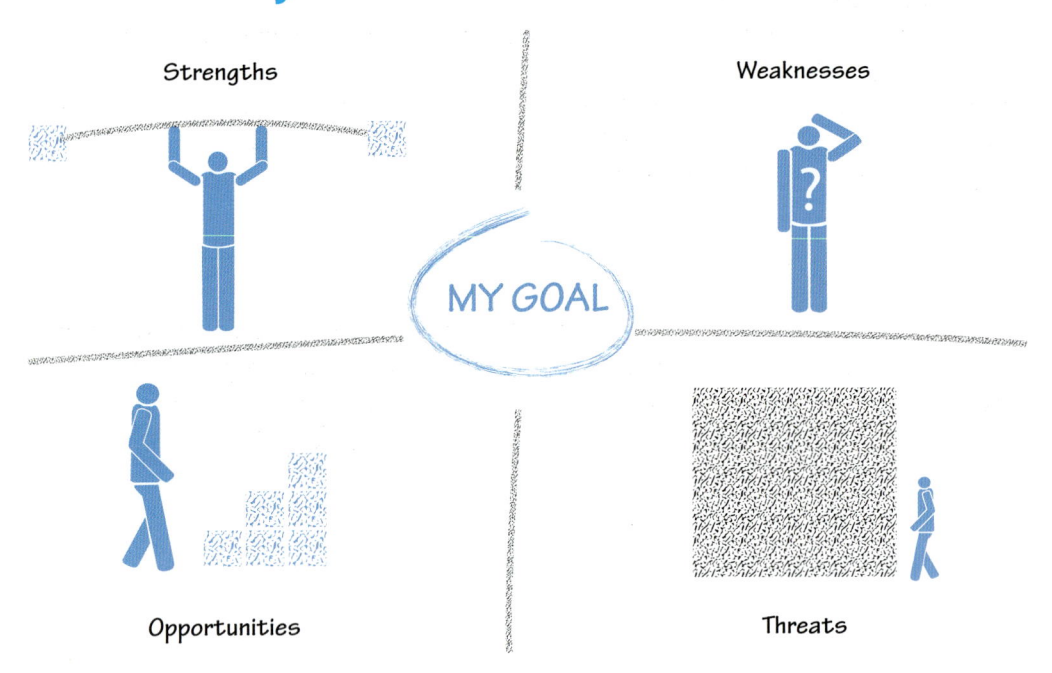

MY GOAL

One tool that management can use to help with decision making is SWOT analysis.

It is used to evaluate where the organisation is now and where it should be in the future.

SWOT analysis helps with planning, deciding the way forward for the organisation and looking at strategies that could be used.

It looks at all internal and external factors. Internal factors are the resources within the organisation. External factors are those things within the organisation's environment that are happening now or are likely to happen in the future.

Strengths and weaknesses are *internal factors*. Opportunities and threats are *external influences*.

Strengths

Weaknesses

Opportunities

Threats

SWOT analysis is a tool that can be used effectively for any decision making. Many businesses will have a running SWOT analysis that is kept up to date and will regularly refer to it, perhaps once a week, to see if they need to take action. By doing this, the business can avoid rash decisions as most of the information needed is already there.

- SWOT analysis should not be seen as a one-off exercise.
- It should be part of the continuing process of evaluating how the organisation is doing now and what it should be doing in the future.
- It analyses the internal areas of an organisation to indicate where it is performing well.

- It analyses the internal areas of an organisation to indicate where it is weak and needs to improve.
- It examines external areas that could be used to improve performance or profitability in the future.
- It examines possible threats that can exist externally, which means an organisation is ready for any eventuality.
- It gives more/better information and so results in better decisions.

Role of a manager

You could say the manager's job is to manage, but that doesn't really describe the different tasks that managers have to undertake as part of their responsibilities. Henry Fayol identified five key areas in the role of a manager: plan, organise, control, command, co-ordinate. However, we can add others as shown below.

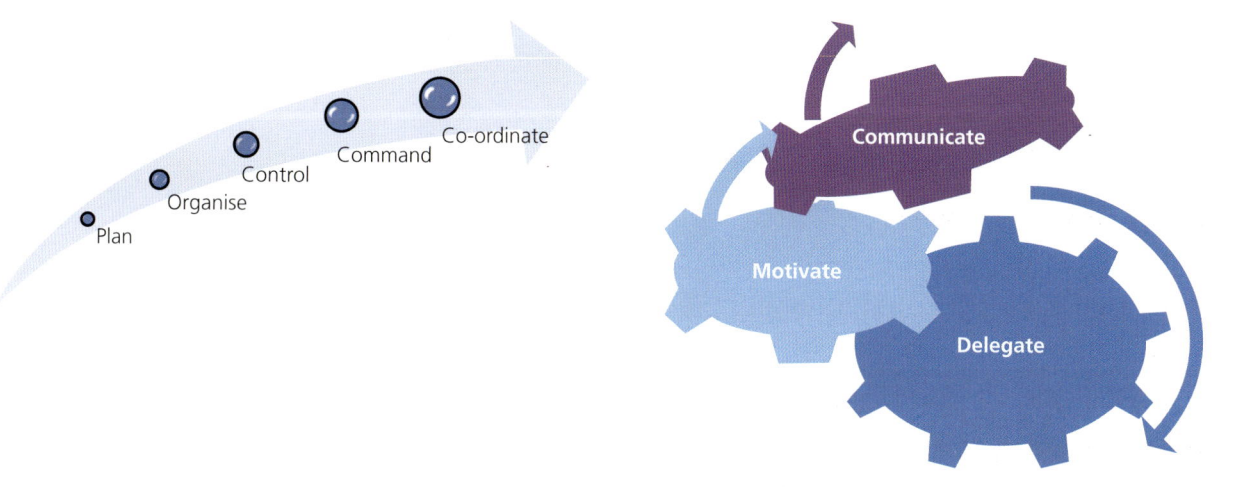

Plan	Looking ahead, seeing potential opportunities or problems and devising solutions, setting targets and setting aims and strategies.
Organise	Arranging the resources of the organisation to be there when people need them and acquiring additional resources if required.
Command	Issuing instructions, motivating staff and displaying leadership.
Communicate	Ensuring all staff are informed of decisions and reasons for them.
Co-ordinate	Making sure everyone is working towards the same goals, that all the work being done fits together and people are not duplicating work or working against each other.
Control	Looking at what is being done, checking it against what was expected and making any necessary adjustments. This is the monitoring and evaluating role of management.
Delegate	Giving subordinates the authority to carry out tasks. This helps with motivation and reduces the manager's workload. The overall responsibility will still lie with the manager who delegated the authority.
Motivate	Encouraging workers by helping them to enjoy their tasks through teamworking, participation in decision making and by giving them some responsibility.

Evaluating and measuring decisions

An important part of decision making is evaluating how well your decision worked.

- Were the objectives of the decision met?
- What happened that was not expected?

If things did not go to plan, then some changes may be needed. All decisions may not be successful, for several reasons. They could be due to internal factors such as poor employee relations, or external factors such as changes in the economy. It is important that managers evaluate their decisions and adjust if necessary.

Quality decision making depends on checking at all stages, so any necessary changes can be made and the organisation can best meet its objectives.

To find out how effective the decision was you could:

- see if profits have increased
- see if sales have increased
- survey customers
- survey employees
- see if the share price has increased.

Research task

Carry out a search to find out how managers in your school or college help achieve success.

Revision questions

1. Compare the different types of decisions made in a business.
2. Describe factors that will impact on the quality of a decision.
3. Explain the role of a manager within an organisation in helping achieve its objectives.
4. Describe the use of SWOT analysis.

Section Assessment: Understanding Business

This segment aims to test your knowledge of the preceding section with exam-standard questions. It is recommended that you answer the questions based on the standard timing for the external examination, which allows around two minutes per mark. There is a selection of questions that you might expect to find in both Section 1 and Section 2 of the question paper.

Section 1 is worth 30 marks in total and the allocation of each question can range from 1–8 marks. Section 2 has four questions of 15 marks each, containing individual questions in the range of 1–8 marks. The difference with Section 2 is that it specialises in individual topics, so there could be a 15-mark question on Understanding Business, as exemplified below. Remember that Section 2 questions tend to dig a little deeper into your knowledge of particular areas of the course.

Once you have attempted these questions, it would be a good idea to ask your teacher to mark them or go over appropriate responses to them.

Section 1 questions

		Marks
1	Explain the benefits of having a strong corporate culture for an organisation and its employees.	4
2	Explain the advantages of internal (organic) growth for an organisation.	4
3	Discuss the use of functional grouping.	3
4	Distinguish between strategic and tactical decisions.	3
5	Describe possible conflicts that may arise between the stakeholders of an organisation.	4
6	Discuss the benefits of de-layering.	4
7	Compare tall structures with flat structures.	3
8	Describe the impact of internal factors on an organisation.	3
9	Describe the role of the manager.	5
10	Explain the role of business in society.	2

Section 2 questions

			Marks
11	a	Describe the benefits for a business in diversifying its product range as a method of growth.	4
	b	Discuss methods of external growth (integration).	4
	c	Describe possible disadvantages in the use of outsourcing.	3
	d	Describe the objectives of a third-sector organisation.	4
12	a	Describe the impact of economic factors on a business.	2
	b	Describe other external factors.	6
	c	Describe the purpose of a mission statement.	3
	d	Describe what is meant by 'corporate social responsibility'.	4
13	a	Explain the benefits of using a decentralised structure.	4
	b	Compare the objectives of an organisation in the public sector with those in the private sector.	4
	c	Describe how the objectives in the private sector may conflict within the organisation.	2
	d	Discuss the use of SWOT analysis as a decision-making tool.	5
14	a	Discuss the impact for a business of introducing new technology.	5
	b	Describe the benefits for a business of using a matrix structure.	3
	c	Discuss the use of a customer grouping within an organisation.	3
	d	Describe the benefits of product grouping.	4
15	a	Discuss the benefits for an organisation of becoming a multinational company.	5
	b	Describe what is meant by the term 'quaternary sector'.	2
	c	Describe the benefits of franchising for the franchisee.	5
	d	Explain what is meant by 'managerial objectives' within an organisation.	3

Section 2

Management of Marketing

Once you complete this section you will be able to:

✓ apply knowledge and understanding of how the marketing function enhances the effectiveness of large organisations

The Management of Marketing section of this book looks at how a business uses marketing to identify, anticipate and satisfy the consumers of its products. Successful marketing is essential to the success of a business. It needs to be able to identify its consumers, what they want from the product and how much they are willing to pay. A business cannot stand still and simply assume its product will continue to sell. It has to look at ways of developing its products to meet the changing needs of consumers, as well as exploring new markets to develop.

SECTION 2 MANAGEMENT OF MARKETING

Topic 2.1 Customers	You should be aware of: • the role of marketing in a business to achieve objectives • what is meant by market led and product led and the differences between them • consumer behaviour • social classifications.
Topic 2.2 Market research	You should be aware of: • the different methods of field research and their costs and benefits • the different methods of desk research and their costs and benefits • the use of sampling in market research • the use of market research information to a business.
Topic 2.3 Marketing mix	You should be aware of: • how the combination of price, product, place, promotion, people, process and physical evidence ensures a product is successful and the impact of one element another.

Topic 2.4 Product	You should be aware of:
	
	• the sales revenue and profit levels at each stage of a product's life cycle
	• using extension strategies to enhance product sales and profits
	• product portfolios:
	  • costs and benefits
	  • the Boston Matrix and its use
	• product life cycle:
	  • research and development
	  • introduction
	  • growth
	  • maturity/saturation
	  • decline.

Topic 2.5 Price	You should be aware of:
	
	• pricing strategies:
	  • cost-based (cost plus)
	  • skimming
	  • penetration
	  • price discrimination
	  • destroyer/predatory (an illegal practice)
	  • loss leaders
	  • promotional
	  • psychological
	• advantages and disadvantages of each strategy.

Topic 2.6 Place	You should be aware of:
	
	• the overall channels of distribution available to organisations:
	  • reasons for choosing different channels
	  • costs and benefits of different channels
	• the costs and benefits of using:
	  • wholesalers
	  • different types of retailers
	  • direct sales (including different methods).

SECTION 2 MANAGEMENT OF MARKETING

Topic 2.7 Promotion	You should be aware of:
	
	• into-the-pipeline promotions (offered by manufacturers to retailers), for example:
	   • point-of-sale materials
	   • sale or return
	   • dealer loaders
	   • promotional gifts
	   • staff training
	• out-of-the-pipeline promotions (offered by retailers to consumers), for example:
	   • BOGOF
	   • free trial/sample packs
	   • vouchers/money-off coupons
	   • competitions
	• public relations.

Topic 2.8 People	You should be aware of:
	
	• the way people can be used as part of an extended marketing mix when providing a service, for example:
	   • delivering customer satisfaction
	   • providing after-sales service
	   • training staff in customer service
	   • having helpful staff.

Topic 2.9 Process	You should be aware of:
	
	• the processes that can be used as part of an extended marketing mix when providing a service, for example:
	   • the process of delivering the product or service
	   • the impression left on the customer
	   • short waiting times
	   • user-friendly websites
	   • helpful information given to customers.

Topic 2.10 Physical evidence	You should be aware of:
	
	• the physical evidence that can be used as part of an extended marketing mix when providing a service, for example:
	   • the physical environment experienced by the customer
	   • the layout and design of premises
	   • the layout and design of websites
	   • ambience.

Topic 2.11 Technology	You should be aware of:
	
	• how technology can be used in marketing and the costs and benefits of using it, for example:
	   • electronic point of sale (EPOS) for market research
	   • online survey
	   • internet advertising
	   • e-commerce
	   • email
	   • databases
	   • social media
	   • desktop publishing (DTP)
	   • text alerts
	   • apps
	   • quick response (QR) codes.

2.1 Customers

Market led v. product led

Market-led approach

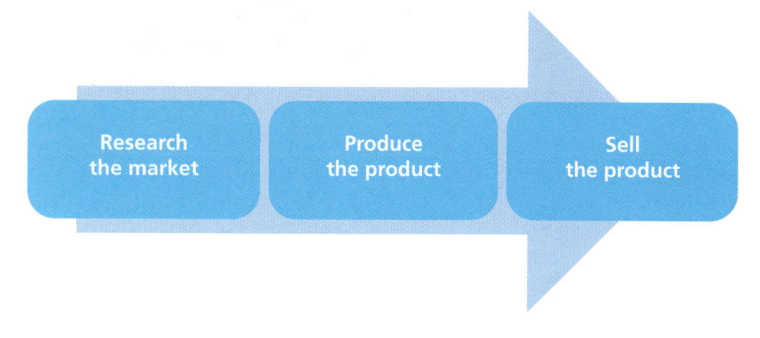

Research the market → Produce the product → Sell the product

Market-led (orientated) products are based on the business going out and finding out what consumers are looking for. They are common in highly competitive markets, and developing products based on market research is the only way to be successful in meeting customers' needs.

A business will look at possible innovations in its products and ask consumers what they think. If the feedback from market research is positive it will then decide if it can develop the product in a profitable way. It needs to make its products stand out from the competition.

- The focus is on customer wants and producing a product to satisfy them.
- A lot of market research is carried out before production starts.
- The organisation focuses on market testing.
- The product is one that consumers want or need.
- Market research is central to a market-led approach.
- A market-led approach is more able to meet and respond to consumer changes in fashion or tastes.
- Supermarkets are commonly market led.

Product-led approach

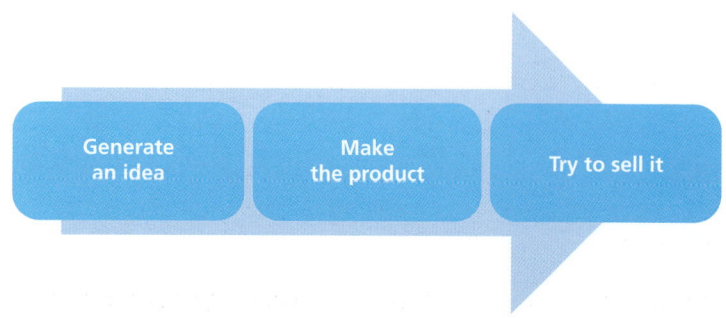

Generate an idea → Make the product → Try to sell it

A product-led approach is when an organisation produces a product first and then tries to sell it to customers. This is more risky for producers. While market-led producers are not guaranteed success, product-led organisations have no real way of knowing how successful they will be. These businesses often involve products that are highly technical, where the research is focused on the product development rather than on the market.

Many of these companies will sell their products directly to other manufacturers rather than try to sell to consumers. For example, a small medical drugs company will focus on developing a new drug, and once it shows signs of being successful they will sell the patent to a larger drugs company which will go through the process of carrying out trials and achieving approval before putting it on the market. This is because getting drugs licensed for prescription is hugely expensive.

- Very little market research is carried out with a product-led approach.
- The organisation focuses on product research and testing.
- Product-led products have little competition in comparison to market-led products.
- Drug companies are often product led.

Consumer behaviour

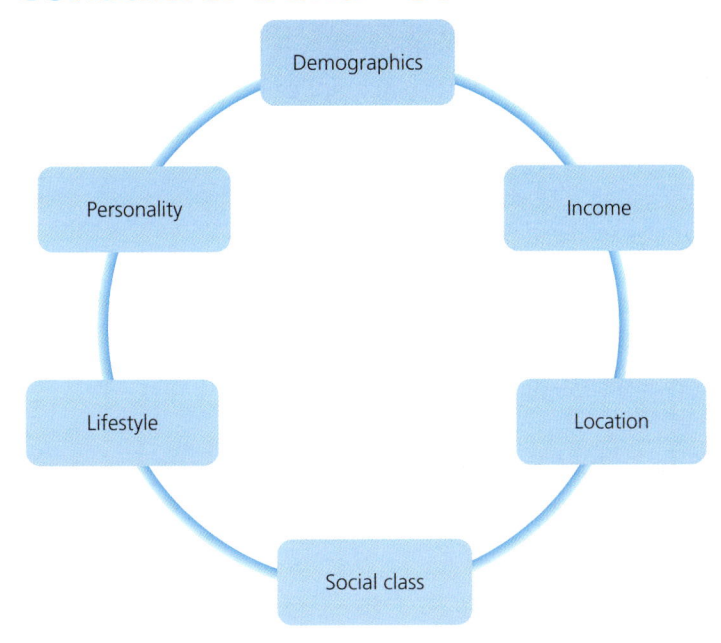

Here we will look at the factors that affect how consumers behave and how their buying preferences change with their circumstances.

You could say that it will be down to each individual's tastes, what they like and don't like, but research shows that similar groups have very similar buying preferences.

A whole area of study in marketing is focused on this, called demographics. This is the study of the structure of the population, in terms of age, gender, household income, buying patterns and lifestyle.

Using demographics allows the business to tailor products to each group's needs and helps with recognising market segments, and so achieves greater profitability and better customer service.

Some of the groupings are shown in the following table.

Household income	The more income in the household, the higher the quality and quantity of products they will buy.
Location	Consumers living in different parts of the country/world will have different needs and spending patterns for food, clothing, travel.
Social class	Consumers tend to have similar interests and tastes within broad classifications.
Lifestyle	Consumers' lifestyle affects what products they buy. For example, those who are interested in a healthy lifestyle will be much more conscious of what they eat and drink, and of exercise.
Personality	Consumers' personality will dictate what products they will be interested in buying. Extroverts are more concerned about getting themselves noticed and will opt for products that make them stand out from the crowd, such as unusual clothing.
Political	Many consumers have strong political views and this will influence their purchases.

Consumer behaviours can also be linked to the habits/decisions displayed by individuals. Therefore, organisations may attempt to acquire or research information or data sets which will help them inform their marketing and tailor it towards certain groups.

Consumer decision styles:
- Routine/habitual
- Informed
- Impulsive
- Confused
- Brand conscious
- Price/quality conscious

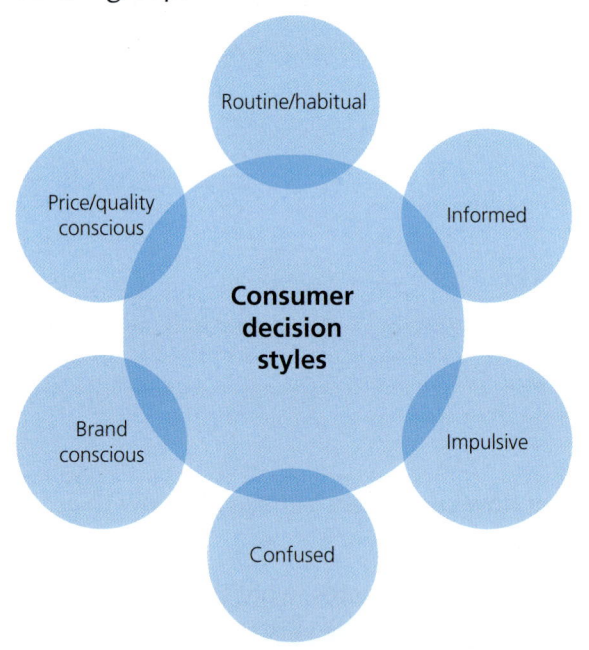

Consumer decision style	Definition
Routine/habitual	The consumer purchases a particular product simply as a result of routine/habit/always having purchased this in the past.
Informed	The consumer has made an informed and educated choice, perhaps carrying out their own research before coming to a decision on which product to purchase.

Impulsive	The consumer has acted on their feelings and without much thought as to their actual needs, the price, the quality, etc.
Confused	The consumer has purchased the product without any particular decision-making information to hand and has perhaps even purchased something that they did not intend to purchase.
Brand conscious	The consumer has, most likely, made an informed purchase because what they are most concerned about is the brand/image, e.g. designer trainers by Valentino.
Price/quality conscious	The consumer cares most about the price and/or quality. It may be that a low price is the most important decision or that the quality has to meet a certain standard expected by the consumer before they are willing to make the purchase.

Social classifications

These classifications are used by market analysts and governments to group together members of the public who tend to behave in certain ways due to their income and social status.

They are useful in marketing because again the spending patterns of these groups tend to be broadly similar. For example, those in the A and B classifications are more likely to buy organic food, holiday in more exotic locations and drive more expensive cars.

So the marketing department in a business needs to know the best places to advertise its products where the target market is most likely to see the adverts, such as in certain newspapers, websites, magazines, etc.

Classification	Description	Example
A	Upper or upper middle class – senior managerial/professional	Company director, surgeon, professor
B	Middle class – intermediate managerial/professional	Bank manager, head teacher, accountant, lawyer
C1	Lower middle class	Shop manager, bank clerk, sales representative, nurse
C2	Skilled working class	Electrician, heating engineer, mechanic
D	Working class – semi-skilled	Machine operator, slater, driver, call-centre worker
E	Lowest subsistence level – unskilled, low paid	Cleaner, porter

Report
Prepare a report on how consumer behaviour affects buying choices.

Research task
Search for a product-led business and a market-led business. Justify your choices.

Revision questions

1. Compare a market-led approach to a product-led approach in the development of new products.
2. Describe the influence of consumer behaviour on the success of a business.
3. Explain why social classification information is a useful marketing tool.
4. Describe three different consumer decision styles.
5. Justify the marketing of a pair of designer trainers costing £800, making reference to consumer decision styles.

2.2 Market research

Market research methods

There is a wide variety of methods for gathering market information. There are two categories of methods:

- field research, where the business collects the information itself (primary information)
- desk research, where the business uses someone else's information for its own purpose (secondary information).

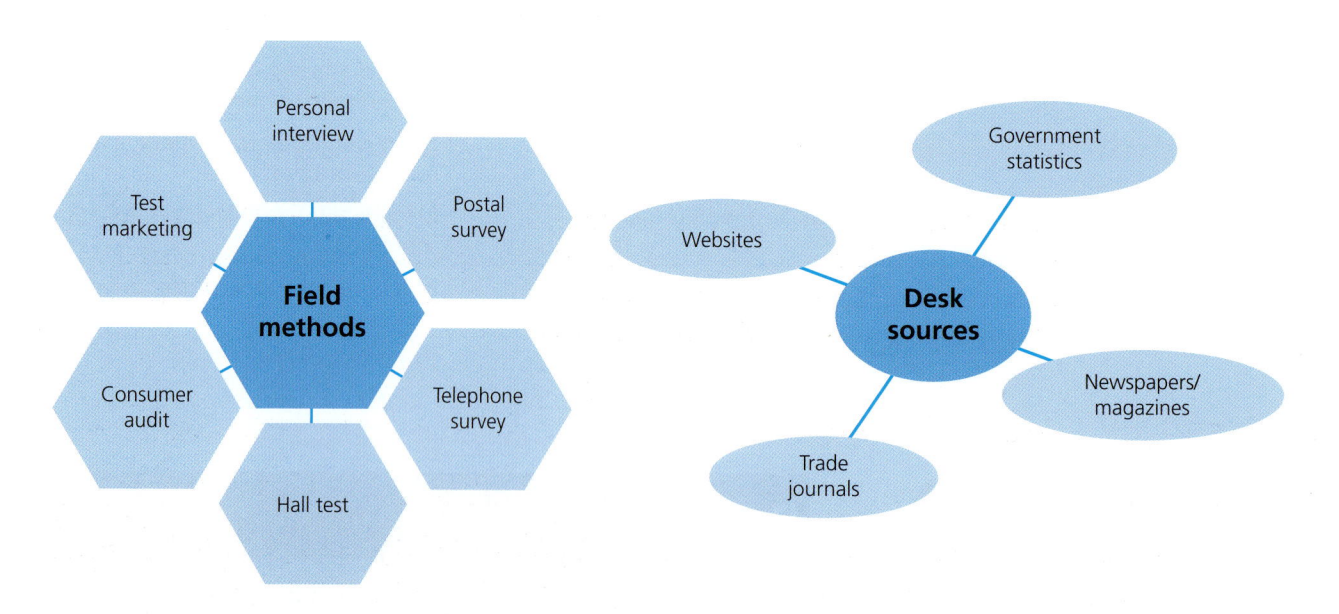

Field methods: Personal interview, Postal survey, Telephone survey, Hall test, Consumer audit, Test marketing

Desk sources: Government statistics, Newspapers/magazines, Trade journals, Websites

2.2 MARKET RESEARCH

Report
Prepare a report comparing desk and field research.

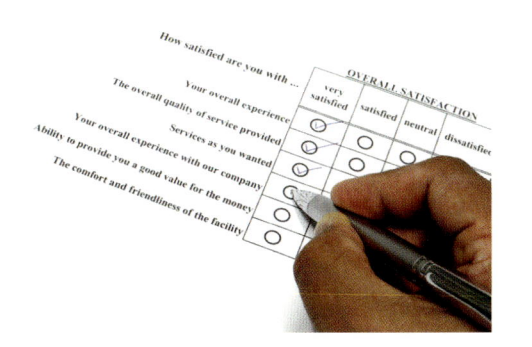

Field research is more expensive and time-consuming to collect. A large enough sample must be taken to ensure its accuracy. However, it should be more accurate than desk research and will be up to date.

The method chosen will depend on the finance available, how quickly the information is needed, and how accurate or precise the information needs to be for the decision to be made.

Field research methods

Street survey/personal interview

This involves stopping people in the street or visiting them at home. Street surveys are often briefer, and do not allow for as many follow-up questions as home interviews do.

Advantages of street survey/personal interview
- Allows the organisation to directly gain the views of customers.
- Allows two-way communication between the interviewer and the interviewee.
- The interviewer can clarify any questions to aid understanding.
- Specific market segments can be targeted.

Disadvantages of street survey/personal interview
- Interviewers have to be trained to ensure accurate information is received.
- It can be very time-consuming to collect enough information.
- It is a very expensive method compared to others as it can be labour intensive to collect and analyse the data.
- People don't like to be stopped in the street or disturbed at home.

Postal survey

This involves sending out questionnaires by post for people to complete and return. Because it is a relatively cheap method, a much larger number of people can be approached to respond, although few will reply. Postal surveys tend to be simple tick-box questionnaires, which are easy to collate.

Advantages of postal survey
- Survey forms can be sent out to all customers.
- Reaches a large geographical area.
- Focus can be on customers in a targeted area.
- Relatively cheap method.

Disadvantages of postal survey
- Usually has a very poor response rate as it can be seen as junk mail.
- May have to add incentives such as prizes to get a response.
- Questions need to be fairly simple and easily understood.
- Design costs may be high.

Telephone survey

This involves phoning people at home or work to ask their opinions.

Advantages of telephone survey
- Instant feedback from customers.
- Focus can be on certain groups of customer.
- It can be used as part of after-sales service.
- Large numbers can be contacted quickly.

Disadvantages of telephone survey
- Sometimes gains a hostile response from the person called.
- People are often unhappy with being called at home.
- Cold calling can lead to a poor reputation for the business.
- There are increasing legal restrictions on cold calling.

Hall test

Here a larger number of consumers are invited to comment on a range of products. Most major cinema releases are first shown to a test audience who will then be asked to discuss what they thought of the film. On the basis of the feedback, modifications can be made or scenes re-shot – even changing the ending is common. Once the test audience's changes are made, the film will be put into general release.

Advantages of hall test
- Gives consumers the chance to see or try a product and to be questioned on their opinions of the product.
- Allows product to be demonstrated.
- Fairly cheap method.

Disadvantages of hall test
- Can be difficult to analyse qualitative information.
- Consumers often give favourable replies simply to be polite.

Consumer audit

This is the process of determining who your ideal customer is, measuring their real experience with your product and using that data to make decisions which will enhance customer experience. You would consider who was looking at your product and why, then try to meet their expectations of the product.

Advantages of consumer audit
- This can provide accurate information on consumer buying patterns.
- It can be used to predict consumer trends.

Disadvantages of consumer audit
- Consumers get fed up quickly, resulting in a high turnover of respondents and inaccurate data.
- Consumers may not complete the journals accurately or on time.
- It is a very expensive method as many consumers receive payments to complete diaries.

Test marketing

This involves selling the new product in one small market sector before launching it fully into the wider market.

Advantages of test marketing
- Allows for the product to be amended or improved before national launch.
- Saves the cost of a national launch if the product does not receive good reviews in the test market.

Disadvantages of test marketing
- Regional tastes may not represent the nation as a whole.

Observation

Watching how consumers shop and behave in-store, and their reactions to products on display.

Advantages of observation
- Provides accurate quantitative information.
- There is no direct contact with the customers so no bias can be introduced.

Disadvantages of observation
- Cannot clarify any situations or ask for explanations.

Internet survey

Businesses can now contact customers directly once they have made a purchase online. The business has their email address and most also ask them to register their details.

Advantages of internet survey
- Customers are more likely to respond as it is less hassle to fill in a questionnaire online.
- Business can create a database of customers' details to help analyse the results.
- Lower cost than many other methods.

Disadvantages of internet survey
- Cost of designing the online questionnaire can be high.
- Customers may still not respond.
- Can end up in spam folder.

Report
Prepare a report comparing the different types of survey.

Social media

Many businesses now have teams set up to monitor comments on products that appear on Twitter, Facebook, etc.

Advantages of social media
- Usually honest opinions are likely to be seen.
- No direct contact with the customer is needed.
- Businesses can respond quickly to negative comments.

Disadvantages of social media
- Costly to set up and run.
- Information will be available to competitors.

Loyalty cards

Advantages of loyalty cards
- Up-to-date information on consumer buying habits is obtained.
- Can encourage customers to remain loyal to the store.

Disadvantages of loyalty cards
- Expensive to set up and run.
- Need to provide discounts to encourage customers to keep using them.

Mystery shopper

- Conducts undercover research to gain a realistic customer experience.
- Can give immediate feedback to management or employee.
- May be used to assess competitors' services.
- Used primarily to discover areas of weakness or praise strengths.

Desk research methods

Desk research can give the business detailed information about market conditions and changes in the external environment, so is essential for PESTEC or SWOT analysis (see pages 23 and 54–55). It can be obtained fairly quickly and cheaply, but its value is limited.

The information that is obtained is difficult to verify. It may be wrong, biased or out of date; and there is often no way for the business to find out how accurate it is. This could mean that decisions based on it may well be wrong.

The information is also available to competitors so the business does not gain any competitive advantage.

Desk research methods are described in the table below.

Internet search	Viewing competitors' website can give very useful information on their marketing mix and their plans for the future.
Government statistics	The government will collect a huge range of data about consumers' income, buying patterns, opinions and changes in the markets.
Newspapers/magazines	These can give useful information on changes in consumers' opinions and trends that are likely to affect the market. They can also give early warnings of possible good or bad publicity.
Trade journals	These have good information about the market and possible future changes, including overseas competition.

Research task

Search for government information on consumer spending habits.

Uses of market research

Organisations can use market research in the following ways:

- Ask customers their opinions and use the information to make alterations to existing products.
- Allow groups of customers to test out products and give feedback to ensure new products meet customers' needs.
- Use the internet to research information on the market to gain a better understanding of the size and profile of the market.
- Use information on the market contained in government statistics/reports to ensure advertising is targeted at the correct market segment.
- Ask customers their opinions and use the information to enter new markets or to increase market share.
- Use feedback from customers to ensure advertising is targeted at the correct market segment and that it is cost effective.

Sampling

There are three decisions to be taken when planning a sample to research.

- Who is to be surveyed?
  This is the population to be targeted in the research. Once this has been established, a sampling frame is developed – this is a way to make sure that everyone in the population being targeted has a chance of being included in the sample.
- How many people/companies should be surveyed?
  The larger the sample, the more accurate the survey will be; however, it will also be more expensive. It has been shown that samples of less than one per cent of a population can provide sufficiently reliable information if the sampling frame is correctly developed.
- How will people be selected for the survey?
  There are two main methods – random sampling and quota sampling.

Random sampling

Random sampling involves producing a random list of individuals to survey. Those picked for inclusion in the sample could be generated randomly, using a computer and the telephone directory or the electoral register.

Advantages of random sampling
- There is no chance of bias being introduced when selecting individuals for the sample.
- It is simple to draw up the sample.
- Random sampling reduces possible bias compared to quota sampling, which profiles respondents.

Disadvantages of random sampling
- It may not be focused on any particular market segment.
- It assumes that all members of the group are the same, which is not always the case.
- It is an expensive method to administer and run.

Stratified sampling is a method of random sampling that divides up the sample into segments based on how the population as a whole is divided up.

Quota sampling

This type of survey is preferred when carrying out research. Here, those chosen to be surveyed are selected in proportion to the whole population by social status, gender, age, etc. Once the quota for, say, males aged between 15 and 21 has been reached, no more are surveyed.

Advantages of quota sampling
- Quota sampling selects respondents based on criteria, whereas random sampling selects respondents indiscriminately.
- Statistics are available showing the proportions of different groups within the population that are readily available.
- Interviewers can substitute someone else if the interviewee is not at home at the time of the visit or phone call.
- Quota may be cheaper as less respondents may be sampled, whereas random often needs greater sampling to create an accurate profile.

Disadvantages of quota sampling
- Results can be less representative than using the random sampling method.
- It is easier to introduce bias which may affect results.

Revision questions
1. Describe the advantages and disadvantages of primary information.
2. Discuss methods of secondary research.
3. Describe methods of sampling used in market research.
4. Describe the use of market research within an organisation.

2.3 Marketing mix

Product Promotion People Physical evidence
Price Place Process

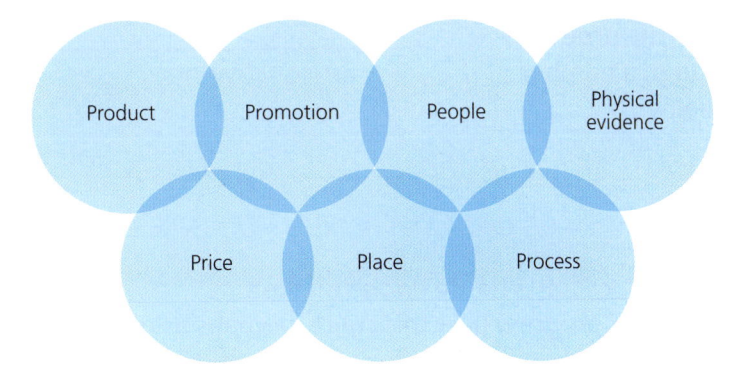

In order to market or sell its product successfully, a business must develop a strategy based on seven key elements as shown in the artwork above. How these elements are combined in the marketing strategy is called the marketing mix.

It is important to appreciate that all elements of the marketing mix are dependent on each other. When one element changes, it has an impact on other elements that are present in the mix. The marketing mix will be different for every product in every business.

Some examples are given in the table below. Note that this is not an exhaustive list.

Change in marketing element	Potential impact	Key elements affected
Selling online for the first time	Selling price of products may need to be lower in order to compete	Place, promotion
Developing a new product	The product may not sell or be competitive/profitable	Price, place, promotion, people, process
Stop using social media	Loss of customers	Place, people, product
Diversify the product range	Customers may not 'buy into' different products that are not core	Price, place, promotion, people, process
Process – new manufacturer is to be used to manufacture an existing product	Quality and reputation may suffer unless there is no difference in the product	Product, people, place

2.4 Product

The product life cycle

It is said that a product has a natural 'lifespan' through which it passes until it is withdrawn from the market. It may be that some products have a much longer lifespan than others or that the manufacturer has been very successful in using extension strategies to prolong the life of the product. However, all products go through a number of distinct phases as shown below.

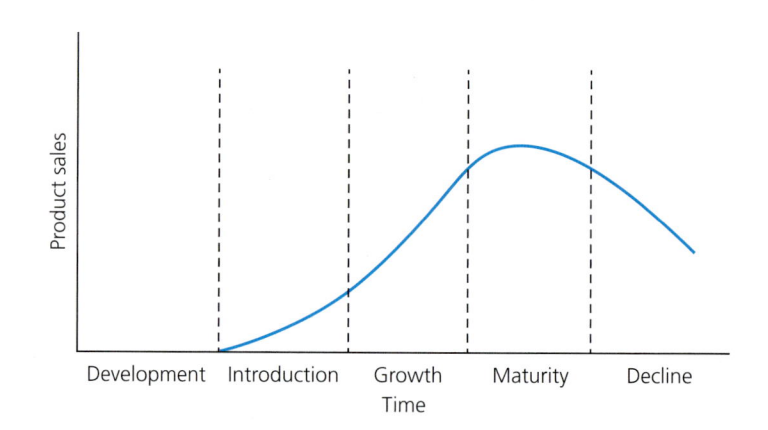

Development stage

- This takes place before the product starts its life on the market.
- A large number of products never progress past this stage, perhaps as much as 80 per cent.
- Product development is essential for most businesses in order to bring out new or improved products.
- The costs involved can be very high.
- The product will initially make a loss for the organisation as there have been no sales.

- Before launching the product onto the whole market, the business may decide to test-market the product.
- Modifications can be made to the product as a result of consumers' reaction to it, prior to the launch on the whole market.
- The product is not for sale on the market at this point, so there will be no profits generated.

Introduction stage

- This is when the product is launched onto the market.
- Heavy spending on advertising is necessary at this stage to raise awareness.
- Sales are slow and the selling price at this stage does not cover the development and start-up costs, so losses are usually made on sales.
- The product may not yet have broken even and there may still be losses because it is newly launched on the market.

Growth stage

- During this stage consumers become more aware of the product and sales start to grow rapidly.
- It is also during this stage that the product begins to become profitable.
- Advertising is maintained to continue to raise awareness of the product.
- Profit is generated/increasing as sales increase due to advertising/promotion.

Maturity stage

- This is when sales reach their peak.
- This is the highest level of sales that the product will achieve without the business taking some action.
- Spending on advertising can be much less as the product is fully established on the market.
- Development costs should have been repaid, and the product will be at its most profitable.
- These profits can then be used in part to fund development of new products.
- The business will work to keep the product in this stage for as long as possible.
- Competitors will start to emerge.
- The market will eventually become saturated with many similar products – sometimes referred to as the saturation stage.
- Profits may be high as sales are at peak point due to brand loyalty.

Decline stage

- Sales and profits start to fall.
- New and better products emerge.
- When the business sees profits fall to a level where they will affect the overall profitability of the organisation, the product will be withdrawn from the market as resources could be better used on other products.
- Profits decline/possible losses as sales lower due to change in customers wants.

Market saturation

This is sometimes included in the product life cycle, but it has more to do with the market than the product. At market saturation, potential new markets or consumers have been exploited by the industry. Any growth in sales will be at the expense of competitors, so advertising will be high, competition fierce, and the risk of failure will drive continuous development of additional features.

The mobile phone market has been at saturation point in most of the world for some time and so manufacturers have to keep bringing out new models of their products to maintain sales from existing customers and to try to attract new customers.

With market saturation new products are introduced to the market (for example, Microsoft and Google phones) and experience growth, and other products go into decline and will eventually be withdrawn from the market (for example, Nokia). The product life cycle focuses on the individual product that the business provides. This allows the business to ensure that it continues to attract customers to the product, and to know when to replace it on the market.

Research task

Search for a product at each of the different stages in the product life cycle. Justify your choices.

Extension strategies

These are the methods employed by businesses to prolong the life of their products and stop them going into the decline stage. The most successful extension strategies will actually lead to periods of sales growth.

Each of these will increase interest in the product, which should lead to increased sales – if successful. They can also be used to keep competition out of the market.

The business could also increase the product line by adding new versions or flavours.

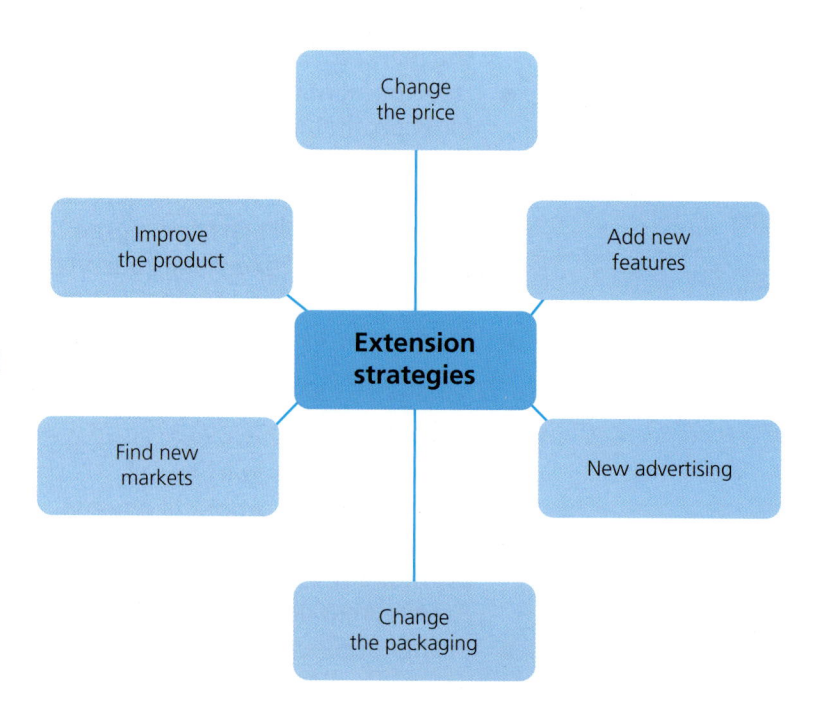

Extension strategies:
- Change the price
- Add new features
- New advertising
- Change the packaging
- Find new markets
- Improve the product

2.4 PRODUCT

77

Report
Prepare a report on the methods of extending a product's life cycle.

Product life cycle graph: Product sales vs Time, showing stages Development, Introduction, Growth, Maturity, Decline, with a Product extension curve during maturity.

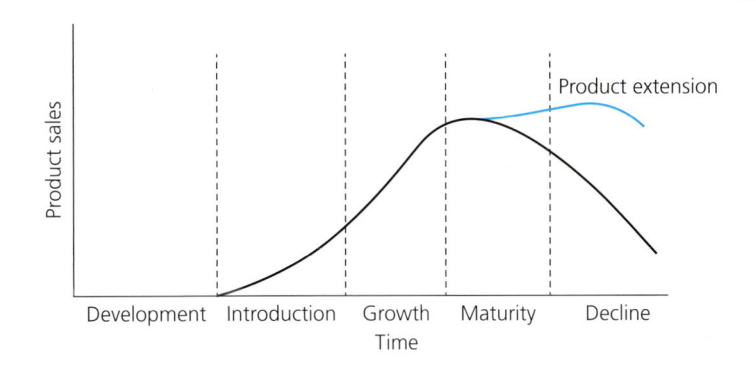

Product portfolio

This is the range of different products a business sells, usually under the same brand name. However, the business could also decide to move into very different product ranges. For example, Unilever makes ice cream and soap powder under different brand names.

Advantages of selling a range of products
- There are increased profits from selling a variety of different products.
- Brand awareness will increase.
- It will be easier to launch new products.
- Allows the business to spread the risk – not relying on a single product.
- The business can more easily cope with seasonal fluctuations.
- The business can meet the needs of different market segments.
- New products can replace those products at the end of the product life cycle.
- It will enhance the status of the business.

Disadvantages of selling a range of products
- Advertising costs can be higher to ensure customers know about all the products.
- Research and development costs can be high to maintain a variety of new products.
- If one product under the brand name has a problem it can affect the whole portfolio.

Research task
Visit the Arcadia Group website (www.arcadiagroup.co.uk) and list the different brand names in the group. Explain why each will appeal to a different market segment.

Boston Matrix

The Boston Matrix is one method a business can use to analyse its product portfolio. It focuses on each product's market share and market growth.

It identifies four types of product:

Cash cows

- These are at the maturity stage in the life cycle.
- They will need little investment and profits can be 'milked' to generate cash for the business.
- Cash cows need to be managed to maintain strong cash flows.
- They can support the development of stars.

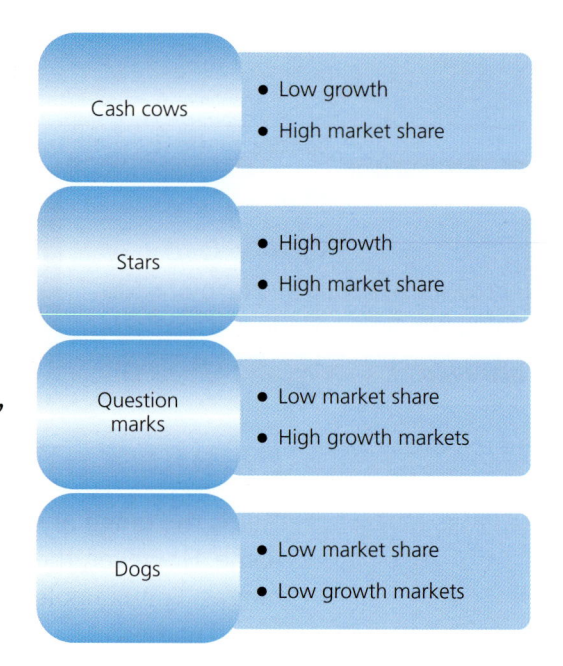

Cash cows	• Low growth • High market share
Stars	• High growth • High market share
Question marks	• Low market share • High growth markets
Dogs	• Low market share • Low growth markets

Stars

- Stars are in the growth stage of the product life cycle.
- They need heavy investment to maintain growth.
- Profits will be growing and stars can eventually become cash cows.

Question marks/problem children

- These are still at the introduction stage of the product life cycle.
- They need substantial investment to grow market share.
- A decision needs to be made over whether or not it is worth continued investment.
- Profitability cannot be guaranteed.

Dogs

- These products are in the decline stage of the product life cycle.
- They may continue to break even or make a small profit.
- Dogs are no longer worth investing in.
- They will eventually be withdrawn from the market.

The matrix allows the business to evaluate the range of products it has available for customers, and focus resources where the business will gain the highest sales and profit.

Although the matrix is seen as a useful tool for analysing the business's product portfolio, there are several problems associated with it:

- It only provides a snapshot of the current position.
- It cannot measure what is going to happen in the future.
- The product life cycle varies over time.
- It does not take account of external factors such as competitor actions.

- Market growth is an inadequate measure of a market's attractiveness.
- Market share is only an adequate measure of a product's ability to generate cash.
- It ignores issues such as developing a sustainable competitive advantage.
- It takes no account of internal factors such as company policy.

Revision questions

1. Explain extension strategies that a business could use for its products.
2. Describe the benefits of a wide product range.
3. Describe the impact on sales and profit of each stage in the product life cycle.
4. Discuss the use of the Boston Matrix when analysing the product portfolio.

2.5 Price

This is how much consumers will be charged for the product. It may be that different groups of customers will be charged different prices, or different prices at different times. The price will affect the buying decisions of the customers so it is important to choose the right price at the right time for each group of customers.

There are a number of different pricing strategies that the business can adopt as shown below.

Pricing strategies

- High/premium price
- Low price
- Market/competitive price
- Skimming
- Penetration
- Promotional
- Destroyer
- Cost based (cost plus)
- Price discrimination
- Psychological

Premium/constantly high price

- Price is set higher than competitors to give the image of quality and exclusiveness.
- It is used to maintain interest from the target market.
- Product has appeal to consumers looking for a particular image.

Low price

- Price is set lower than competitors to attract customers to the product.
- It is used for value-for-money products.
- Consumers are less interested in image.

Market/competitive pricing

- Price is set at the same level as competitors.
- Normally used for products that are identical.
- Consumers don't see much difference between competitors so other elements of marketing mix must be used to compete.

Skimming pricing

- Price is set high initially when no competition exists.
- Used when the product is new or unique.
- Used in a market with little or no competition.
- This will appeal to certain market segments that want the product in the introductory stage.
- It allows the business to make high profits prior to competitors entering the market.
- When competitors enter the market, the price is lowered to market price.
- This allows people on lower incomes to purchase the product.

Penetration pricing

- Price is set slightly lower than competitors to attract customers.
- Used to entice consumers to switch from other brands.
- Once a customer base has been created, the price is slowly increased to the same as competitors.
- Used in a highly competitive market.

Promotional pricing

- A low price is set for a short period of time to boost sales in the short term.
- Sometimes a loss can be made on the product.

Destroyer pricing

- Price is set very low compared to competitors.
- Once there is no competition in the market, the price is then put back up to the normal market level or higher.
- Used mainly by larger organisations to destroy competition.
- The organisation must have large reserves to sustain this over any length of time.

Other pricing strategies

- Cost-based (or cost-plus) pricing is where the selling price is set by adding a percentage to the cost of production. The business can choose (within reason) the percentage that it wishes to add.
- Discriminatory pricing is when the business will charge different prices to different customers for basically the same product. Examples could be Boots charging higher prices where there is no Superdrug close by; train companies charging different ticket prices at different times of day; Tesco charging different prices depending on where the store is located.
- Psychological pricing is where the price appears lower than it actually is, for example, £299 instead of £300 or £9.99 rather than charging £10.00.
- Goldilocks pricing is where the most profitable product is priced between a very low-priced one and a very high-priced one. The product is seen as reasonable quality for the price being charged.

Loss leaders

This is more of a promotional activity than a pricing one. Supermarkets use promotional pricing for some of their sales lines as loss leaders. They will advertise the low price for these products, attracting customers into the store in the hope that they will buy a whole range of other goods at the same time.

> **Report**
> Prepare a report on why pricing strategies would change over time for a business.

The supermarket can increase profits overall while making a loss on the promoted products.

2.6 Place

Channels of distribution

This refers to the marketing strategy used to make products available to customers.

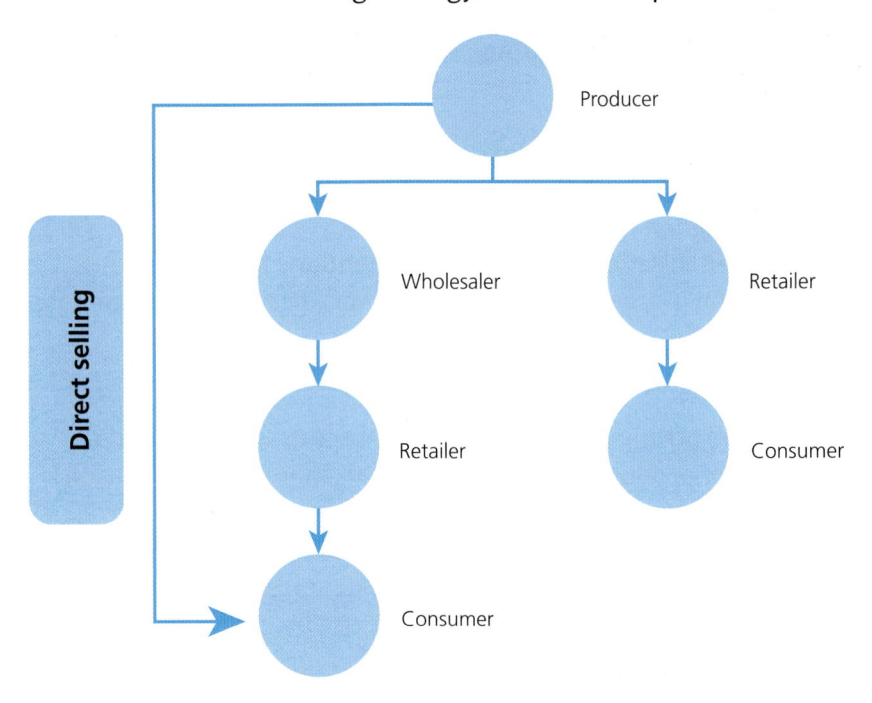

```
                    Producer
                   /        \
            Wholesaler       Retailer
                 |              |
             Retailer        Consumer
                 |
             Consumer
```

Direct selling (Producer → Consumer)

The chosen channel depends on:

- The product – for example, a new computer system would go direct from producer to consumer.
- The size of the market – mass-produced products would need wholesalers and retailers to get the product to the consumer.
- The target market – local markets may be best catered for directly.
- The size and age of the business – new or small businesses may only be able to sell direct to consumers.
- The costs involved – it's cheaper for Cadbury's to use wholesalers and retailers than to try to distribute its products itself.
- The finance available within the organisation – may not have the finance to set up its own e-commerce.
- The image of the product – premium products would only be sold at selected retailers.
- The reliability of the other companies in the chain – it may be seen as safer to sell direct.
- Legal restrictions that may apply – for example, alcohol, petrol and medicines can only be sold by licence holders.

- Where the product is in the life cycle – for example, if Cadbury's launches a new product, it will want it to be as widely available as possible.
- The organisation's own distribution capabilities – it may have its own shops, for example, Hollister.
- Durability of the product – perishable products must get to the consumer as quickly as possible.

Direct selling

Direct selling is where the producer sells directly to the consumer without the need for shops (retailers) or wholesalers.

Mail order

Mail order is goods that are sold via catalogues.

Advantages of mail order
- Offers credit facilities.
- Can be exclusive and the only way to purchase some products.
- Saves expensive high-street locations.

Disadvantages of mail order
- Consumers may not like the lack of personal service and many goods require to be returned.
- Involves high advertising costs.
- High levels of bad debts occur.

Internet selling

This is where firms sell their products or services over the internet.

Advantages of internet selling
- Consumers can order online from the comfort of their home.
- Saves the time and hassle of travelling to high-street stores.
- Goods are delivered direct to home of consumer.
- Saves on overhead costs.
- Available 24/7.
- Cheaper prices.
- Can reach wide geographical areas.
- Customers in rural areas who are unable to visit a physical shop are able to purchase products.

Disadvantages of internet selling
- Delay between purchase and receiving goods.
- Lack of personal contact.
- Customers unable to 'try on' clothing so may not purchase.
- Some concerns over the use of credit cards and the security involved.

Direct mail

Direct mail is where companies send letters or leaflets advertising their products for sale directly to the homes of possible consumers.

Advantages of direct mail
- Consumers within specific market segments can be targeted directly.
- Can reach wide geographical areas.

Disadvantages of direct mail
- Consumers do not respond well to vast amounts of junk mail.
- Very few responses.

Specialist magazines

Specialist magazines are used to describe and sell specialised products direct to consumers.

Advantages of specialist magazines
- Consumers can submit an order by telephone or by completing an order form.
- Consumers who purchase the magazine are interested in that area, so sales are more likely.

Personal selling

This is where products are sold door to door or by telesales.

Advantages of personal selling
- Can be direct to retailers or consumers.
- Allows the product to be demonstrated.

Disadvantages of personal selling
- Consumers are not keen on being disturbed at home.
- Sales costs can be high.

> **Research task**
>
> Visit the website of the Direct Selling Association (www.dsa.org.uk) and describe its code of business ethics.

Retailers

There are a number of different types of retailer. One type is the independent retailer, usually with just one shop, such as your local corner shop. However, they do sometimes join forces in order to buy in bulk and offer some competition to the larger chains, e.g. Spar.

Multiple chain stores have a number of outlets spread across the country. They are usually well known, such as Next or Marks & Spencer.

Supermarkets offer a wide range of groceries, and now more commonly clothing, household and electrical goods in their bigger stores.

Department stores, such as John Lewis, offer a range of goods in the different departments within the store. They tend to specialise in higher-priced premium brands.

Local stores

As well as the corner shop, the major supermarket chains now operate small local units, such as 'Tesco Metro' and 'Sainsbury's Local', to meet the changes in shopping habits.

Advantages of local stores
- Convenient for the consumer; close to home or on their way home from work.
- Can provide specific services such as cash machines and payment services.
- Loyal repeat customers.

Disadvantages of local stores
- More expensive to operate.
- Cannot normally compete on price.

Mobile shops

Advantages of mobile shops
- Allow participants and spectators at events to purchase goods.
- Increase brand awareness as they travel the country.

Disadvantages of mobile shops
- Will only be able to hold a limited amount of inventory.
- Narrow target market.

High-street stores

Advantages of high-street stores
- Customers more likely to impulse buy in physical stores.
- In-store customers can connect to the online store via their mobile and view, compare and order from the entire range of products the business has on offer. This is particularly useful if the size/colour/model is not available in the store.

Disadvantages of high-street stores
- Competitors selling similar products.
- Best locations are expensive.

Report
Prepare a report on the advantages and disadvantages of using a retailer for a manufacturer.

Wholesalers

The wholesaler buys in bulk from a manufacturer and breaks the product down into smaller quantities for selling on to retailers or even direct to the consumer.

Advantages of wholesalers
- Saves the manufacturer from making lots of smaller deliveries which, in turn, saves them on transport costs.
- Saves on administration costs.
- Saves the manufacturer from having high stockholding costs as a lot of the inventory is held by the wholesaler.
- If there are changes in trends and fashions, the manufacturer will not be left with unsold inventory.
- Wholesalers can help label and package the product for the manufacturer, which is less time-consuming/less work for the manufacturer.
- Retailers can buy from wholesalers in smaller amounts, which can help increase overall sales of the manufacturer's product.

Disadvantages of wholesalers
- By using wholesalers, manufacturers lose control over the image of their product, which could mean the product not being presented the way the manufacturer would want.
- Profits are lost to the wholesaler which otherwise could be kept by the manufacturer to improve their financial position.

Case study: Modern retailing

When asked about retailers, we most often think about the shops on the high street with big name brands, with outlets in many town centres. Or we might think about the retail parks with big stores and plenty of parking, or the shopping mall. In any case we'd be right, but modern retailing is much more complicated than that.

Many town centres are now filled with charity shops, betting shops, fast-food restaurants and money shops; that is, the ones that aren't empty. We are told that the high street is dying, that it is only a matter of time before retail parks go the same way, as we move to online shopping. Is this true?

Overall sales for retailers are increasing, and then only 5 per cent of those sales are lost to online purchasing. The reality is that 70 per cent of shoppers like to touch before they buy and they can only do that in-store. Added to that is the fact that, for many people, shopping is a social activity that can't be done on your phone, or in your house. This has led to some of the most successful online retailers opening physical stores.

Oak Furniture Land started as a small eBay retailer; within three years it became eBay's biggest retailer and eventually set up its own website and moved away from eBay. It then found its customers were asking if it had showrooms so they could actually feel the product before they bought, and within a few years the company had opened more than 40 stores with plans to open a new one every month for the next three years.

Now 65 per cent of its sales are made in-store. Customers use the website to find what they want, check it out in-store and then make the purchases. Oak Furniture Land does not need a lot of staff in-store because the customers already know what they want; the company takes sites where there are good deals on renting premises, so this keeps the costs of the stores low.

This has allowed Oak Furniture Land to overcome the problem of 'showrooming', where customers go to the shop to look for the product, get advice from specialist staff, and then go home to buy it cheaper online. This was the problem for Jessop and Comet that forced them out of business. Research shows that 70 per cent of customers will shop online to get the best price.

Screwfix is another online retailer that has now opened shops. It found that the customers' demands could not be met online. Now it finds that customers sit in their cars outside the store, order what they want on their phones, and then go in and collect their orders. Some traditional retailers, such as Marks & Spencer, work with their websites in-store to show their whole range of products, rather than just what they have available in the store on that day.

So, online or in-store?

The answer for new retailers seems to be a small number of low-cost shops with a very good website. That's expensive to set up for a new business. They could, like Oak Furniture Land, become an eBay retailer and join the likes of Argos, BT, Superdry, Office and Kookai, who also use eBay. Or they could use Amazon, who will charge a small fee for each item sold but will also provide inventory control, use of Amazon's logistics, 1-click purchasing for customers, and the chance to be a featured seller for its European market. Gone are the days when you would just look for a shop to rent close to your customers.

Revision questions

1. Describe the types of retailers available to a manufacturer.
2. Discuss the role of the wholesaler.
3. Discuss methods of direct selling.

2.7 Promotion

Promotion

Marketing is about communicating with consumers, and promotion is the method used to pass information to the consumer. It is an essential way of keeping existing customers and getting new ones.

Promotions into the pipeline

These are promotions that a manufacturer offers to the wholesaler or retailer that sells its products. They can include:

- Dealer loaders, where the wholesaler/retailer receives an extra amount free, such as five boxes for the price of four.
- Providing the wholesaler/retailer with staff training.
- Providing the wholesaler/retailer with point-of-sale displays.
- Allowing goods to be purchased on a sale-or-return basis.
- Running competitions.
- Providing credit facilities – buy now, pay later.
- Giving bulk-buying discounts.
- Payments/fees for favourable displays or just for selling the product in the stores.

Most supermarkets demand fees from producers for selling their products and if they want the best sites on the shelves then they will be expected to pay extra. They may have to make further payments if the supermarket sells more than expected.

Promotions out of the pipeline

These are promotions that a manufacturer, wholesaler or retailer offers to consumers to encourage them to buy more of the product. They can include:

- Free samples or trial packs that are given away in store or with other products.
- Bonus packs where, for example, 50 per cent is given free.
- Price reductions, which are short-term pricing strategies to encourage sales. For example, a pack may carry '50p off' on its packaging.
- Premium offers where one product is given free when another is purchased.
- Direct mail to selected customers.
- In-store demonstrations or tastings. Tastings are common in supermarkets where customers are allowed to taste and try new products.
- Social media can be used to show adverts, recommendations and celebrity endorsements.

Research task

Identify promotions out of the pipeline currently available in supermarkets.

Public relations

Public relations (PR) is used to improve the image of the business. Examples of PR methods that could be used are:

- Using a press release to counteract bad publicity.
- Giving donations to charities.
- Sponsoring events locally and nationally.
- Obtaining product endorsements/celebrity endorsements.
- Issuing publicity literature.
- Giving out company merchandise.
- Using a press conference – inviting media to attend allows a two-way interaction.

Research task

Search for three different examples of public relations in the media.

Product/celebrity endorsement

Advantages of product/celebrity endorsement
- Consumers buy the product in an attempt to be like the celebrity.
- Photographs of the celebrities are used to create visual connections to the product.
- Higher prices can be charged due to the endorsement.
- Brand loyalty may be created due to the endorsement.
- Statements can be used in promotions to further enhance the product.

Disadvantages of product/celebrity endorsement
- It can cost large amounts of money to retain the celebrity.
- If the celebrity gains bad publicity, the product is also tarnished.
- Product endorsement does not guarantee a quality product.

Ethical marketing (diagram):
- Must not mislead the consumer
- Promises must be there in the product – it must 'do what it says on the tin'
- Adverts must not be indecent or obscene
- Should not offend the customers' beliefs or moral sense

Ethical marketing

Brands that can promote their ethical values are likely to be more successful than those that can't, as consumers have greater trust in those businesses.

Revision questions

1. Discuss the importance of public relations to an organisation.
2. Describe methods of promotion into the pipeline.
3. Describe methods of promotion used by business.
4. Discuss the use of out-of-the-pipeline promotions to increase sales.
5. Discuss the use of celebrity endorsement.

2.8 People

The extended marketing mix/service marketing mix

In addition to the traditional four Ps of price, product, place and promotion, it is now necessary to add three more Ps to the mix to give us seven Ps.

These have been added because today marketing is far more customer oriented than before, and because the tertiary sector of the economy now dominates economic activity in this country.

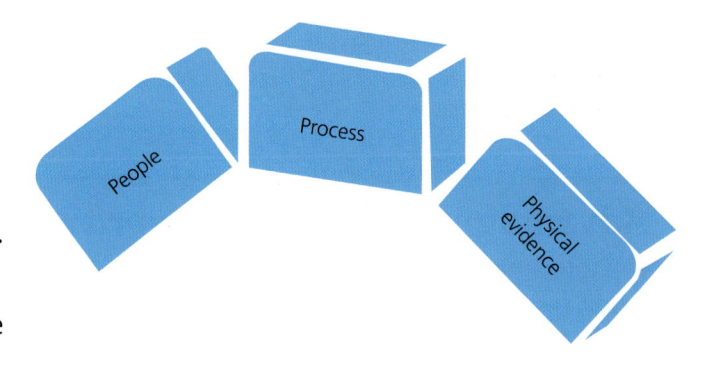

Customer satisfaction

Customers are more likely to be loyal to organisations that serve them well. Managers must make sure that all staff are kept up to date and are behaving the way that is expected of them towards customers.

Anyone who comes into contact with customers will have an effect on the level of customer satisfaction.

A high level of customer satisfaction can be achieved by:

- creating a culture of customer service, so that all employees understand the job they have to do
- looking at the way that telephone calls are handled
- looking at the way customers are treated in face-to-face situations
- taking notice of customers' view of price in relation to the quality they receive.

Level of after-sales service

Not all customers will complain in person; they may phone, or they may use the business's website. It is important to make sure that customers do not get more frustrated.

Some call centres simply do not have enough staff to deal with complaints or questions, and some websites are difficult to navigate, so these should be considered carefully to ensure that customers have a good experience when using them.

- Create a culture of customer service, so that all employees understand the job they have to do.
- Develop a customer-care strategy.
- Recruit and train good employees.
- Ensure all employees are trained to a high standard.
- Ensure there are enough employees to deal with customer service.
- Have the right infrastructure in terms of website and call centres.

Report
Prepare a report to show how excellent customer service can be achieved through the employees of a business.

2.9 Process

Associated with customer service are a number of processes or systems involved in making marketing effective in an organisation. These are the ways of delivering the service and should include:

- processes for handling customer complaints
- processes for identifying customer needs and requirements
- processes for handling orders
- providing innovative mobile scan-and-go facilities in stores
- providing e-commerce for customers to purchase anytime, anywhere
- using loyalty cards to maintain customer satisfaction
- offering customers targeted promotions
- providing nutritional information on food products
- providing home delivery service

- date and time slots for deliveries
- tracking of online orders
- warranties and guarantees
- price match promise
- fair refund policy.

There should also be a formal procedure in place detailing what should be done, and by whom, in the event of a complaint, as shown below.

Customer		Organisation	
How the complaint should be made and to whom	Transparent process	Stages of the complaint are monitored by management	The same employee should process the complaint
How long it will take to deal with	Relevant ombudsman	All complaints should be acknowledged in writing	Training given Guidelines for compensation, refunds, etc.

Research task

Visit Amazon (www.amazon.co.uk) and search for processes it uses to ensure customer satisfaction of its services.

2.10 Physical evidence

This is evidence that an organisation uses to verify that it keeps promises to customers.

Today consumers typically come into contact with products in retail units – and they expect a high level of presentation in modern shops, for example:

- bright and modern premises
- easy to navigate around the store
- good standard of presentation of displays
- attractive physical layout not only in shops, but also in the layout and structure of virtual stores and websites
- self-checkout tills
- ample and convenient parking
- recycling facilities for customers.

Combining the three Ps in business

How these three elements combine can be seen in the hotel industry to ensure customer satisfaction and competition with rivals.

People	Process	Physical evidence
Friendly greeting at check-in	Online booking	Modern appearance to rooms
Helpful and knowledgeable staff	Quick and easy check out	Comfortable bed
Will arrange taxis for residents	Immediate action if something is at fault	Clean and well presented
Cleaning staff well trained	Rooms cleaned and tidied each day	All rooms en-suite
Prompt service	Questionnaire on service provided in all rooms	Tea/coffee making facilities
		All facilities working properly
		Customer parking
		Wi-fi available

Benefits of good customer service

- Customer loyalty
- Improved reputation
- Easier to attract new customers
- Higher sales/profits
- Lower staff turnover
- Fewer complaints/returns which can be expensive to administer
- Less chance of legal action
- Easier to attract high-quality employees
- Can create competitive edge

Case study: Apple and McDonald's

Sitting eating your hamburger while checking your phone. Sound familiar? What has this to do with business management? Well, let's look at your phone first.

So why are Apple products so expensive?

Well, Apple has a premium product, so it can charge a premium price. Many people think Apple products are the best, nothing else will do, so are willing to pay a higher price. Having the latest version of the phone makes them happy and improves how they feel about themselves.

How has Apple achieved this?

It's all about marketing.

- **Promotion** – You won't see too many adverts for the latest phone. Apple doesn't have to advertise them. National news media across the world takes care of that for it, with worldwide PR launch events showing customers queuing for days to be first to get the latest phone.
- **Product** – There is no doubt that the product itself is very good; it has to be to keep the customer loyal. The software and hardware create very few problems for the user. Apple has been clever enough to keep the product user friendly with its upgrades, unlike Microsoft with its Windows upgrades.
- **Place** – Apple has managed to keep control of the supply chain to ensure its products get to the customer when they expect it. However, it may reduce supply of the latest products to increase customer demand, as their most loyal customers rush to snap up the latest version before it runs out.

- **Price** – Although its products are premium priced, Apple is not averse to a little market skimming. After the initial launch, it will supply slightly cheaper versions, and eventually the price will be lowered on all products prior to the launch of the next version, which will be even more expensive. After all, it needs to bring in new customers in order to keep growing.
- **People** – Apple employs a very successful corporate culture. Its staff are fully trained to ensure customer satisfaction, from the 'experts' in-store to the helplines and online customer support. All are designed to keep its customers loyal.
- **Physical evidence** – Apple stores have more the look of a high-end jewellery store than an electronics shop. Customers are welcome to come in and try all the products with staff available to provide support. The company has less control over others that sell its phones such as network providers, but will limit who can sell the latest versions.
- **Process** – Setting up and running iTunes and the app store have allowed Apple to create very profitable revenue streams, and a very user-friendly source of continuous entertainment and social media for the customer. Only Apple-approved apps can be downloaded, which ensures few problems for the customer. Apple also makes sure there are apps for all the most popular products such as Twitter, Snapchat, Facebook, etc.

What about your burger?

McDonald's doesn't even have contracts with its suppliers, and can change to a different one whenever it wishes. It's all done with an agreement. For new suppliers this can be very profitable, but at the same time, that profit may disappear tomorrow unless they make sure McDonald's is happy, and it will only be happy if the customers are happy.

- **Product** – Every burger is made from one breed of cattle, so farmers have to specialise in that breed. McDonald's restaurants all have the same grills and all must cook the burger in exactly the same amount of time. Staff in the restaurants can't change it, and this ensures consistency of product quality. It's the same with fries, chicken, etc. The company has the process down to a fine art so that the customer should never have to complain.
- **Process** – Any cooked products that lie for more than a set period of time are thrown out. And all customers should be served within a set time period. Inspectors regularly visit, sometimes as 'mystery shoppers', to make sure that all restaurants are doing exactly as told.

McDonald's owns very few restaurants; most are franchises, so tight control is necessary to keep customer satisfaction high. Customer loyalty is essential for McDonald's success. With restaurants being run by owners rather than managers, they are much more likely to be successful.

Revision questions

1. Describe pricing strategies that could be used to increase sales for an existing product.
2. Discuss the use of loss leaders by a supermarket.
3. Describe pricing strategies that could be used to launch a new product on the market.
4. Explain the importance of after-sales service for a retailer.
5. Discuss the importance of customer satisfaction for a manufacturer.
6. Describe methods used to help ensure customer satisfaction.
7. Discuss the use of e-commerce to increase customer satisfaction.
8. Describe how poor physical evidence can affect the sales of a business.
9. Describe how the elements of the extended marketing mix are combined to ensure customer satisfaction.

2.11 Technology

Technology has an increasing number of uses in marketing. Here are some specific examples that relate to the marketing function:

Technology	How it is used in marketing
EPOS (electronic point of sale)	Information can be collected from this form of electronic payment in order to inform market research.
Online survey	Organisations can use their own online surveys or online survey tools such as Survey Monkey to carry out market research.
Internet advertising	Organisations can reach wide audiences by choosing to advertise on the internet, e.g. on social media or related websites.
E-commerce	E-commerce allows organisations to reach new markets by using their own or third-party websites to market and sell their goods and services.
Email	Using email as a means of business communication makes the organisation more efficient in its ability to communicate and carry out marketing activities.
Databases	The creation and use of customer databases allows organisations to hold useful marketing information.
Social media	The use of social media such as Facebook, Twitter and Instagram allows organisations to reach out to their customers in new ways, bringing new opportunities for marketing. It also helps with creating a strong brand image.
Desktop publishing (DTP)	Desktop publishing can be used to create online and hard-copy marketing and advertising media.
Text alerts	Making use of customer mobile numbers and contacting them using a text service is a good way to alert them to new products and offers, direct to their smartphone.
Apps	Many organisations invest in the development of an app to link into the advertising or selling of their products/services.
Quick response (QR) codes	The use of smartphones has allowed the development of QR codes, which are an effective way of communicating information about a particular product.
Shipment tracking	In the past, if you wanted to track a shipment for something that you had ordered you had to call the company. Most distribution companies now allow you to track your order online or using an app.
Analytics	Website analytics tools such as Google Analytics allow organisations to track detailed information about their website, e.g. who visits it, where they're from, how long they spend on each page, etc.

Role of technology in marketing

Although marketing still relies heavily on customer engagement, often face to face, consumers expect the business to provide up-to-date, reliable technology. It also allows the marketing department itself to operate much more efficiently.

Benefits of e-commerce in marketing

- The full range of an organisation's products can be shown on a website.
- This saves the need for large outlets or costly high-street shops to display them.
- It reduces costs because large numbers of shop staff are not required.
- Customers can purchase online from their own home.
- It allows worldwide sales – access to global economy.
- Sales can be made 24/7.
- Customers can leave comments on the website.
- Businesses can make use of customer details for market research purposes by email to contact customers with promotions.
- Text alerts can be used to inform customers of new products and special offers.
- Apps can be used to give customers easier access to products and services.

Benefits of technology in marketing

- It improves communication through use of email, which speeds up sending files to colleagues throughout the world and can have attachments for colleagues to view.
- The use of videoconferencing allows meetings to take place without travelling and corresponding travel costs.
- Increased access to information through the use of the internet allows organisations to look at competitors' websites.
- The marketing department can find suppliers anywhere in the world.
- It increases productivity and speed of work as computers often work faster than humans.
- File sharing can be carried out anywhere in the world through the organisation's network, which will improve decision making as files can be accessed at the same time by colleagues worldwide.
- Labour costs will be reduced as use of computers will reduce labour requirements.
- It improves the quality of products or services to customers.
- It will reduce the number of errors and wastage.
- It allows for more flexible working with staff as they can work from home and stay in contact via technology – leading to better relationships.
- It improves the business's image and competitiveness.

Section Assessment: Management of Marketing

This segment aims to test your knowledge of the preceding section with exam-standard questions. It is recommended that you answer the questions based on the standard timing for the external examination, which allows around two minutes per mark. There is a selection of questions that you might expect to find in both Section 1 and Section 2 of the question paper.

Section 1 is worth 30 marks in total and the allocation of each question can range from 1–8 marks. Section 2 has four questions of 15 marks each, containing individual questions in the range of 1–8 marks. The difference with Section 2 is that it specialises in individual topics, so there could be a 15-mark question on Marketing, as exemplified below. Remember that Section 2 questions tend to dig a little deeper into your knowledge of particular areas of the course.

Once you have attempted these questions, it would be a good idea to ask your teacher to mark them or go over appropriate responses to them.

Section 1 questions

		Marks
1	Describe what is meant by market share.	1
2	Describe the advantages of having a varied product portfolio.	5
3	Describe the promotional strategies that may be used by an organisation.	4
4	Describe the market research methods that an organisation might use to gather information about its customers.	6
5	Describe the use of technology in driving sales.	3

Section 2 questions

			Marks
6	a	Describe the tactics that an organisation might use when launching a new product.	5
	b	Discuss the factors that might influence the selection of a channel of distribution.	4
	c	Compare the use of random and quote sampling.	3
	d	Discuss the influence of technology in retailing.	3
7	a	Describe the benefits of market research.	3
	b	Describe the extension strategies that can be used on a product.	4
	c	Discuss the role of social media in marketing.	4
	d	Describe the use of the following pricing strategies: • destroyer pricing • penetration pricing.	4
8	a	Describe the elements of the marketing mix.	7
	b	Discuss the roles of the wholesaler and the retailer.	4
	c	Justify the use of different market research methods.	4

Section 3

Management of Operations

Once you complete this section you will be able to:

✓ apply knowledge and understanding of how the operations function contributes to the success of large organisations

The Management of Operations section of this book studies how the operations side of things looks at the whole process, from selecting the right suppliers, choosing the right production methods to final delivery to the customer, in a way that allows the business to be successful. This requires a balance between maintaining high-quality products and cost efficiency to avoid unnecessary spending.

The operations will be the most costly aspect of the business so it is essential that the process is as efficient as possible, keeping costs as low as possible.

SECTION 3 MANAGEMENT OF OPERATIONS

Topic 3.1 Inventory management	You should be aware of: • the features, costs and benefits of just-in-time inventory control • the storage and warehousing of inventory • the logistical management of inventory.
Topic 3.2 Methods of production	You should be aware of: • the costs and benefits of capital-intensive production • the costs and benefits of mechanised production • the costs and benefits of automated production • the costs and benefits of labour-intensive production • the reasons for production choices.

Topic 3.3 Quality	You should be aware of:
	
	• the importance of quality to organisations and customers
	• the distinction between quality control methods (inspection) and quality assurance methods (prevention)
	• quality standards and symbols as a way of documenting and displaying quality, for example:
	  • CE Marking
	  • BSI Kitemark
	  • trade logos
	• the costs and benefits of a range of methods of ensuring quality, for example:
	  • quality control
	  • quality assurance
	  • benchmarking
	  • quality circles
	  • mystery shoppers
	  • continual improvement of process and system.

Topic 3.4 Ethical and environmental issues	You should be aware of: • the costs and benefits of fair-trade activities • the costs and benefits of environmental responsibility • the costs and benefits of ethical operations.
Topic 3.5 Technology	You should be aware of the costs or benefits of using technology, including: • computer-aided design (CAD) • computer-aided manufacture (CAM) • electronic point of sale (EPOS) • robotics • barcodes and QR codes • email • internet • databases.

3.1 Inventory management

Inventory (or stock) is the materials held by the business that it needs to produce the final product for the customer.

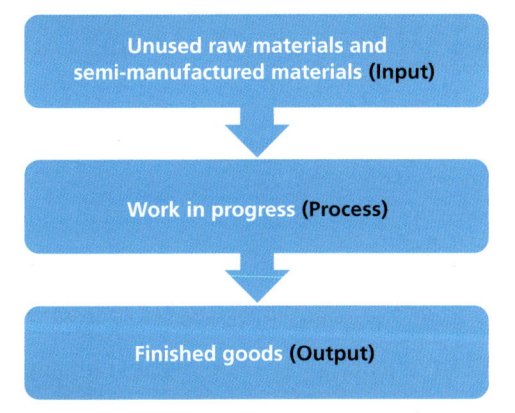

Unused raw materials and semi-manufactured materials (Input)

↓

Work in progress (Process)

↓

Finished goods (Output)

Inventory management systems

Inventory represents a large investment by the business, so methods must be employed to ensure that the costs of holding inventory are as low as they can be while ensuring inventory is available for production when needed.

Purpose of inventory control systems

- To anticipate running out of inventory before it happens.
- To ensure the production line will always be able to run if there is inventory.
- To ensure that customer orders are not delayed through lack of inventory.
- To control the admin costs of ordering as inventory is ordered at regular intervals.
- To avoid the high costs of storage and maintenance by avoiding over-stocking.
- To minimise insurance costs for inventory in storage.
- To reduce the security required – less inventory stored means less security needed.
- To minimise the storage space required.
- To minimise the money tied up in inventory which could be used more profitably elsewhere in the business.
- To minimise the chance of inventory deteriorating or becoming obsolete.

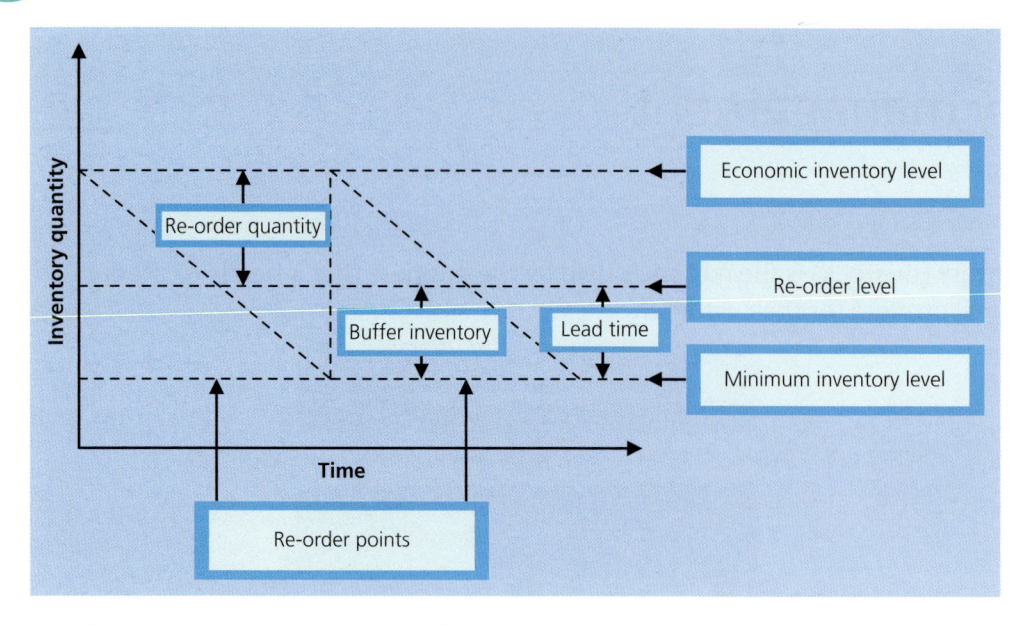

The illustration above shows the following aspects of inventory control:

- Maximum/economic inventory level – the highest level of inventory that should be held to minimise costs, bearing in mind storage space and finance available.
- Minimum inventory level – the level that inventory should not fall below in order to avoid shortages.
- Re-order level – the level at which inventory should be re-ordered, taking account of usage and lead times.
- Re-order quantity – the amount that is ordered to take the inventory back up to maximum/economic level.
- Lead time – the time between ordering new inventory and its arrival.
- Buffer inventory is a cushion supply of inventory in excess of the forecast demand.

Problems with under-stocking

- The business may run out of inventory and have nothing to sell, or may have to stop production.
- Repeated re-ordering means increased ordering admin costs.
- Unable to take advantage of bulk-buying discounts.
- Customers have to go elsewhere to buy.
- Reputation is damaged when customers are unable to buy the product.
- Customers may stop coming all together.
- Loss of sales and profits.

Problems with over-stocking

- Additional storage costs (for example, security, space, insurance).
- Money tied up in inventory could be used elsewhere.
- May cause cash-flow problems.
- Inventory may perish or go out of date.
- Changes in demand could mean it goes to waste (becomes obsolete).
- Increased risk of theft.

Electronic inventory management

Using barcodes allows all inventory to be tracked electronically from the moment it arrives with the manufacturer until it is delivered to the customer. The same EPOS (electronic point of sale) equipment that is used at the till when you buy something in the shop is used in the warehouse.

This brings a number of benefits to the organisation:

- It provides managers with instant, up-to-date information on inventory.
- It also allows for automatic re-ordering of inventory when the re-order level is reached.
- There is a reduction in instances of human error.
- It highlights changes in demand from customers.
- It alerts management to theft of inventory.

Just in time

A just-in-time (JIT) system is a popular method of operation for mass manufacturers as it limits the amount of inventory held by the organisation to near zero. It works best where there is a very close relationship between the manufacturer and its suppliers.

In practice, JIT is very simple: the inventory is held by the supplier and is only brought to the factory as and when it is needed. The whole production process has to be geared to working with the JIT system.

The cost savings can be very high as there are none of the usual inventory-holding costs:

- Capital is not tied up in inventory – money can be used for other purposes or removed entirely from the manufacturer's expenditure.
- Reduced storage costs – space, equipment, warehouse and stores staff, services, etc.
- Fewer inventory losses/less wastage – for example, theft, accidental damage, inventory exceeding its shelf life, inventory obsolescence.

In a JIT system these costs are paid by the suppliers.

The whole production operation works on the JIT system where nothing is produced unless there are customers to buy the products. The marketing department will give figures on expected demand or actual orders, and only then will production take place. Supplies are ordered 'just in time' to become parts for the final product; these component parts are assembled 'just in time' to become finished products, 'just in time' to be sold to the customers.

> **Report**
> Prepare a report on the costs and benefits of introducing a just-in-time system.

Advantages of JIT
- Reduces storage costs as inventory is delivered as it is needed.
- The organisation is more responsive to consumer demand.
- Money is not tied up unnecessarily in buying large volumes of inventory.
- Improves cash flow.
- Can also result in less wastage of inventory.
- Capital can be used elsewhere in the organisation.
- There is less warehouse space needed for inventory.
- Theft will be reduced as inventory is more tightly controlled.

Disadvantages of JIT
- Organisations can lose out on bulk-buying discounts.
- Relies heavily on suppliers' co-operation in delivering inventory when it is needed.
- Can result in high admin and delivery costs as there are many small deliveries.
- Production may be interrupted or halted if there is a delay with a delivery.
- The organisation may be unable to meet sudden increases in demand.
- Heavy reliance on suppliers to ensure quality.

Storage

Centralised inventory control

Here the inventory is held in a central store making the inventory secure, with specialist staff to receive, check and issue inventory.

Advantages of centralised inventory control	Disadvantages of centralised inventory control
• Standard organisational procedures can be developed for ordering, receiving and issuing inventory. • Storage costs can be better controlled. • It can reduce costs as bulk purchasing uses economies of scale. • Fewer smaller purchases are necessary. • It reduces duplication of inventory held throughout the organisation.	• Recruitment, training and salaries are required for the specialist staff. • The cost of creating an area for storage. • Time delays between ordering and receiving the inventory. • It can be time-consuming to receive inventory when needed in departments. • If large amounts are held there is an increased likelihood of wastage. • Specialised requirements of departments is harder to maintain. • Central inventory may be remote from production – time is required to move materials. • Moving inventory from remote store has cost implications.

Decentralised inventory control

Here inventory is held at various locations within the organisation. Each branch or department is responsible for ordering and maintaining its inventory. This type of inventory control:

- allows for better decisions to be made about what inventory to buy and how much to order
- makes sure that inventory is always available for production
- can be more expensive.

Warehousing

Companies will often make use of warehousing facilities to bulk store their goods. Warehouse space may be owned by the company, leased or rented.

The main reason for utilising warehouse space is because most businesses will be unable to exactly match their output to the demand for their products. Inventory of finished goods will be stored in the warehouse in order to meet demand quickly.

It is important that the warehouse space is of suitable quality and offers security for the protection of inventory. It should also offer the correct environment for the storage of inventory, for example, dry, temperature maintained.

The main aspects of warehousing are discussed below.

Design and layout

Warehouses should be on ground level only as storage and retrieval of inventory from floors above ground level will increase handling times. A system of inventory rotation should be in operation to avoid deterioration of inventory quality.

Mechanical handling

Some businesses may decide to utilise specialist inventory handling equipment that can be incorporated into the design of a new building. This may be costly, but there are substantial benefits to be gained in terms of the space used and time required to move inventory.

Pallets are often used in warehouses and they are a relatively cheap method of organising inventory – they can be easily moved using a forklift truck and enable inventory to be stored off the floor. They can also be reused.

Advantages of warehousing
- Large amounts of inventory can be securely stored which can reduce theft – cost savings are made if theft is reduced.
- Inventory types can be better categorised in a warehouse, making management of inventory easier and navigation of inventory quicker.
- May allow for easier access, resulting in more efficient delivery and larger quantities of inventory able to be transported from one location. Fewer runs may be needed saving expense on fuel/travel times.
- The warehouse may break down bulk orders from suppliers and distribute these to customers/outlets, saving the manufacturer time.
- Allows for stockpiling in advance of periods of high demand so that sales will not be lost.

Disadvantages of warehousing
- Expensive to run due to overhead/energy/rent/security costs.
- May be located in a rural area due to land/premises costs.
- Fire/flood/contamination, etc., can affect the entire inventory reserve.

Logistics

Businesses have a choice in the transportation that they use: their own, hired or public transport. The decision on which type of transport to use will be based on the needs of the particular business and the costs involved.

The advantages and disadvantages of each are summarised in the table below.

Type of transport	Advantages	Disadvantages
Own	Complete control	High initial investment and continuing running costs
Hired	No capital investment, ability to change requirements quickly	Less control
Public	No capital investment, cheaper	Less control. Unreliable, poor value for money, little control

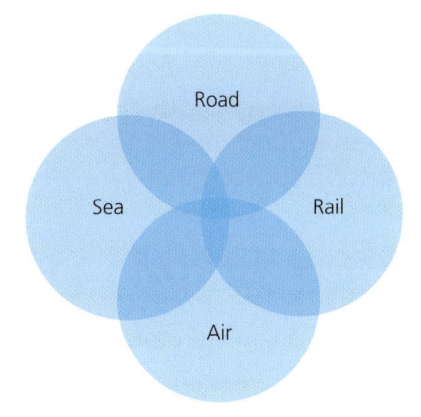

Physical distribution

The type of transport used to deliver products to the market will vary depending on the product being sold and the value of the product. The method chosen needs to be suitable for the product and for the customer. Things the business should consider include:

- ensuring shops do not lose sales because of supply problems
- ensuring the product does not go off or out of date during transit
- cost.

Road

- Road transport is often the best method in terms of cost and convenience.
- Deliveries can be made straight to the shop or the customer at a relatively low price.
- Refrigerated vehicles can be used to transport perishable items.
- It is an easy way to get directly to a customer's location.
- As road networks improve, it is a quick method.
- It is relatively cheap.
- However, there can be problems with delays, roadworks and weather.
- Increases in fuel prices make the overall cost dearer.
- It is not suitable for all products.

Rail

- Rail is convenient for bulky products.
- Railways don't suffer the problems of traffic jams.
- It can often be faster than by road where restrictions on the length of time a lorry driver can stay at the wheel means long-distance deliveries have to be broken down into stages.
- It is more environmentally friendly than road.
- However, it requires specialised freight terminals to load products.
- It is not suitable in rural areas with no rail network.

Air

- Air travel is usually the fastest method of transport across long distances for products that are less bulky and have a limited shelf life.
- It is perfect for long distances or more remote areas.
- For many products air travel is too expensive compared to other forms of transport.
- It often still requires road transport for the initial and final stages of delivery.

Sea

- Sea is normally best for international trade.
- It is less expensive than air for large loads.
- The increasing sizes of container ships allow huge amounts to be transported over long distances.
- It is good for items that don't have a short shelf life.
- Is a slower method than the others.

Case study: ASDA

Asda uses a 900-vehicle fleet to deliver products from its 21 distribution centres around the UK to its 18,000 stores. ASDA uses a sophisticated software system that enables it to:

- ensure on-time delivery so that inventory is available for sale to customers
- reduce mileage, fuel costs and vehicle emissions
- make more efficient use of its drivers and fleet.

The system allows the company to track its vehicles around the country. The result is a better service to its customers, reduced operating costs and a lower carbon footprint.

Revision questions

1. Describe the benefits and disadvantages of just-in-time inventory management.
2. Describe factors to be considered when setting up an inventory-management system.
3. Describe the importance of logistics in operations.
4. Describe factors that a business should consider when designing its warehouse.
5. Describe the benefits of a centralised storage system.

3.2 Methods of production

The production method used will depend on a number of factors as detailed below.

- The skills of the workforce – where low-skilled labour is employed, a mechanised process may prove more effective.
- The finance that the organisation has available – capital-intensive production can be very expensive to set up.
- The technology available to be used in the production method.
- The size of the business.
- The actual product being made.
- The amount of product required for the market – high demand will require capital-intensive/mass production methods to create large volumes for sale.
- The standard of quality required – high quality may require labour-intensive production or robotics to ensure standard.

Capital-intensive production

Capital-intensive production is common in mass production in a factory with a production line, where the product being produced flows through various stages with parts being added at each stage.

This is common where a standard product is being produced. Production tends to be capital-intensive where it is carried out using mainly machinery, often involving a highly automated production process.

Examples of this type of industry include car production.

This type of production results in a continuous output of products that are essentially the same.

Advantages of capital-intensive production
- Economies of scale can be achieved.
- Automated production lines save time and money.
- Quality systems can be built into the production.
- Uses standardised machinery so can work 24/7.
- Labour costs are lower as fewer skilled workers are required.
- Production costs will be lower than labour-intensive production.

Disadvantages of capital-intensive production
- A standard product is produced that may not suit all customers.
- High costs are associated with the set-up of an automated production line.
- Work can be repetitive and boring for workers.
- If production runs are high, there may be too much produced and supply will exceed demand.

Automation/mechanisation

The continuing developments in technologies such as CAM (computer-aided manufacture), CAD (computer-aided design) and automation (robotics to replace workers) allow firms to quickly design, develop and produce products. It also allows firms to produce a much wider variety of similar products to appeal to different segments of the market.

Advantages of automation/mechanisation
- Machines can carry out very complicated tasks very quickly, and with a high degree of accuracy.
- Machines can perform in seconds jobs that may take even the most skilled workers hours or days to achieve; indeed, machines can do jobs that are impossible for human workers.
- There is far less waste when machines are used, and the quality is usually consistent.
- Robots can operate in hazardous conditions.
- Robots or machinery will perform repetitive tasks that human workers would not enjoy.

Disadvantages of automation/mechanisation
- Machines are harder to replace than humans if they break down.
- They will be able to carry out only a very narrow range of tasks.
- They are very expensive to install and maintain.

3.2 METHODS OF PRODUCTION

111

Many firms will face problems when introducing machines:

- Workers will be unhappy and demotivated as they are worried about their job security.
- Some workers will have to be made redundant, and may be due redundancy payments.
- Workers will need to be trained to use the machines.
- Mistakes will be made until the workers are fully competent in their jobs.

Labour-intensive production

Labour-intensive production is where the use of labour is greater than the cost of capital or machines.

Advantages of labour-intensive production

- It is often easier to organise production on a small scale.
- 'One-off' orders can be easily accommodated to meet the customer's exact requirements.
- The order can be changed during the production process to meet the customer's requirements.
- This will mean increased customer satisfaction, which will improve an organisation's competitiveness.
- Workers will see the results of their labour, which can be motivating.
- There is higher quality of product due to skilled workers being used, giving increased customer satisfaction.
- The business can charge a higher/premium price due to it being a unique product.

Disadvantages of labour-intensive production

- Production costs are likely to be higher for the job costing as there are few economies of scale.
- Production time may be longer than using other methods as individual requirements of the job have to be met.
- Costs may be higher as specialist machinery may be required.
- Skilled workers will be required, adding wage costs to production.
- There can be higher than average research costs which again will be reflected in the price charged to the customer, and this may be off-putting.
- Costs are high as a variety of machinery or tools is required which may often be laying idle.
- Lead times can be lengthy and this means that customers cannot simply walk in and purchase the product; again this may be off-putting.

Research task

Identify three businesses that would use labour-intensive production, justifying your choices.

Labour-intensive v. capital-intensive production

As already mentioned, labour-intensive production is where the cost of labour is greater than the cost of capital. Capital intensive is when machines are used in production rather than workers. In most cases capital intensive is preferred because it can be a lot cheaper.

There are advantages and disadvantages of using skilled workers instead of machines as shown below.

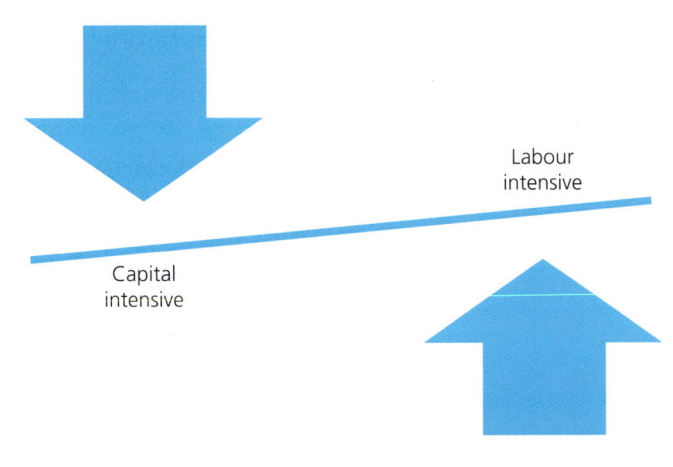

Advantages of using skilled workers

- A niche market can be created and higher prices charged because the product has been made by skilled workers.
- As skilled workers have a great deal of experience, they can spot mistakes quickly. They will pay attention to detail and are able to produce unique products.
- Machines are expensive and a lot of money is needed at the outset to buy them.
- Skilled workers will produce quality products.
- Skilled workers can adapt what they are producing to suit the changing needs of the customer.
- Personal touch – customers like dealing with people who they can talk to, rather than machines.

Disadvantages of using skilled workers

- Skilled workers take their time – machines are much faster.
- Skilled workers are very expensive in terms of wages, etc.
- They can make expensive mistakes.
- They cannot work long hours and can get tired and stressed.
- Workers need to be motivated, managed and supervised.
- Machines do not phone in sick and do not need holidays.
- Workers need safe working conditions.
- Skilled workers have to be paid higher wages than semi-skilled machine operators.

Research task

Identify two businesses that would use capital-intensive production, justifying your choices.

Revision questions

1. Compare labour-intensive and capital-intensive production methods.
2. Justify the use of automation for large-scale production.
3. Describe the costs and benefits of introducing robots to a production line.
4. Discuss the merits of employing only highly skilled workers.
5. Discuss the impact of increasing use of automated production.

3.3 Quality

What quality means to an organisation depends on customer requirements and expectations. In order to be successful an organisation must meet, and try to exceed, customer requirements from the goods or service.

Quality is important because it brings a number of benefits to the organisation.

- It increases customer satisfaction.
- It improves the reputation of the business.
- It can increase sales and profits.
- It generates fewer complaints or returns as customers will benefit from quality services and products.

There are a number of different quality measures that the business can take to ensure the quality of its products.

Quality control

Quality control involves checking a sample of the raw materials at the start of production and then checking the final product; it is a simple inspection system. Although it is a relatively cheap method, it has a number of disadvantages as shown on the next page.

> **Disadvantages of quality control**
> - It is an historic concept and assumes that there will be a degree of waste up to 25 per cent.
> - The system of quality checking at the end of the manufacturing process can lead to a whole batch being discarded if errors are found.
> - It can lead to significantly increased costs of production.
> - Goods that are tested for quality-control purposes need to be destroyed.
> - Sampling does not ensure that all goods that leave the production line are of the highest quality.
> - There can be a high level of customer complaints or returns as customers will not be happy to accept goods that are below standard, having slipped through the quality checks.

Quality assurance

This focuses on the prevention of errors, and takes place throughout the production process.

- Quality is checked at every stage of the process instead of just at the end.
- This reduces waste to levels as low as five per cent.
- It can be an expensive system to set up.

For some organisations, quality control and quality assurance mean the same thing; however, in Higher Business Management we differentiate between them.

Quality management

(Diagram: A cycle showing Quality management at the top, connecting to Benchmarking, Mystery shoppers, Quality circles, and Quality standards/symbols.)

Quality management is the most effective way of ensuring quality in the goods or service for the customer. It combines with other existing approaches to quality, to focus all aspects of the business on quality.

The eight principles of quality management

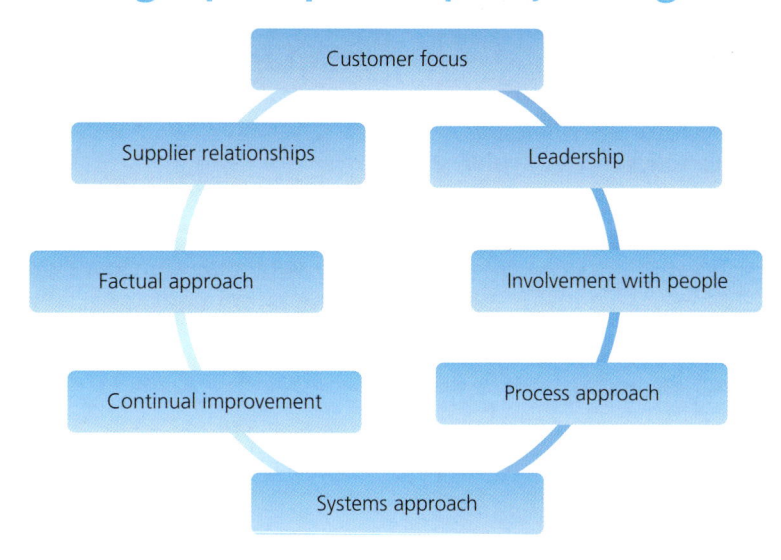

- Customer focus
- Leadership
- Involvement with people
- Process approach
- Systems approach
- Continual improvement
- Factual approach
- Supplier relationships

Customer focus	Ties in with the marketing mix, putting the customers' needs at the heart of the quality process. The aim is to exceed both external (consumer) and internal (rest of the organisation) customer requirements.
Leadership	Creating an ethos to ensure all people involved in the process are focused on achieving the quality objective.
Involvement with people	Complete involvement of staff in using their abilities for the benefit of the organisation.
Process approach	All activities and resources are managed as a process.
Systems approach	Identifying, understanding and managing all processes involved as a single system to achieve the organisation's aims.
Continual improvement	Using process-performance measures to continually try to improve the processes and system.
Factual approach	All decisions are based on the analysis of data and information available.
Supplier relationships	The relationships between the organisation and its suppliers are seen to be interdependent, so developing a mutually beneficial relationship between them increases their ability to add value.

Quality-management systems are developed to benefit the organisation, employees, suppliers and the customer. They aim to provide a consistent, high-quality product or service, allowing the organisation to achieve success.

In the quality-management process:

- The business has clearly defined policies on quality so that the whole organisation is focused on achieving it.
- All staff are involved and committed to ensuring high quality in their work.
- The organisation is focused on customer satisfaction.
- All processes are evaluated on a regular basis to ensure quality.
- Staff training is an ongoing process.
- Products are checked at all stages of the production process.
- Quality circles are set up to make the processes more efficient.
- Teamwork is important at all levels.
- The business constantly strives to make processes more efficient and reduce waste.

Benefits of quality management
- Motivated staff should ensure a high-quality product or service.
- Using high-quality raw materials will lead to a high-quality product or service.
- Highly skilled staff will result in good customer services.
- Using up-to-date machinery will help standardise product quality.
- It should result in fewer products being faulty or not of a proper standard.
- It should result in fewer customer complaints.
- It should result in repeat sales.
- It should result in the organisation having a good reputation.

Disadvantages of quality management
- It may mean higher purchasing costs for raw materials.
- It can result in high staff-training costs.
- There may be higher staffing costs.
- There may be slow production due to constant checking.

Quality standards and symbols

BSI (British Standards Institution) certification is internationally recognised as demonstrating to customers, competitors, suppliers, staff and investors that the business is committed to being the best it can be.

BSI not only carries out audits but also provides training and business-improvement software to improve quality in many areas of business from manufacturing to health care, each with its own standard.

CE Marking

This mark shows that a product meets European Union (EU) safety, health or environmental standards, which allows businesses to gain fast and easy access to the European markets.

CE Marking by manufacturers can offer customers a measure of reassurance about the quality and safety of their products. The 'CE' Mark on a product means that a manufacturer claims that it conforms to minimum legal requirements – for instance, in respect of health and safety – as laid down by EU regulators.

BSI's Notified Body status for many European Directives and Regulations enables it to offer third-party testing and factory production-control assessments, where products require it.

BSI Kitemark

This mark also shows that a product or service meets certain safety, quality or security standards. It also provides ongoing reassurance to the end user as it means that the product or service has been checked not once, but regularly, to prevent standards slipping over time.

ISO 9000

This International Organisation for Standardisation (ISO) award is in recognition of standards for quality management in the business.

Benefits of BSI certification
- BSI awards are used to show quality has been approved.
- A specific standard can then be met for all the organisation's products.
- Levels of quality can be guaranteed to customers.
- The Kitemark symbol can be used as a marketing tool.
- Certification will give customers confidence when purchasing a product.
- Higher prices can then be charged.
- Fewer customer complaints or returns.
- Limits waste.
- It can lead to increased sales, repeat sales or gain of sales from competitors.
- Many other businesses will only deal with companies that are BSI certificated.

Disadvantages of BSI certification
- It is an expensive process to go through.
- It is time-consuming to go through initially.
- Rigorous checks and paperwork must be kept, including records of purchases and production.
- Agreed standards need to be maintained at all times.
- It will require thorough checks and audits by BSI staff to prove the standards have been met.

Research task
Find three other trade logos that are used in business.

Trade logos

Logos such as Fairtrade or ABTA (Association of British Travel Agents) are given to organisations that meet specific standards. This assures consumers that they can rely on these products in meeting certain standards or give assurances that buying from that business is safer than others without the logo.

All ABTA members act on an agreed code of conduct in the standard of service they provide. In the event that the travel company goes out of business, the customer is assured they will be reimbursed for the cost of the holiday. All advertising should be accurate, they have fair terms of trading and they aim to provide a fast and efficient complaints procedure.

The benefits and disadvantages of trade logos are similar to those of BSI. For example:

Benefits of trade logos
- They give the business a better reputation.
- Customers are more likely to purchase.
- Higher prices can be charged.
- Show products meet industry standards.

Disadvantages of trade logos
- It can be expensive to meet the requirements.
- The organisation has to comply with inspections.

Benchmarking

Benchmarking is a process of quality assurance that uses the best performers in a particular industry to set standards for others to meet. This means that organisations from the same business sector can compare their performance to the market leaders in the same field.

It can be difficult to decide who to benchmark against. The setting of benchmarked standards is somewhat subjective as it may be identified from sources such as customers, journalists and business analysts.

Using best methods identified through best practice in industry would help raise the quality of products or services.

Benefits of benchmarking
- Identifies best practice in the market, so will improve the performance of the organisation if those techniques are adopted.
- It enhances competitiveness.
- It is a continuous process of improvement.
- Can act as a motivator for employees, giving them goals to achieve.
- May identify other functions that could be improved in the business.

Disadvantages of benchmarking
- It can be difficult to gather all the relevant information needed as it is often not available.
- It can be time-consuming to study and analyse competitors' techniques.
- The organisation may be unable to adopt techniques due to internal constraints.
- Can only be as good as the benchmark set.

Quality circles

This is where small groups of workers, including managers, meet to discuss where improvements can be made in production.

It allows the actual workers doing the job to make the suggestions which are then put forward for approval. This results in a more motivated workforce.

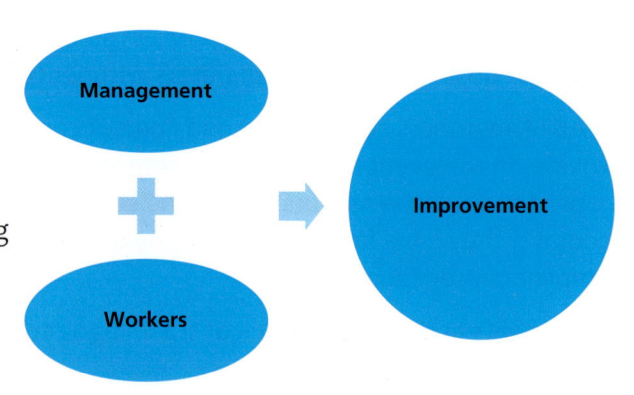

Management + Workers → Improvement

Workers doing the job can often have a better idea of how to improve than management.

Mystery shoppers

Mystery shoppers are outside specialists trained to measure how well a business performs in its treatment of customers. Mystery shoppers can be used to ensure managers and staff are focused on the key issues of customer care.

In customer service a mystery shopper will look at:

- How the service they received compared with the service they expected.
- How much they trust the business and its product.
- How customer service compares with competitors.
- How much loyalty they feel towards the business as a result of their last transaction.
- How much they feel the business values them as a customer.
- How much they feel they are treated like an individual person.

In employee performance a mystery shopper will look at:

- Whether all staff complied with legal requirements.
- Whether staff were honest.
- Whether staff followed company laid-down standards and procedures.
- How the business's service compared against the best companies in the industry.
- Possible training needs.

Whichever quality method is chosen, it will rely heavily on the staff involved in delivering the quality product or service.

Fully trained staff will be needed to ensure that quality is met at each stage of the production and delivery process, including after-sales service, and they will need to be motivated to ensure that quality is maintained.

Revision questions

1. Justify the use of benchmarking.
2. Explain how quality management benefits an organisation.
3. Discuss the use of mystery shoppers to ensure quality.
4. Describe the benefits and disadvantages of achieving BSI certification.
5. Discuss the disadvantages of introducing quality management for an organisation.

3.4 Ethical and environmental issues

Ethical behaviour and corporate social responsibility can bring significant benefits to a business. For example, they may:

- attract customers to the firm's products, thereby increasing sales and profits
- make employees want to stay with the business, reduce staff turnover and increase productivity
- attract more employees wanting to work for the business, reduce recruitment costs and enable the company to get the best employees
- attract investors and keep the company's share price high, thereby protecting the business from takeover.

Unethical behaviour or a lack of corporate social responsibility, by comparison, may damage a firm's reputation and make it less appealing to stakeholders. Profits could fall as a result.

Waste management/control

All businesses create waste. If it is not dealt with correctly by the business, it will face a number of problems.

- Consumers won't want to buy from a business whose products are polluting their environment.
- It gives the business a bad reputation, which will affect their sales.
- There are a number of legal obligations in terms of waste that the business needs to meet.

By law, businesses have a duty of care: first, to reduce the amount of waste they create and second, to deal with the waste they create in an environmentally sensitive way. The laws require them to:

- consider alternatives to just disposing of the waste, such as recycling
- store all waste products safely and securely
- keep records of all waste that they transport
- obtain a licence to transport, store, treat, recover or dispose of the waste themselves.

3.4 ETHICAL AND ENVIRONMENTAL ISSUES

Duty of care responsibilities

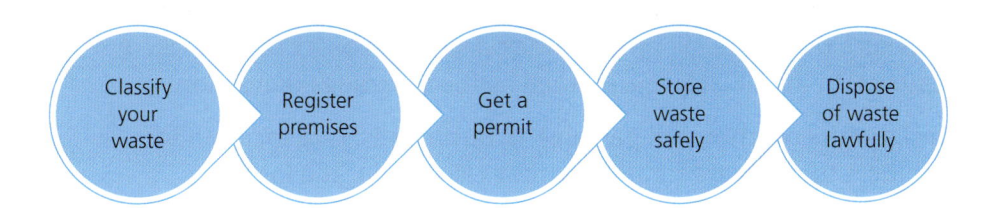

Classify your waste → Register premises → Get a permit → Store waste safely → Dispose of waste lawfully

Businesses will want to keep the cost of waste disposal as low as possible to ensure profitability. Most businesses will use a specialist firm to do this for them, but they have responsibility to ensure that the firm they use is fully licensed.

The government is also concerned with the packaging that businesses use, and has laid down guidelines that businesses must follow when designing their packaging:

- They must reduce the amount of packaging for their products in order to reduce the amount of waste created.
- They must only use the minimum weight and volume needed to keep the product safe and hygienic.
- The packaging must not contain high levels of hazardous substances.
- The packaging must be designed so that a certain amount of it can be recycled.
- Any packaging that is intended to be reused has to be designed so that it can be reused several times, not just once.

Strategies for reducing wastage:
- Train staff so fewer mistakes are made
- Provide less packaging in products
- Purchase inventory with little packaging
- Quality assurance to identify errors early
- Advertisements to encourage recycling
- Provide recycling points within the factory
- Purchase only what is required to prevent inventory deteriorating
- Use ethical suppliers and biofuels

Fair trade

All organisations should aim to trade fairly with all suppliers. The terms of trade should not adversely affect the viability of suppliers.

The Groceries Code Adjudicator (GCA) regulates and investigates stores that are seen to breach the Groceries Supply Code of Practice. Large retailers could be fined up to one per cent of their annual turnover if they are found to be breaching the code. This could include delaying payments to suppliers, adding unnecessary costs to suppliers and excessive terms of trade.

Fairtrade is a global movement that works to achieve better prices, decent working conditions and fair terms of trade for farmers and workers. It supports small-scale farmers and workers who are marginalised from trade in a variety of ways. It makes sure they get a fair price for their product in order to allow them to stay in business. In the UK, it is represented by the Fairtrade Foundation.

Fairtrade works with governments, parliament, businesses, civil society and other stakeholders to advocate for policies that will make trade fair.

In order to use the Fairtrade mark on its products, a business must meet international fair-trade standards. These are set by the international certification body, Fairtrade International. The business will have to pay its suppliers an appropriate rate to ensure they can continue to operate. This may add to the cost of production. The process itself will take time and money to secure the Fairtrade mark, and also to maintain it.

By putting the Fairtrade mark on its products, stocking Fairtrade goods or serving them to customers, the business can demonstrate its ethical commitment to customers, have a positive impact on the producers of the commodities with which it works and get closer to its supply chain.

Report
Visit the Fairtrade website (**www.fairtrade.org.uk**) and produce a report on how it can help a small business.

Environmental problems and solutions/ethical issues

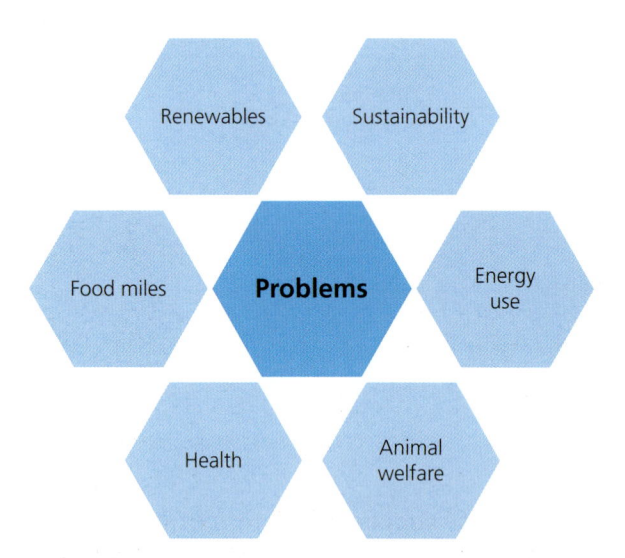

Renewables · Sustainability · Food miles · **Problems** · Energy use · Health · Animal welfare

There are a number of problems that businesses must handle well in the eyes of their customers in order to maintain confidence in their products. They should:

- use materials from sustainable sources
- ensure their food products do not contain unhealthy ingredients
- provide safety and/or nutritional information with their products
- work to reduce their carbon footprint by reducing pollutants

- use and support renewable energies
- support the local communities where they operate
- use local suppliers where possible to reduce food miles
- have high standards for animal welfare
- avoid the use of unnecessary pollutants
- meet and try to exceed government targets for recycling.

To help with this, many businesses have installed solar panels and wind turbines at their premises. Supermarkets will now try to source more of their supplies from local businesses. They will now check their supply chain to ensure that their suppliers operate to the same standards that they do.

Businesses will have set policies for dealing with waste and recycling, product safety and community engagement.

Revision questions

1. Describe the ethical issues faced by organisations.
2. Discuss the benefits of fair trade for a retailer.
3. Discuss methods a business could use to reduce the environmental impact of its operations.
4. Describe the link between waste management and environmental responsibility.

3.5 Technology

Role of technology in operations

Technology now plays an important part in all manufacturing systems, and keeping up to date with the latest innovations is essential to ensuring the business remains competitive.

The use of barcodes and EPOS (electronic point of sale) systems at the tills allows the business to track goods from production to warehouse to retailer and finally to customer in real time. Technology can also be used to indicate peaks in demand for a product, or areas where it is selling well, to make sure inventory is always available for sale by increasing production.

If the product is not selling well in a particular area then a business can increase promotional activities to try to increase sales.

Benefits of technology in production

- It increases productivity due to the use of machinery which can allow more products to be made.
- Unit costs of production are reduced.
- It reduces waste as technology makes fewer mistakes than humans and this increases profit.
- A consistent quality of product is made, which can increase customer satisfaction.
- It improves production methods through use of robotics and CAD/CAM.
- Technology can be used in situations that are hazardous to workers, which results in fewer accidents to the workforce.
- Accuracy should be increased as technology results in fewer mistakes, especially when carrying out large calculations, resulting in improved customer satisfaction.
- It improves efficiency in administrative functions.
- It enhances reputation with potential customers.
- It reduces staffing costs.
- It increases the speed of information handling.
- It allows purchase orders to be placed online and email confirmation of orders to be sent/received.
- The internet can be used to compare supplier prices before placing purchase orders.
- It improves the speed of communication due to the use of email or intranets, which makes decision making quicker.
- It increases the access to information which should result in a more informed, better decision being made.

Benefits of technology in inventory management

- Databases can be used to keep balances of inventory which are automatically updated.
- Total inventory values and store sales can be checked easily at any time of the day.
- Linked to tills through EPOS.
- Inventory can be ordered automatically when it reaches the re-order level.
- Decisions on slow-moving inventory or viewing bestsellers can be made by managers from their computer.
- Regional variations in inventory can be highlighted from head office.
- It reduces the danger of inventory going out of date.
- It reduces staff theft of inventory.

Costs of using technology

- Initial and recurring costs of hardware and equipment.
- Ongoing cost of replacing and upgrading obsolete systems.
- Installation costs – for example, the cost of installing a network infrastructure – can be quite high.
- New furniture to house equipment.
- Staff training – this will inevitably lead to a loss of working time.
- Losses in efficiency as even staff who have been trained to use the new system will be unfamiliar with it for a period of time and more likely to make mistakes.
- Teething problems will also contribute to inefficiencies.
- Possibility of losing information.
- Computer viruses.
- Increased risk of commercial espionage and hacking.
- Health and safety issues for staff such as repetitive strain injury and backache.
- The continued use of technology leads to a dependency culture which becomes more and more difficult to escape.

> Remember, introducing new technology has a cost, and the business will want to keep that cost as low as possible. It should, however, ensure that it takes account of possible negative effects, particularly when it is first introduced.

Revision questions

1. Describe the impact on operations of using outdated technologies.
2. Describe the benefits of using modern technology in operations.
3. Describe the use of technology in inventory control.
4. Explain the impact of introducing new technology to the operations department.

Section Assessment: Management of Operations

This segment aims to test your knowledge of the preceding section with exam-standard questions. It is recommended that you answer the questions based on the standard timing for the external examination, which allows around two minutes per mark. There is a selection of questions that you might expect to find in both Section 1 and Section 2 of the question paper.

Section 1 is worth 30 marks in total and the allocation of each question can range from 1–8 marks. Section 2 has four questions of 15 marks each, containing individual questions in the range of 1–8 marks. The difference with Section 2 is that it specialises in individual topics, so there could be a 15-mark question on Operations, as exemplified below. Remember that Section 2 questions tend to dig a little deeper into your knowledge of particular areas of the course.

Once you have attempted these questions, it would be a good idea to ask your teacher to mark them or go over appropriate responses to them.

Section 1 questions

		Marks
1	Explain the importance of ethical business operations.	4
2	Compare centralised and decentralised warehousing.	3
3	Discuss the use of automation to produce complex products.	5
4	Describe the benefits of using a mystery shopper to gather information.	3
5	Explain the advantages of using just-in-time inventory control.	3

Section 2 questions

			Marks
6	a	Describe the impact on an organisation of not being environmentally responsible.	4
	b	Describe the problems of holding too much inventory.	4
	c	Compare quality control and quality assurance.	4
	d	Discuss the use of quality circles.	3
7	a	Describe the quality methods that an organisation may use.	6
	b	Describe the costs of ensuring that business operations are environmentally responsible.	4
	c	Justify the production methods that an organisation could use for high-volume, high-quality production.	5
8	a	Describe the costs and benefits of: • benchmarking • quality circles • quality control.	6
	b	Describe the use of: • CE Marking • BSI Kitemark.	4
	c	Explain the importance of quality to customers.	3
	d	Describe the impact of robotics on operations.	2

Section 4

Management of People

Once you complete this section you will be able to:

- ✓ analyse factors influencing human resource management and suggest strategies for improved performance in this functional area

- ✓ apply knowledge and understanding of key business theories and concepts relating to human resource management in familiar and unfamiliar contexts

The Management of People section of this book looks at how businesses are managed in terms of the people who help to run them.

People are the single biggest investment of any organisation in terms of both time and money. It is therefore important that they are managed properly. Each individual employee makes a valuable contribution towards the success of the organisation by helping to achieve organisational objectives. Employees can be viewed as a business resource, and the organisation aims to make the most efficient use of its resources in order to be successful.

SECTION 4 MANAGEMENT OF PEOPLE

Topic 4.1 Workforce planning	You should be able to describe approaches that could be used to manage human resources effectively, making reference to any of the following:
	
	• elements of workforce planning, for example:
	  • skills analysis of current staff
	  • staffing forecasts to meet demand
	  • planning internal and external supply of staff
	  • costs and benefits of internal and external recruitment
	  • costs and benefits of selection methods.

Topic 4.2 Training and development	You should be aware of:
	
	• the relevance of staff development and training to organisations and employees
	  • different ways of training staff, for example:
	    • apprenticeships
	    • graduate training schemes
	    • corporate training schemes
	    • work-based qualifications
	    • continuing professional development (CPD)
	• the costs and benefits of different ways of training staff
	• different types of appraisal, for example:
	  • one to one
	  • 360 degree
	  • peer to peer
	• the costs and benefits of appraisal to organisations and employees.

Topic 4.3 Motivation and leadership	You should be aware of:
	
	• motivation theories:
	  • Maslow
	  • Herzberg
	• the benefits of motivation
	• the role of management in motivating employees
	• styles of leadership and their costs and benefits:
	  • autocratic
	  • democratic
	  • laissez-faire
	• how leadership styles are used and justified in a given business scenario.

Topic 4.4 Employee relations	You should be aware of:
	
	• the meaning of employee relations
	• the impact of positive employee relations
	• legal and company policies and processes, and their impact on employee relations, for example:
	  • grievance
	  • discipline
	  • dismissal
	  • absenteeism
	  • redundancy
	• the role of external institutions and their impact on organisations and employees, for example:
	  • trade unions
	  • ACAS
	• how organisations use employee participation and their costs and benefits, for example:
	  • works councils
	  • worker directors
	  • consultative committees.

Topic 4.5 Legislation	You should be aware of:
	
	• the impact of current employment legislation on organisations and employee relations, for example:
	  • Health and Safety at Work Act
	  • Equality Act
	  • National Minimum Wage Regulations
	  • National Living Wage Regulations.

Topic 4.6 Technology	You should be aware of:
	
	• how technology can be used in human resource management, for example:
	  • databases
	  • video conferencing
	  • online application forms
	  • job advertising
	  • e-diary
	  • presentation software
	  • virtual learning environment (VLE) training
	  • electronic testing
	• the costs and benefits of using technology.

4.1 Workforce planning

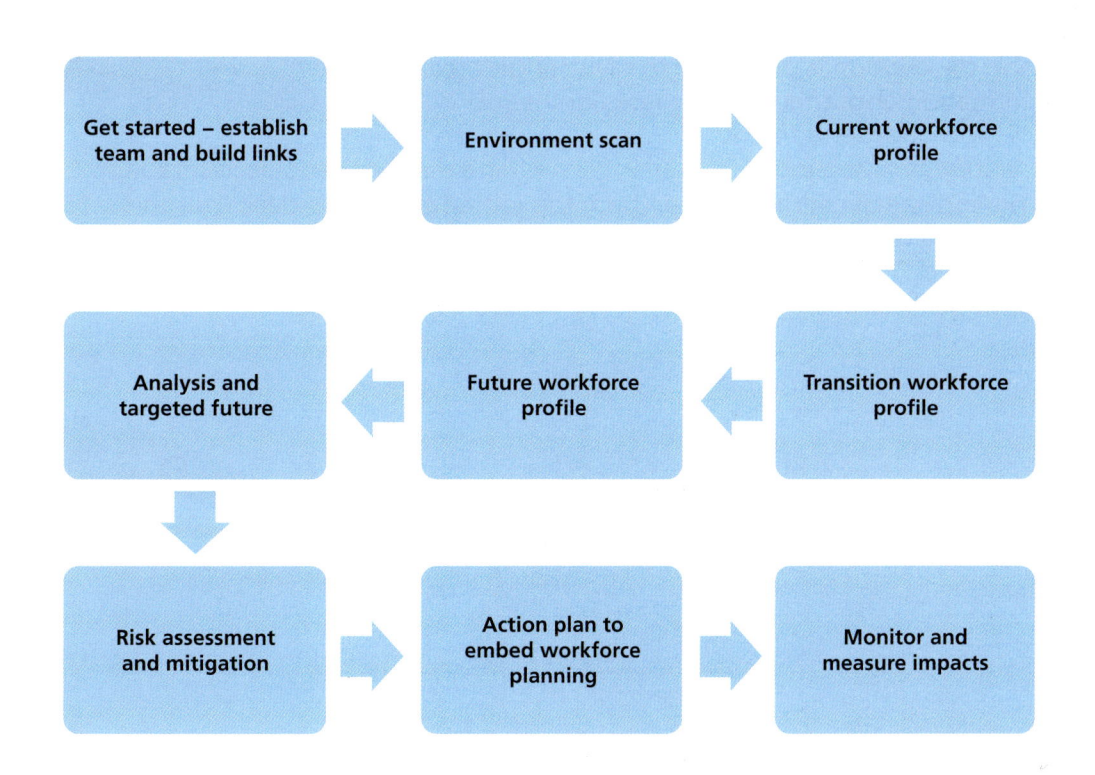

Get started – establish team and build links → Environment scan → Current workforce profile → Transition workforce profile → Future workforce profile → Analysis and targeted future → Risk assessment and mitigation → Action plan to embed workforce planning → Monitor and measure impacts

Workforce planning is a continual process that is used to align the needs of the organisation with those of its workforce in order that the organisation can meet all of its objectives.

Strategic workforce planning usually operates over a three- to five-year period and links into the strategic business objectives.

Operational workforce planning typically covers the immediate twelve- to eighteen-month period and should align with the business planning cycle.

Workforce planning will involve a skills analysis of all current staff. This involves collecting information from all employees about their individual skills to enable the organisation to build a complete picture of its workforce, its particular strengths and weaknesses.

It is also important to be able to plan ahead, so staffing forecasts will be drawn up to enable demand to be forecast and planned for. This links to the need for planning the numbers of internal and external staff that will be required and to arrange for their recruitment.

The recruitment process is detailed below.

The recruitment process

A job analysis is conducted by the human resources department, which looks at the duties and responsibilities of the job and records the skills required to do the job effectively.

Using the job analysis, two documents used in recruitment are created:

1. A job description is produced to give candidates more information about the specific tasks of the job:
   - job title/department
   - duties of the job
   - responsibilities
   - line manager and accountability.
2. A person specification is written from the job analysis. This describes the ideal candidate the employer is looking for to fill the post:
   - skills
   - qualifications
   - experience
   - personal qualities.

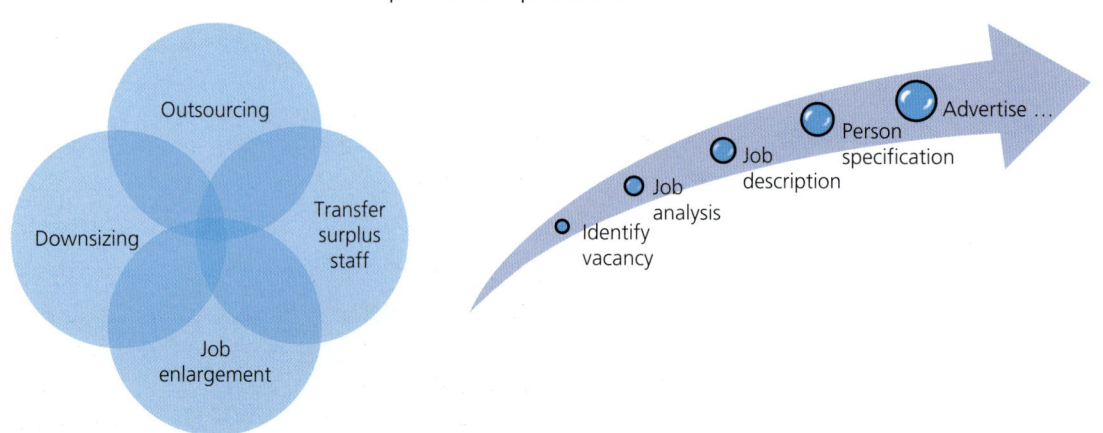

However, organisations may not always want to fill a job vacancy. Instead, they may see this as an opportunity to reduce staffing costs.

Internal versus external recruitment

Organisations and the recruiting manager will often need to make a decision on whether to advertise a vacancy internally or externally. A suitable candidate may already have been identified internally, in which case the expense of 'going external' can be avoided.

There are other advantages to recruiting internally as shown below.

Advantages of internal recruitment
- Lower costs than external recruitment.
- The person is already known – risk of appointing the wrong person is reduced.
- Induction training is not required.
- Existing investment in the employee is not lost if they are retained and promoted.
- The prospect of internal promotion is a strong motivator for existing employees.

Disadvantages of internal recruitment
- The choice of candidate is restricted.
- A better person for the job may exist in the external pool.
- The opportunity for new workers to bring new ideas and skills to the organisation is missed.
- Internal promotion often just creates a 'domino effect' – it creates another vacancy to be filled.

The use of external recruitment opens up a different range of possibilities. There is a wide range of methods of recruiting staff from outside the organisation and the method used will often depend on the nature of the vacancy.

Benefits of using external recruitment
- Unskilled and semi-skilled labour can be recruited using the local job centre.
- Many temporary posts are filled using an employment agency.
- More senior and management posts are often recruited using a specialist recruitment agency.
- Specialist staff can be recruited via trade magazines or a specialist agency.
- The internet plays a vital role in modern recruitment, whether this is an advert on the organisation's website or on a jobs website such as www.s1jobs.com.

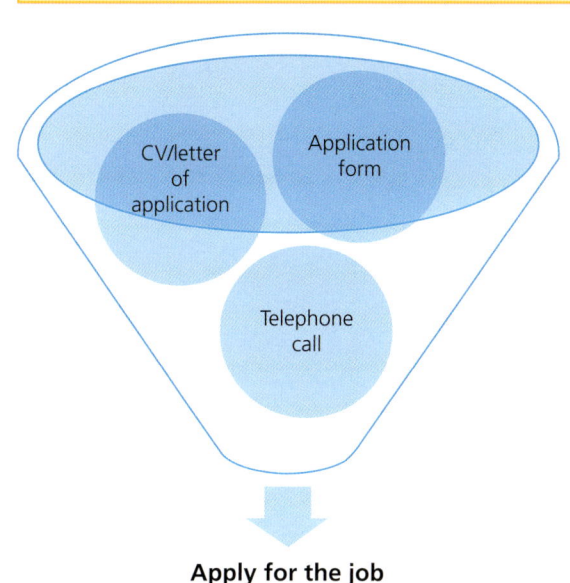

Methods of selection

Different organisations will choose different methods when it comes to selecting the best person to fill a vacancy. The first step in selection is deciding what form the application for the vacancy will take.

The organisation may stipulate how applicants are allowed to apply. For example, this may be by use of the organisation's application form only. In this way, the organisation can control the type and flow of information about each applicant and it can make it easier to carry out an initial screening of those who have applied for the vacancy.

[Funnel diagram: CV/letter of application, Application form, Telephone call → Apply for the job]

An application form is popular as it gives all applicants the same questions and opportunities to sell themselves for the position in question. The application form should be used in conjunction with the person specification when making a decision about which applicants will progress to the next stage and which applicants will be rejected. Applicants who will not progress to the next stage of the selection process should be notified by email or letter. It is increasingly common for organisations to advise applicants prior to application that should they be unsuccessful at any stage of the selection process then they will not be informed and to use a timescale to define this. For example, they may advise that following the closing date for applications, if the applicant has not received notification of progress to the next stage within three weeks then they have been unsuccessful. This is usually due to issues surrounding company time and cost.

Some organisations still favour the submission of a curriculum vitae (CV) as a means of application for a vacancy. This may be done by hard copy or electronically (soft copy). There are some advantages to the applicant when applying with a CV, such as the fact that it can be completely personalised and may offer a better opportunity to 'sell yourself' as being most suited to the vacancy.

In any instance, the organisation will use the information provided to select those applicants who are most suited to the job and move them along to the next stage of the selection process. This usually means that the best candidates for interview will be listed on a short leet or a long leet. A long leet is an initial list of candidates who have been selected for interview. It will be a best guess at who is to be interviewed based on the information provided in the application and who best meets the criteria for the job. A short leet is a final list of candidates for interview. It may be reached following interview of those on the long leet or the organisation may proceed directly to the short leet stage.

A long leet will usually have around ten suitable candidates listed. Following interview of the candidates on the long leet, a decision may be made on who to appoint or else this may result in the production of a short leet. A short leet will usually have five or fewer suitable candidates who are closely suited to the vacancy on offer. As mentioned earlier, these candidates may have reached this point as a result of strict screening at the application stage or they may have arrived at this point as a result of surviving the long leet stage.

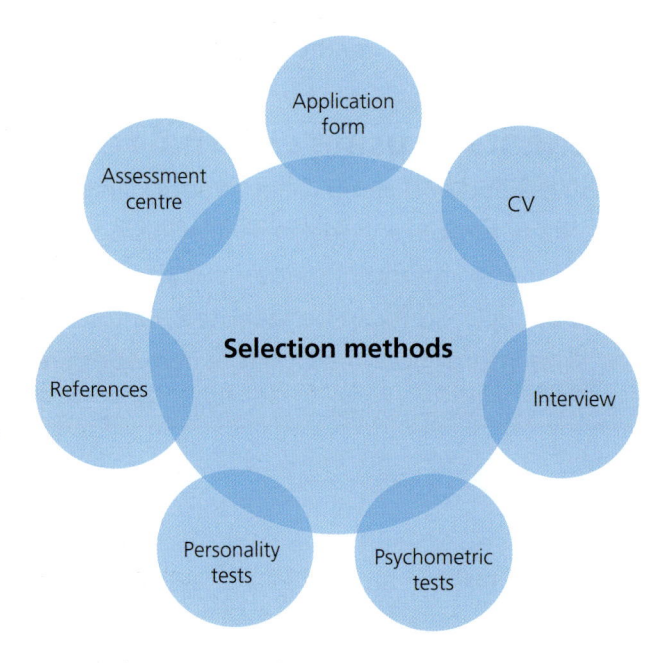

Selection methods
- Application form
- CV
- Interview
- Psychometric tests
- Personality tests
- References
- Assessment centre

Interviews

Interviews are the most common method used to make the final decision on which applicant will be offered the job. The decision will be based on who most closely matches the person specification and also performs best on the day of the interview.

It is increasingly common for organisations to use competency-based interview techniques. This means that the interview is conducted using questions that only relate to the particular competencies of the job.

However, regardless of the questions used at interview or the style of the interview itself, ongoing research shows that interviews are not a very successful way of predicting how well a person will perform in a particular job.

It is normal business practice for interviews to be carried out by the line manager to whom the person being recruited will report. Such employees will be trained by the human resources department to ensure that they are fully aware of the rules and regulations relating to recruitment. The recruiting manager will normally be accompanied at interview by another member of staff from the organisation. This may be a more senior member of staff or it could be a member of staff from another department. It is important that the people carrying out the interview are suitably qualified as they may be too easily persuaded by the appearance, personality or interview technique of a candidate.

The interview also represents an opportunity for the applicant to find out more about the job and the organisation. It may be that on conclusion of the interview they feel that they would not fit into the organisation.

A successful interview happens when the interviewer(s) has prepared beforehand. Many human resource departments have a process in place with accompanying documentation to assist with this. Good interviews should elicit the best responses from the candidates and make them feel welcome and relaxed in the business environment. Interviews are a good way to identify the personality and personal characteristics of the applicant and also get a feel for how they match up with their application (application form or CV) and any references that have been taken up prior to interview.

However, interviews are not always the best way to appoint people. Some applicants get very nervous and may not perform well at the interview. Sometimes, the people carrying out the interview can make unfair judgements based on performance at the interview or even based on the appearance of the applicant.

Four different interview styles are identified on the following page. The type of interview used will depend on the job being interviewed for and the policies of the organisation itself.

One to one
- Usually a face-to-face interview with one interviewer asking the questions.
- Can be less stressful for the applicant than a panel interview.

Panel
- Several interviewers sit on a panel and take turns to ask questions.
- May involve an interviewer who is external to the organisation.

Successive
- Several interviews one after the other with a different interviewer each time.
- Each interviewer may choose to specialise their questions and target different areas and skills.

Telephone
- Conducted over the phone or using video/audio conferencing.
- May be recorded for future review.
- Saves money on travel and accommodation.

Group task

Have you ever been interviewed? As a group, discuss the interview process and make a list of questions that you think might be asked at a typical interview.

Testing

Aptitude tests

These are objective tests that may also be used in the selection process. This means that each applicant's performance can be measured and compared. Sometimes they will be used prior to interview or as part of the interview process to aid the scoring applied to each individual applicant. Each test is designed to test a particular skill.

Psychometric tests

Psychometric tests are designed to measure the abilities of the applicant. They can be used prior to interview as part of the selection process or as part of the interview process itself, providing information that the interviewer(s) will use in order to further inform their decisions.

These tests typically focus on verbal and numerical reasoning and take the form of timed multiple-choice tests which are sat under examination conditions.

Recently, many large organisations have started to move away from using such tests as their accuracy and validity have been called into question.

Personality tests

Personality tests are designed to 'measure' the personality of the applicant and give an insight into their values and beliefs. They are also typically used to ascertain whether the applicant is a team player or holds any particular strengths or weaknesses within their personality. This allows the organisation to make a more informed judgement when it comes to deciding who should get the job.

Medical tests

Medical tests determine whether or not the candidate is fit and healthy for the purposes of the job. They are often used by the army and police as part of their selection process.

Different types of testing can have different impacts on different applicants. Some people react well to the challenge of tests while others may struggle to give their best in the test environment. There are advantages and disadvantages in using testing as shown below.

Advantages of testing
- Good for making comparisons.
- Tests suitability of the applicant against the person specification.
- Verifies the claims made by the applicant.

Disadvantages of testing
- Applicants can be affected by nerves.
- Poor testing can lead to discrimination.
- Results can be unreliable if not managed by properly trained staff.

WWW
Try out some psychometric tests on yourself at www.allthetests.com.

Group task
As a group, discuss the use of testing as part of the interview process and how the results of testing might be used. Do you think it is fair to all candidates?

An applicant may need to attend a specialised **assessment centre** to undertake a series of tests as part of the interview process.

References

A reference is usually requested after a person has been offered a job and accepted it. The reference is used to confirm that the person applying for the job is who they say they are. References are normally written statements from previous employers or other reliable persons who can give information about the applicant to the potential employer. Any reference provided should be honest, open, truthful and unbiased.

Flexible working

Flexible working is supported by most organisations, but the opportunities will be determined by the needs of the business. It is a way of working that is designed to suit the needs of the employee. This could include flexible start and finish times or working from another location, such as home.

Every employee that has worked for the same employer for at least 26 weeks has a legal right to request flexible working. Note that this right is not just applicable to parents and carers. While every employee has the right to make the request, the employer does not have to agree to the request. Employees can only make one request in any twelve-month period.

The government supports flexible working and there is an expectation that employers will deal with all such requests in a reasonable manner. In considering a formal written request for flexible working from an employee, the employer should:

1. Assess the advantages and disadvantages of the request for the organisation.
2. Hold a meeting to discuss the request with the employee directly.
3. Offer an appeals process in the event that the request is denied.
4. Deal with the request and any appeal within three months of the receipt of the original request.

There are several types of flexible working as shown in the adjacent diagram.

All employers have the right to refuse any application for flexible working if there is a good business reason for making that decision.

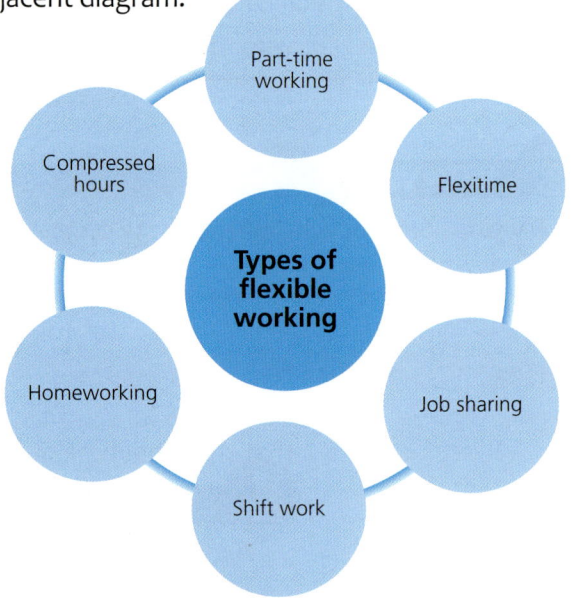

Types of flexible working:
- Part-time working
- Flexitime
- Job sharing
- Shift work
- Homeworking
- Compressed hours

There are advantages and disadvantages to flexible working.

Advantages of flexible working
- Ability to keep talented staff
- Reduction in absenteeism
- Increased employee commitment
- Better work/life balance
- Reduction in commuting – meets green agenda

Disadvantages of flexible working
- Lack of managerial direction for the employee
- Requires high level of personal motivation
- Adverse effect on teamworking
- Potential communication problems

Revision questions

1. Describe the advantages and disadvantages of internal recruitment.
2. Describe the advantages to an organisation of using external recruitment to fill a vacancy.
3. Discuss the advantages and disadvantages of using an interview as a method of selecting and appointing someone to a job.
4. Explain why some organisations choose to use tests to assess the suitability of candidates for a job.
5. Discuss the importance of flexible working in the modern world of work.

4.2 Training and development

Training has always been an important part of business – it helps people to be more effective in their job and to reach their full potential. Continuous training supports the Scottish Government ethos of lifelong learning, which is further supported by Curriculum for Excellence. There is a generally accepted view that, in modern society, education does not stop at completion of school years. There is the option of further and higher education which can contribute to preparation for the world of work. However, once workers enter the world of work, it becomes the responsibility of the employer to ensure that the employee has the correct skills and knowledge in place to be able to carry out their job effectively and efficiently. Most organisations have in place a framework of training and development to support their employees and to ensure that they have a suitably trained workforce.

Staff development

Staff development is the process of helping employees to reach their full potential. This will include training of some sort, but to achieve full development some of the training will not be specific to the employee's existing job. Instead, it will allow the employee to train in other areas of work and to develop new skills.

In this way, the organisation is supporting the overall development of its workforce as a whole. This may prepare some employees for future promotion or movement into different areas of the business. It can also promote a better understanding for employees as to how different parts of the organisation operate.

Staff training

Staff training is the process of teaching an employee how to do their job, how to do it better or how to do a new job in which they have little or no experience. Any training put in place by the employer should serve to improve the efficiency of the employee and make them more productive so that they are more able to contribute to the organisational objectives. A spin-off of training also valued by the employee is that the employee is likely to feel more motivated. Motivated staff are more likely to be loyal to the organisation and have lower rates of absenteeism.

Flexibility

Staff development and training help to achieve the organisational target of flexibility. All organisations hope to achieve a multi-skilled workforce. This doesn't just mean having a well-trained workforce. It also means having a workforce where each member can do a variety of jobs or tasks, and be flexible in meeting the changing needs of the organisation and its customers. Training and development give the opportunity to produce a more flexible workforce that can react quickly to the changing world of business.

Upgrading skills

Successful training helps to update the skills of the workforce and improve employee satisfaction. Employees who are comfortable carrying out their job roles will be less stressed and more at ease with what they are asked to do when they have the correct skills and training in place to support their work.

Employees are any organisation's single biggest asset, so it makes sense that the organisation should invest in that asset and develop it as much as possible.

Organisations that offer good training will find it easier to attract new staff as people will value the opportunity for self-development and learning new skills, which will make them more attractive when applying for promotion or to other organisations.

Organisations that have established training programmes in place are also more likely to attract more business and may qualify for quality awards.

Types of training

Induction training

All new employees should go through a process of induction training. This should be designed to introduce them to the organisation and its operations. It will make them more aware of what is expected of them in terms of the tasks they are expected to perform in their job.

Induction training should cover organisational policies and procedures as well as more practical issues, such as normal working patterns and where the toilets are located. The training may be completed in a few hours or may last a few weeks depending on the type of job and the organisation.

On-the-job training

This type of training takes place while the employee is actually doing the job at their place of work. It may involve a more experienced employee showing another worker how to do a job, or the more experienced employee may watch and offer advice and instruction while the learner worker completes the task. This is known as coaching.

Sometimes this type of training is used to train employees across different departments or areas of the organisation. It is often used to train managers so that they can 'learn the business' and get to know each part of the organisation.

There are many advantages of on-the-job training as shown on the right.

Advantages of on-the-job training
- Employee still does their job – saves money for cover.
- In-house trainers can be used.
- Training can be tailored to the employee and the organisation.
- Training is flexible for employees and the organisation.
- Usually cheaper than buying in training.
- Travel costs are saved.

Off-the-job training

This type of training can take several different forms. The organisation may have its own training department that is used to organise and deliver its own courses, or it may invite specialists to train the employees.

In some instances, the employee may be sent to training courses organised by trade associations or other professional bodies, or they may be sent to college or university to obtain further training and qualifications.

The main difference with this type of training is that it takes place while the employee is not carrying out their job and is usually off-site, away from the normal place of work.

The advantages and disadvantages of off-the-job training are shown below.

Advantages of off-the-job training
- Allows staff networking
- Perception of greater value by employees compared to on-the-job/in-house training
- Employees can return to work and cascade knowledge to colleagues

Disadvantages of off-the-job training
- Can be expensive
- Removes employees from the workplace – costing time and money
- Better trained employees may then leave the organisation

The use of technology in training and development

Technology is increasingly used in staff training and development. This is mainly due to the increasing use and availability of online learning. It is possible for an organisation to operate its own virtual learning environment (VLE). This is an online repository for storing and managing learning materials. It also provides the opportunity to create user accounts and interact with learners. A VLE could be administered with co-operation between the IT and HR departments to facilitate modules of learning for employees. It can also be used as part of induction training for new staff.

Online courses and the use of a VLE are a good way of monitoring employees who are undertaking a course of study or who need to complete time-critical training.

Costs and benefits to the organisation of training and development

Every organisation must make decisions about how to train its workforce. There is always a payoff between the relative costs and benefits, and these will differ between organisations. Some of the main costs and benefits are shown below.

Benefits of training
- Well-trained staff are more motivated to do a good job and be loyal to the organisation.
- It is easier for the organisation to meet its objectives with appropriately trained staff in place.
- The organisation may attract awards such as Investor in People status and thereby attract better staff to apply for vacancies
- Increased flexibility in the workforce.

Costs of training
- While in training, employees may not be as effective.
- An organisation with its own training department will incur additional employment costs.
- Well-qualified and trained staff may seek employment elsewhere once fully trained.
- Training that is not planned may be reactive to a situation – and costly.
- Financial costs.

Training schemes

Training schemes are generally available to those who are seeking employment but perhaps don't have all of the necessary skills to fulfil the job role. The employer undertakes to offer the employee training to enable them to gain the skills and abilities required to carry out the job for which they are being employed.

Some training schemes are open to everyone while others have a specific target market. In recent years, the government has given more financial support to organisations offering apprenticeships. An apprenticeship is generally an entry-point job in an organisation that is offered to someone who does not have a degree qualification. This means that while they are learning the job, the employer will also support them with a structured training programme to give them the skills, abilities and qualifications that are linked to the job role. Typically, this will involve attendance at college or university for an extended period of time during the first couple of years of employment. The benefit of this type of training is that the employee will gain valuable practical experience of the job while also learning new skills and gaining a recognised qualification.

Graduate training schemes are aimed at university graduates who are looking to enter the world of work on completion of their degree programme of study. In some instances this may involve a period of in-house training over a one- to two-year period, or studying for a professional qualification while working and being supported by the employer, for example, accountancy or actuarial work.

Graduate training schemes enable new recruits to settle quickly into a professional work environment, receive relevant skills development and get hands-on experience. Experience may be gained either working in a specific role within an established team or working in a number of different areas of the organisation over a period of time.

The National Health Service (NHS) also operates a graduate training scheme offering four different routes of application: finance, general management, human resources or health informatics.

Research task

Research a selection of training schemes that are offered by at least two different employers and write up a short report to show what they offer and the differences between the schemes.

Continuing professional development

'Continuing professional development' (CPD) is a term used to describe the learning activities that professionals engage in to develop and enhance their abilities and remain up to date in their chosen field of work. This is accompanied by the acceptance that academic qualifications must offer more vocational and skills-based or practical learning.

CPD combines different methods of learning, such as training workshops, conferences and events, e-learning programmes, best-practice techniques and ideas sharing, all focused on the need for an individual to improve and have effective professional development.

Work-based qualifications

Work-based qualifications or work-based learning enables employees to work while they learn, fitting their study around work and enabling them to gain useful practical experience.

Unlike training courses that require employees to be off-site during working hours, work-based qualifications involve either no or limited time away from the workplace. The benefits include:

- a minimum time away from the workplace
- use of the employees' work projects for assessment
- both employer and employee benefit from completion of assignment projects
- increased confidence which makes employee time more effective in the workplace
- a qualification being awarded after a period of study.

Research task

Research Investors in People (IIP) by visiting the IIP website at **www.investorsinpeople.co.uk**. Write a short report on the purpose of and benefits to an organisation of having IIP status.

Staff appraisal

Appraisal is the main method used to establish an employee's training and development needs. Appraisals can be used for other reasons, for example, linked to performance and pay and to measure objectives.

An appraisal will normally take place on a one-to-one basis between the employee and their line manager. The main focus of this meeting is to discuss and measure performance in their job role and agree on a set of goals for the forthcoming year. The main objectives of using appraisal for the organisation are to:

- identify future training needs
- consider personal development needs for the individual
- improve the performance of the employee
- provide feedback and constructive criticism to the employee
- identify individuals who have the potential for promotion or who have additional skills that could be utilised now or in the future
- review pay.

The appraisal meeting needs to be taken seriously by both sides and the employer needs to have proper processes in place to follow up actions from the meeting.

At the end of the appraisal meeting, there should be a clear set of objectives and training needs identified with a course of action and timeline in place to achieve it.

Organisations may use different types of appraisal depending on the group of employees being appraised or depending on the time and facilities that are available to carry out the appraisal as shown below.

One to one
- Face to face with direct line manager
- Usually part of a formal process
- Often occurs annually
- May be linked to a review of pay

Peer to peer
- A colleague in the same or a similar position carries out the evaluation
- More informal
- Encourages effective buddying

360 degree
- Involves self-evaluation
- Allows for a more rounded evaluation with contribution from a number of different people, e.g. peers, managers, customers, etc.

Report
Write a short report to management on the advantages and disadvantages of introducing an appraisal system.

Revision questions

1. Explain why appraisal is important to both the organisation and the employee.
2. Describe the different methods of appraisal.
3. Describe the costs and benefits of training.
4. Explain why it is important for an organisation to offer induction training to new staff.

4.3 Motivation and leadership

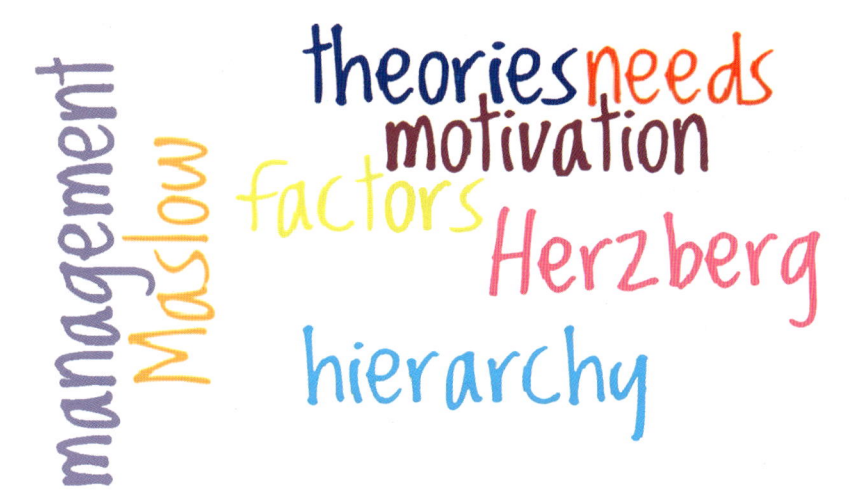

management Maslow theories needs motivation factors Herzberg hierarchy

SECTION 4 MANAGEMENT OF PEOPLE

There are many theories of motivation and management that are relevant to business today. We will focus on the theories developed by two well-known theorists: Maslow and Herzberg.

Abraham Maslow

Maslow's hierarchy of needs

Abraham Maslow was a well-known American psychologist during the 1940s and 1950s when he developed a hierarchy of needs. This was designed to show the five innate needs of humans and was displayed in a hierarchy or pyramid, as shown below.

Abraham Maslow

Self-actualisation
personal growth and fulfilment

Esteem needs
achievement, status, responsibility, reputation

Belonging and love needs
family, affection, relationships, work group, etc.

Safety needs
protection, security, order, law, limits, stability, etc.

Biological and physiological needs
basic life needs – air, food, drink, shelter, warmth, sleep, sex, etc.

Maslow's hierarchy of needs

Maslow theorised that management methods should be appropriate and reflect the level on which employees currently operate. The hierarchy of needs theory remains valid today for understanding human motivation, management training and personal development. The pyramid shows the different stages of need that individuals pass through, with the most basic needs shown at the bottom of the pyramid.

Maslow's theory was further developed in the 1990s with the addition of transcendence needs (helping others to achieve self-actualisation), aesthetic needs (beauty, balance, form, etc.) and cognitive needs (knowledge, meaning, self-awareness), so taking the original hierarchy of five up to a hierarchy of eight needs.

For many people, the original five-stage model remains the most relevant today in demonstrating individuals' motivation.

Frederick Herzberg

Frederick Herzberg was an American psychologist who was famous for promoting the theory of job enrichment and developing the motivator-hygiene theory, which was also known as the two-factor theory of job satisfaction. According to his theory, people are influenced by two sets of factors. The idea is that hygiene factors will not motivate, but if they are not there, they can lower motivation. These factors could be anything from clean toilets and comfortable chairs to a reasonable salary level and job security.

Frederick Herzberg

Motivational factors will not necessarily lower motivation but can be responsible for increasing motivation. These factors could involve job recognition, potential for promotion or even the work in itself.

Herzberg also suggested that employees respond positively to greater responsibility and being recognised for their contribution to the organisation. It is the responsibility of managers to provide positive feedback (satisfiers), such as greater responsibility, and also ensure that hygiene factors are in place (to prevent dissatisfaction).

The motivator and hygiene factors are shown below.

Motivators
- Achievement
- Advancement
- Challenging work
- Empowerment
- Profit sharing
- Promotion prospects
- Recognition
- Responsibility
- Target setting

Hygiene factors
- Administration
- Company policies
- Fair pay
- Interpersonal relationships
- Organisational structure
- Security
- Supervision
- Working conditions
- Working machinery

Research task

Research one of the theories of motivation and management that have just been covered and produce a short report outlining its relevance and impact on business today.

Leadership styles

The definition of leadership is a person's ability to influence the thoughts or actions of others. When we talk about leadership in business, it is usually directed towards the ability of those in a position of influence and their ability to influence those in their control in order to achieve organisational objectives.

However, a good leader is not always a good manager and vice versa. The historic use of the term 'manager' is often in connection with more tangible behaviours that can be easily identified. In the case of a leader, while the same traits as a good manager may be displayed, there is often a more strategic vision involved. We will consider some of the characteristics that define each of these roles even though they are often used interchangeably.

4.3 MOTIVATION AND LEADERSHIP

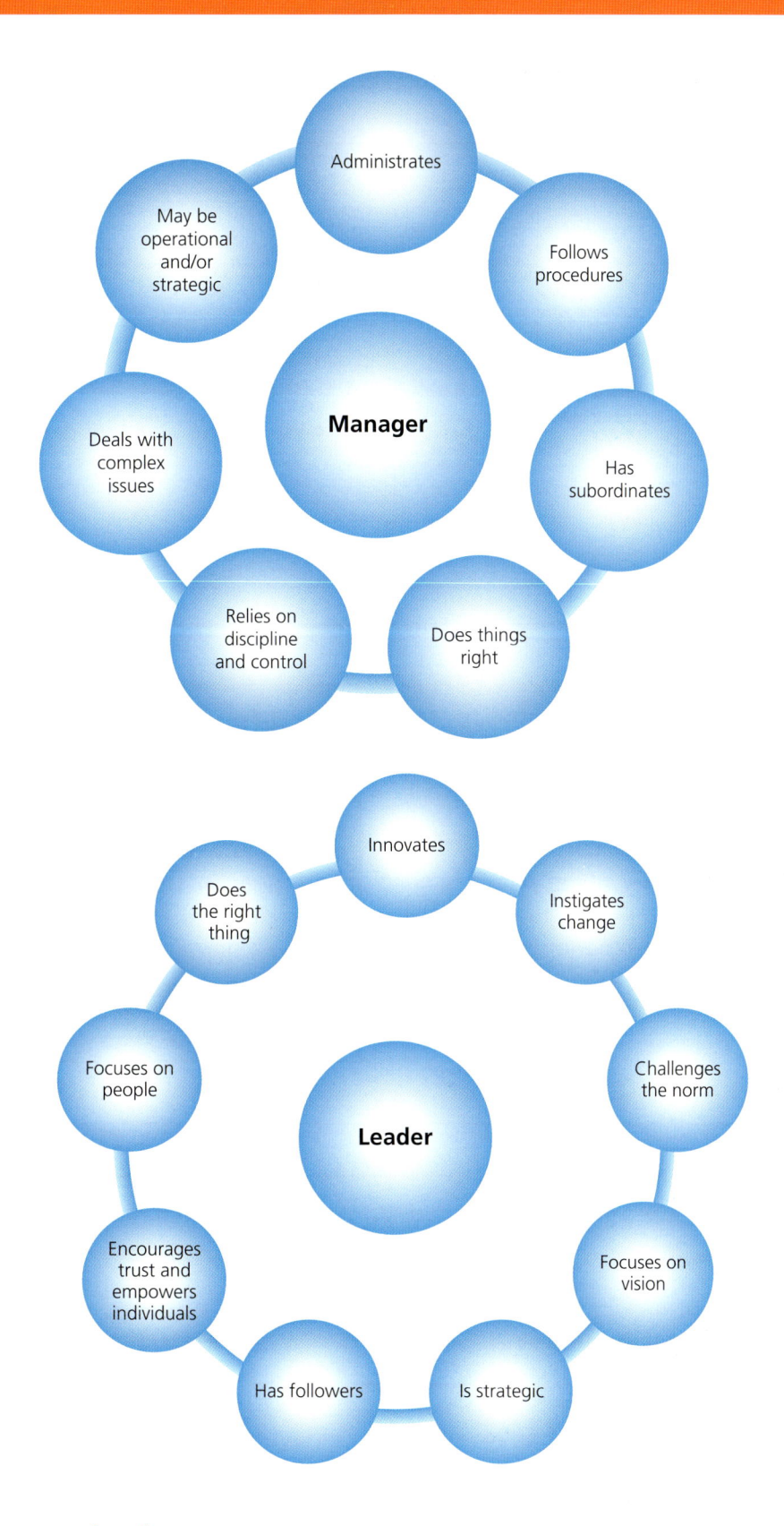

Manager
- Administrates
- Follows procedures
- Has subordinates
- Does things right
- Relies on discipline and control
- Deals with complex issues
- May be operational and/or strategic

Leader
- Innovates
- Instigates change
- Challenges the norm
- Focuses on vision
- Is strategic
- Has followers
- Encourages trust and empowers individuals
- Focuses on people
- Does the right thing

Style theory

Style theory focuses on what successful leaders do rather than focusing on what they are. The thinking behind this theory is that if leaders behave in a certain way then they will be successful.

There are three different styles of leadership: autocratic, democratic/participative and laissez-faire.

Autocratic leadership					
The leader has absolute authority	The leader has no consultation with subordinates	Upward communication is discouraged	The leader dictates what the employees do and how they should act	Obedience is expected without question	The typical view of the leader is controlling and bossy

Advantages of autocratic leadership

- Quick decision making.
- Employees get direct assistance from the top.
- Inexperienced employees may be more motivated through the experience of the leader.

Disadvantages of autocratic leadership

- Lack of input from employees.
- Encourages a blame culture.
- Employees do not get an opportunity to develop.
- Total dependency on the leader.
- Lack of trust.
- Poor motivator.

Democratic/participative leadership						
Good communication between the leader and the employees	Leader shares problems by setting up teams	Leader makes decisions but explains the reasons why	Leader enters into discussion with employees	Upward communication is encouraged	Leader guides but also takes part in team discussions	Achievement is encouraged and recognised

Advantages of democratic/participative leadership
- Employees feel more engaged and motivated.
- Empowerment leads to greater employee job satisfaction.
- Employees are better prepared for promotion if they are exposed to expanded roles and responsibilities.
- Encourages employees to be more accepting of change since they are involved in decision making.

Disadvantages of democratic/participative leadership
- Some employees may require close supervision.
- Only involving employees in small decisions may demotivate them.
- Decision making could take time.
- Requires an effective leader in order to avoid conflict.

Laissez-faire leadership					
Free rein or delegative style of leadership	Leader leaves the employees to it and doesn't interfere	Leader delegates authority and power to employees	The team is expected to set its own goals and resolve its own problems	Requires a very competent leader to set the process in motion	Teams then become largely self-managing

Advantages of laissez-faire leadership
- High degree of trust among employees.
- Increased motivation.
- Managerial wages can be reduced due to less need for management.
- Reduction in stress for managers.
- Employees can improve their skills quickly.

Disadvantages of laissez-faire leadership
- Employees may feel more pressure and become stressed.
- Poor-quality output can occur.
- Competent employees may seek more financial compensation for taking on more responsibility.

Group task

Discuss the type of leadership style that you would prefer in a work situation. Can you justify your preference to the others in your group? Can you identify different styles of leadership among your teachers?

Revision questions

1. Describe the levels of Maslow's hierarchy of needs.
2. Describe Herzberg's theory of job enrichment.
3. Distinguish between a manager and a leader.
4. Describe the difficulties that some employees may have with an autocratic manager.
5. Describe the advantages and disadvantages of having a democratic manager.
6. Describe the impact that a laissez-faire management style could have on the organisation.

4.4 Employee relations

Employee relations is a major role that is fulfilled by the human resources (HR) department in conjunction with managers from across the organisation. It is concerned with how employers deal and interact with their employees, as individuals or as a group.

Positive employee relations help ensure that the organisation meets its objectives. In a positive environment, employees are much more likely to be happy and motivated to help the organisation achieve its objectives. They will be more accepting of change, more flexible in their response to requests and will recognise the need for the organisation to achieve its objectives.

Poor employee relations can lead to conflict and less co-operation from employees and may present a poor image of the organisation to its customers.

The human resources department has responsibility for drawing up and implementing the organisation's employee relations policies. Each organisation will specify what is covered in particular to the organisation itself but the following will normally be included.

HINT

It should be noted that some organisations do not recognise trade unions or may choose only to recognise certain named trade unions.

Collective bargaining is the process by which negotiations with trade unions over pay and conditions or changes to working practices are discussed and apply to all employees.

Employee relations policies:
- Terms and conditions of employment for staff
- Procedures for staff complaints – grievance
- Staff discipline
- Redundancy terms
- Staff involvement in decision making
- Trade union recognition (if applicable)
- Collective bargaining

Advisory, Conciliation and Arbitration Service

The Advisory, Conciliation and Arbitration Service (ACAS) is one of several institutions that has been created to help ensure that disputes between employers and employees are kept to a minimum. The service describes itself as employee relations experts, helping people to work together effectively. Much of the work of ACAS is concerned with advising employers and employees on how best to avoid disputes through the use of best practice and dealing with individual cases.

ACAS can assist in four main ways:

1. Providing impartial advice and help to anyone with a work problem – it deals with over 1 million calls and queries per year to its telephone helpline and through its online service.

2. Preventing and resolving problems between employers and employees and helping settle disputes. The advisory service works with hundreds of companies every year to develop a joint approach to problem solving.
3. Settling complaints about employees' rights. Over 100,000 people a year complain to an employment tribunal. Before reaching this point, ACAS can deal with a referral to see if there is a better and less expensive way to sort out the problem. In cases that involve unfair dismissal, there is also the choice of confidential arbitration instead of using the employment tribunal option.
4. Encouraging people to work together effectively by running workshops and seminars on issues such as basic employment knowledge and the latest developments in legislation. Many events are targeted at small businesses.

> **www**
> You can find out more about the work of ACAS by visiting its website at www.acas.org.uk.

Employers' associations

Businesses in one sector of industry often form an association to look after the interests of all businesses in that particular industry. For example, businesses in the engineering sector may belong to the Engineering Employers' Federation. In doing so, they benefit by having a single strong voice to lobby politicians, deal with negotiations with the engineering unions and give a clear and uniform message to the press and other media.

They can pressure and influence the government in areas such as providing support for research and development, taxation, consumer and employment laws. Market research can be gathered for the benefit of the members, many of which may be small businesses who would otherwise not be able to afford to carry out research.

Research task
Research at least one other employers' association and write up a short report on the activities that it carries out.

Trades Union Congress (TUC)

The TUC represents all trade unions in much the same way as other organisations can represent different groups of employers. It provides information and advice to its members and in recent years the membership of the TUC has risen after a period of decline.

The main activities of the TUC are:

- brings Britain's unions together to draw up common policies
- lobbies the government to implement policies that will benefit people at work
- campaigns on economic and social issues
- represents working people on public bodies
- represents British workers in international bodies, in the European Union and at the UN employment body – the International Labour Organization

> **www**
> Find out more about the TUC by visiting its website at www.tuc.org.uk.

- carries out research on employment-related issues
- runs an extensive training and education programme for union representatives
- helps unions develop new services for their members
- helps unions avoid clashes with each other
- builds links with other trade union bodies worldwide.

Trade unions

Trade unions were originally set up to protect employees from bad working practices and to provide a political voice for the working people of the country. The Labour Party was established by the trade unions. After the success of the party's work in ensuring changes to employment law, the role of trade unions has changed.

Individual workers have less power in their dealings with employers and governments, so by joining a trade union the worker has much stronger resources at their disposal to support their case.

Trade unions are much more interested in working with employers and government for the benefit of their members rather than causing confrontation and industrial action, which could damage the jobs and security of their members. Some unions have joined together to form 'super-unions', thereby representing a very large number of employees.

Benefits of belonging to a trade union
- Obtain good rates of pay for members
- Protect workers' jobs
- Secure appropriate working facilities
- Ensure satisfactory working conditions
- Negotiate employment conditions

Some unions in the UK represent specific sectors of the workforce while others are more general in nature, such as Unite. You will probably have heard of some that represent teachers and lecturers, such as the Educational Institute of Scotland (EIS) which has members from primary and secondary schools as well as college and university lecturers.

Being a member of a trade union often offers a wide variety of benefits. These can include discounts on purchases, insurance services, legal advice and free advice and support on all employment matters.

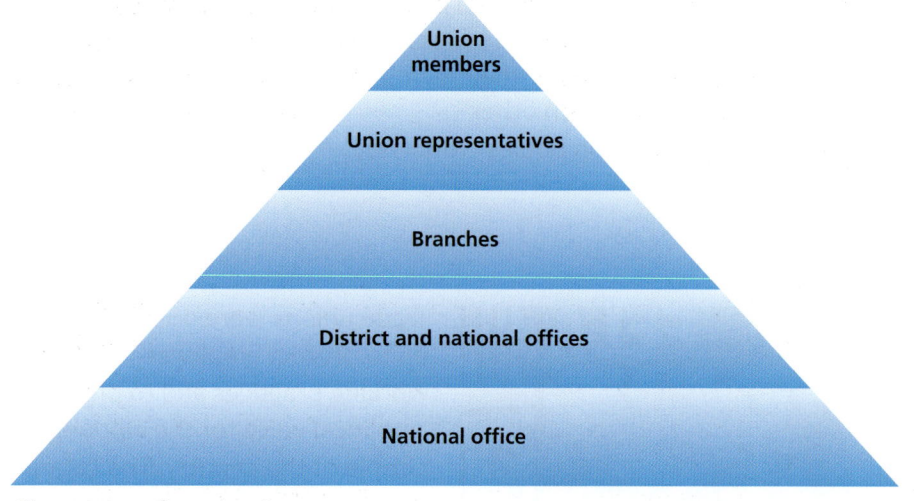

```
         Union
        members

     Union representatives

         Branches

   District and national offices

         National office
```

The structure of a trade union

Different aspects of employee relations

The term 'employee relations' refers to the relationship between employers and employees. It is an important aspect of business as it is vital to have harmony between the employer and the employees. The diagram shows aspects of employee relations and we will consider each in turn.

Employee relations: Negotiation, Consultation, Arbitration, Collective bargaining, Industrial action

Negotiation

The main purpose of negotiation is to come to an agreement between the parties. Employers and employees meet to discuss issues that affect both parties to agree, plan and implement some changes in the workplace. What is negotiated and how the negotiations take place is dependent on the relationship between the two parties and what existing arrangements are in place. Negotiation is often seen as the best method of achieving change in the workplace. Good negotiations should make the employees feel included in decisions that are made and also feel empowered. They should be made to feel that any proposed changes by the organisation will benefit them as much as their employers. During negotiation, employers are seeking 'buy in' (support) from the employees to achieve the organisational objectives.

Consultation

'Consultation' is a term used to describe the legal process that is enforced on employers under employment law for some changes within the organisation. The actual meaning of consultation will differ from one organisation to another. A dictionary definition of consultation means 'the action or process of consulting or discussing'. However, the word can also be interpreted as meaning 'to tell' and in some instances, some organisations will interpret consultation as simply telling employees and/or their trade unions what changes are planned and the reasons for them. Only after this process will the employer listen to views. In the process of consultation, however it is followed up, no agreement is necessary and the employer is under no obligation to take account of the views of the employees.

Arbitration

Where no agreement can be reached between the employer and the employees and a dispute then arises, the situation can reach a stalemate. In such instances, a third party is often engaged to attempt to resolve the dispute. This could involve the use of an independent arbitrator such as ACAS. The arbitrator is unbiased and neutral to the dispute and will listen to both sides, gather other appropriate evidence and offer a solution. The parties may not necessarily decide to agree with the decision of the arbitrator.

Binding arbitration is where both parties agree in advance to abide by the decision of the independent arbitrator. Where no agreement exists, both parties may still try to negotiate around the arbitrator's decision in order to reach an agreement.

Collective bargaining

It is unusual for individual workers to try to negotiate new pay and conditions of employment with their employers. It is much more common for trade unions, staff associations or professional associations to do this on behalf of the employees. Collective bargaining is the process by which the trade union or other body negotiates on behalf of the employees, usually over pay or other changes that are proposed in the workplace.

The process normally starts when either the employees' representatives or the employers propose some change to their existing agreement. For example, the employers could offer a pay rise of one per cent to their employees. The employees' representatives then ask their members whether or not this is acceptable. If it is not acceptable, a counterclaim is made for a different pay rise, for example, three per cent. Negotiations can then take place to try to come to an agreement.

A compromise is usually able to be reached as neither side will wish to have protracted negotiations or a dispute that could involve employee action.

Once both parties have an agreement, the employees' representatives take the offer back to their members with a recommendation that it is accepted. If all goes well then the new pay and conditions agreement will be implemented at an agreed date. In many instances, the employer will attempt to make an agreement that will last for several years to encourage a more settled workforce and save revisiting the agreement on an annual basis.

Industrial action

When we mention the term 'industrial action', the first thing that springs to mind is a strike. However, striking is just one form of industrial action that can be taken by employees.

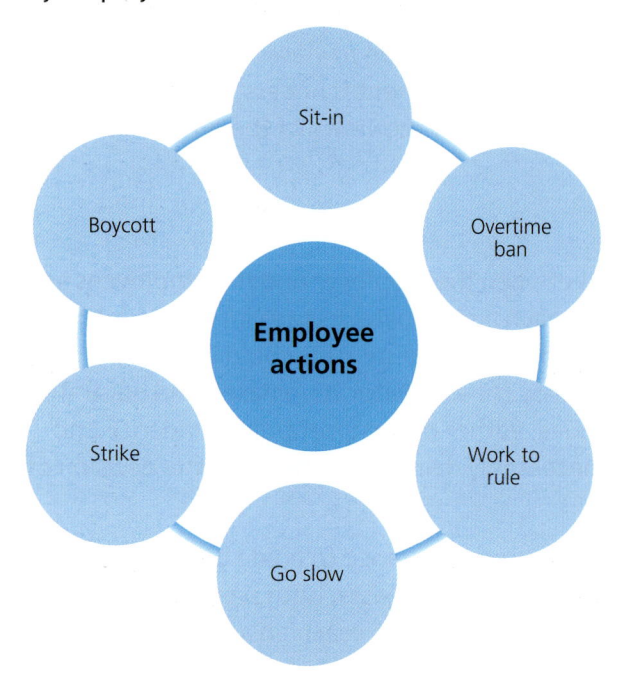

Employee actions:
- Sit-in
- Overtime ban
- Work to rule
- Go slow
- Strike
- Boycott

Strike

When a strike is called, all or most of the workers stop working. This is known as a withdrawal of labour. This is usually only done as a last resort and after all other avenues of negotiation have been followed. Actioning a strike can be counterproductive as it can ultimately threaten the security of the workforce's employment because it will have a negative effect on sales and customers. There is a legally binding set of procedures that a union must go through before it can call a strike. This includes balloting all of its members.

In some cases where a strike has been called, the employer may decide to sack those who go on strike. This is only possible where there is a good supply of available and properly trained replacement workers available on the job market. However, this can cause further bad feeling in the remaining workforce and so may only serve to exacerbate the problem rather than solve it. Sometimes, the organisation may take a more extreme decision and decide to close the factory or move production elsewhere. In such circumstances, this can lead to a sit-in where workers occupy the workplace in an attempt to stop the employer from closing it down.

Work to rule

Work to rule is where employees work strictly in alignment to their terms and conditions of employment and do not allow for any flexibility. This withdrawal of flexibility leads to a reduction in efficiency and output and has a negative impact on the operation of the business.

Overtime ban

A ban on overtime has the same effect as work to rule. This is where the workers refuse to work any overtime hours.

Boycott

A boycott can be used where employers introduce new machinery or duties that the employees disagree with. In this case, the employees refuse to carry out the new duties or use the new machinery.

Sit-in

A sit-in occurs when the employees refuse to leave their place of work and continue to occupy the space outside of normal working hours. They may also combine this with refusing to carry out normal working duties while occupying the workspace.

Go slow

A go slow occurs when employees refuse to work at a normal pace and carry out their duties in a deliberately slow manner. This can have a negative impact on output where the business manufactures goods.

Management of employee relations

It is the responsibility of the human resources (HR) department to try to avoid disputes with employees and industrial action. There are a number of ways of achieving this but whatever method is chosen, communication between the employer and the employees is essential. The employees need to feel included in the decision-making process, so that there is a high degree of buy-in.

Communication should happen at all stages of the process so that a high degree of trust is built up between the employer and the employees.

Works councils

A works council is a group of representatives from the workforce which has the legal right to access information from management and has joint decision-making powers on most matters relating to the employees. The European Works Councils (EWC) legislation states that employers with at least 1000 employees across the EU have to set up a Special Negotiating Body (SNB) in response to a request to do so from at least 100 employees. Employers are not required to take proactive steps to establish an EWC. However, in response to a request from at least 100 employees, an SNB of employee representatives must be convened with the aim of reaching agreement on arrangements for the establishment of an EWC.

Worker directors

A worker-directors initiative involves putting workers into the boards of companies; the individuals are voted for by their colleagues. This improves boardroom diversity, brings worker participation into the boardroom and can lead to better decision making. Such arrangements are not very common in the UK, but it is a popular model in Germany.

Consultative committees

Employers may also use consultative committees to engage with employees. This method is used to make employees feel included in decision making and to gather a wide range of views on particular actions that the organisation may be considering. In some organisations, consultative committees are part of normal business and the organisation may use this model for planning purposes and to inform major decisions. It is much easier to progress decisions and changes in the business when the employees are on board with the process.

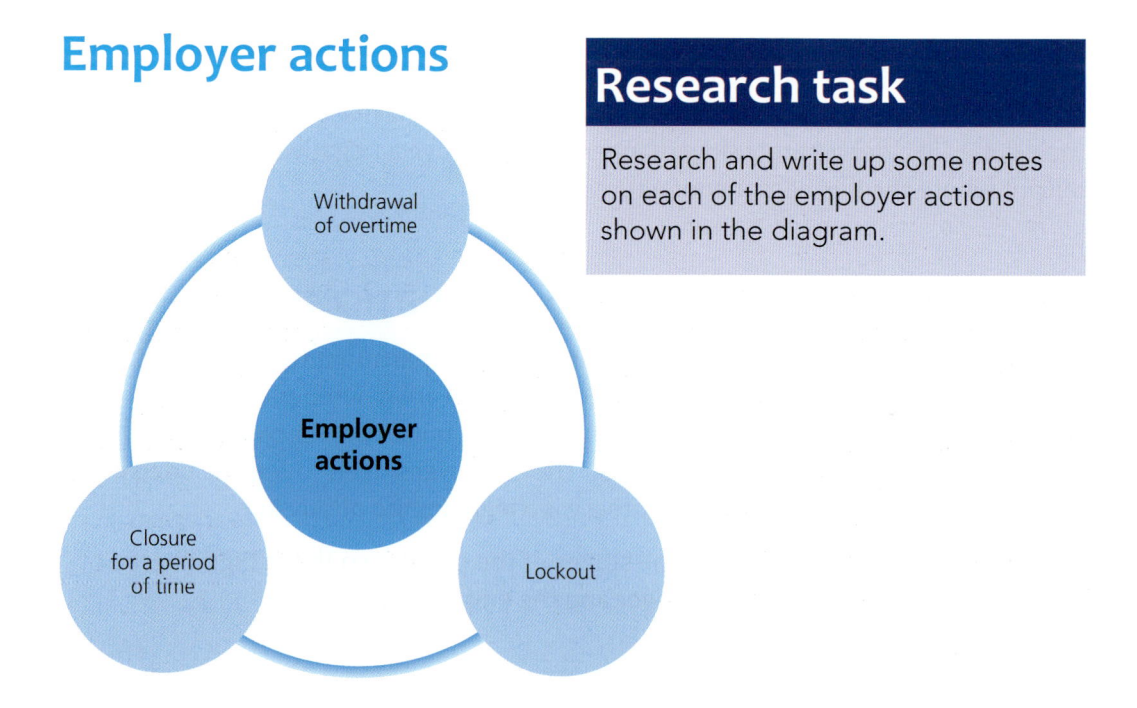

www

You can find out more about works councils at

www.etuc.org/european-works-councils-ewcs

www.european-employers.com/ewcs_in_depth_12.html

Employer actions

Diagram showing Employer actions at the centre, surrounded by: Withdrawal of overtime, Closure for a period of time, Lockout.

Research task

Research and write up some notes on each of the employer actions shown in the diagram.

Company policies that impact on employees

Every organisation will have a set of rules (policies) that employees have to agree to while they are in the employment of the organisation. Many rules are there to ensure that the health and safety of employees is protected. Other rules may be in place to uphold the image and reputation of the organisation by ensuring that all employees act in an appropriate manner. There are three main areas that are covered by company policies, as shown in the diagram below. In each instance, the policy will normally be created, maintained and enforced by the human resources department in collaboration with other senior staff.

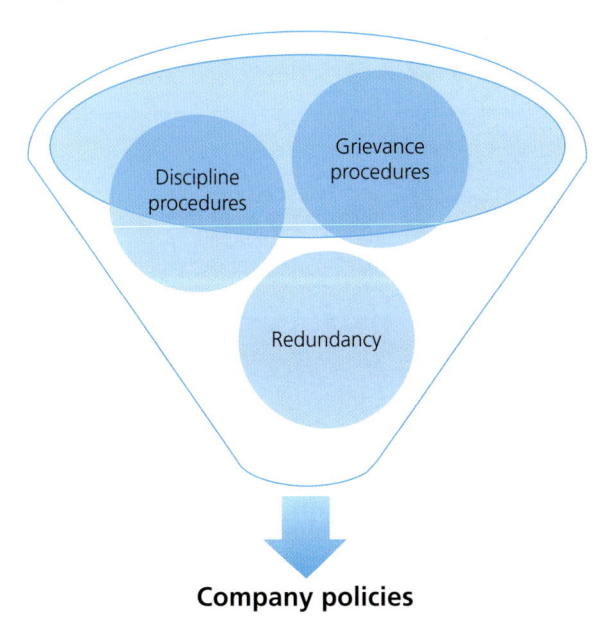

Company policies

- Discipline procedures
- Grievance procedures
- Redundancy

Grievance procedures

Grievance procedures exist to deal with a complaint by an employee against their employer or a complaint by an employee against another employee.

A grievance usually arises because of the way someone has been treated by another member of staff, such as their line manager. All organisations must have a grievance procedure that will be followed and will usually involve the HR department. It is the responsibility of the HR department to enforce the procedure and support the employee through the different stages of the procedure to its conclusion. If the employee is a member of a trade union then they may decide to involve a trade union representative as part of the process. If, on conclusion of the process, the employee is not satisfied with the outcome they may decide to take matters further. This could involve further action or support by the trade union, approaching an organisation such as ACAS for assistance or, more seriously, taking their employer to an employment tribunal.

Discipline procedures

Organisations should have written disciplinary procedures in place so that employees know what will happen if they break the rules set out by the organisation. In most organisations, there will be a scale of warnings which will eventually lead to dismissal, as shown below. All employees should be subject to the same rules and treatment.

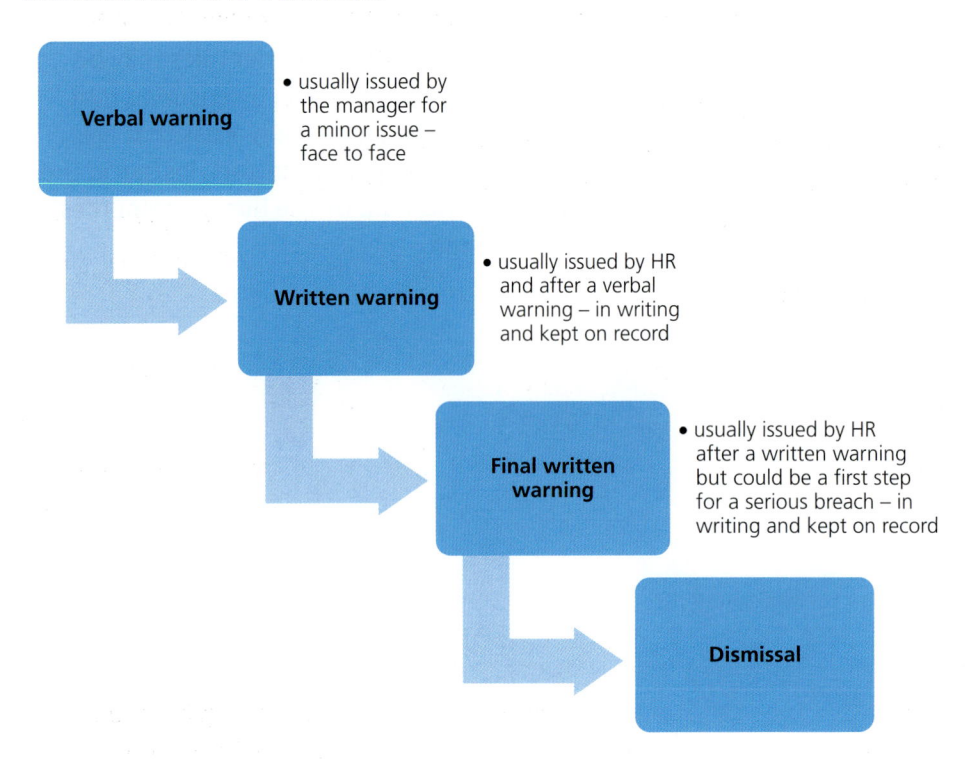

Verbal warning
- usually issued by the manager for a minor issue – face to face

Written warning
- usually issued by HR and after a verbal warning – in writing and kept on record

Final written warning
- usually issued by HR after a written warning but could be a first step for a serious breach – in writing and kept on record

Dismissal

The employer may take other actions or a different route to the eventual dismissal of an employee. Some of these possibilities are shown in the diagram below.

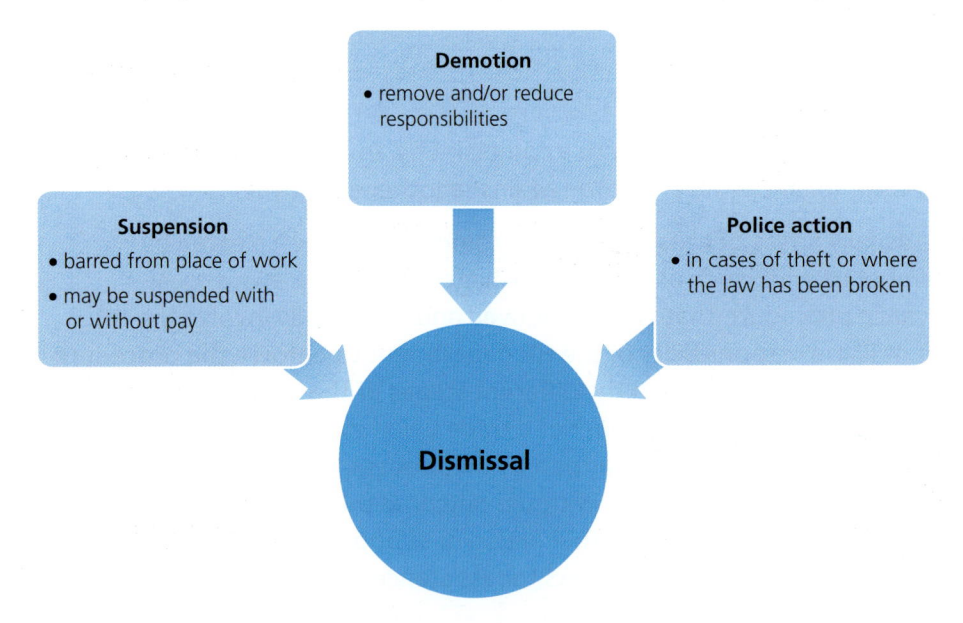

Demotion
- remove and/or reduce responsibilities

Suspension
- barred from place of work
- may be suspended with or without pay

Police action
- in cases of theft or where the law has been broken

Dismissal

Disciplinary procedures are often agreed with the trade unions or employee representatives, but in every case, they must comply with current employment legislation.

Disciplinary procedures are invoked against the employee by the employer to enforce rules or when the employee is thought to have done something wrong. Examples of things that employees can do wrong include lateness, not fulfilling their job role, insubordination and theft. In cases where the action of the employee is very serious, the employee may be sacked on the spot. This is known as summary dismissal as there is no immediate recourse for the employee and no procedure is followed before removing the employee from employment. However, it is more likely that a gradual disciplinary procedure will be followed as outlined previously.

There may be underlying reasons where the behaviour of an employee is giving cause for concern. It is the responsibility of the HR department to manage this aspect of employee support. Unless the breach carried out by the employee is particularly serious, most employers will try to support their staff through difficult times and may offer additional support mechanisms such as counselling or a move to work in another department.

Research task

Explore and discuss different situations where dismissal is considered both fair and unfair by law. Use the internet to research this and present your findings in a table.

Redundancy

Redundancy occurs when the employer finds that they no longer require one or more of their employees. In such a case, the employer will usually have a policy in place that allows for redundancy payments to be made to the affected employees and also gives them a certain amount of notice regarding the time period attached to the redundancy.

The organisation will wish to carefully manage any redundancies as it could attract negative publicity and show the organisation in a bad light.

Once employees have been made redundant, the organisation cannot then employ other workers to do the job previously done by those employees. Redundancy means that the job carried out by these employees no longer exists and, in such a case, the employees would have grounds for unfair dismissal.

Group task

Working in a small group, discuss and list:
- possible reasons for a grievance being raised and how it could be resolved
- possible reasons for an employee receiving a disciplinary procedure notice and the likely level of action by the employer.

All employers need to be aware of the impact that company policies can have on employee relations. For example, where relations between the employer and its employees are generally strained, the announcement of staff redundancies could make matters worse. In another example, the use of disciplinary procedures or the dismissal of an employee can cause anxiety among other employees, particularly if they view the action taken by the employer as being unfair. This can have a negative impact on employee motivation and may affect the day-to-day attitudes of staff as well as the running of the organisation.

Revision questions

1. Explain why it is important for an organisation to maintain good employee relations.
2. Describe the forms of industrial action that may be taken by employees.
3. Discuss the need for a disciplinary policy in an organisation.
4. Describe the impact of redundancy on the employer and the employee.

4.5 Legislation

Legislation is the laws that an employer has to take into consideration. Laws are varied and complex and are often updated. This requires specialist knowledge within the organisation and it is typically managed by the HR department. It is the responsibility of the HR department to ensure that the organisation is fully aware and fully compliant with any relevant legislation by ensuring that employees are appropriately informed and trained.

In large organisations, it may be financially economic to have an in-house legal department in addition to the HR department. This may be due to the fact that the organisation often requires specialist legal advice and it is more financially sensible to have this as part of the normal business operations. In many other organisations, the fundamental legal requirements will be catered for by the HR department and other matters requiring more specialist advice will be contracted out to the organisation's preferred legal advisers. Most organisations will have a link to a firm of solicitors so that they can refer any legal questions to them for advice.

This chapter will look at the following legislation:

- Equality Act 2010
- Health and Safety at Work Act 1974
- National Minimum Wage Act 1998
- Employment Rights Act 1996

Equality Act 2010

The Equality Act 2010 was formed to consolidate and simplify anti-discrimination law in the UK, and to reduce complications arising from having many separate pieces of legislation. It is applicable to organisations of all sizes and types in the UK, so it is essential that all employers are aware of their legal responsibilities.

The Act pulls together the following main pieces of legislation:

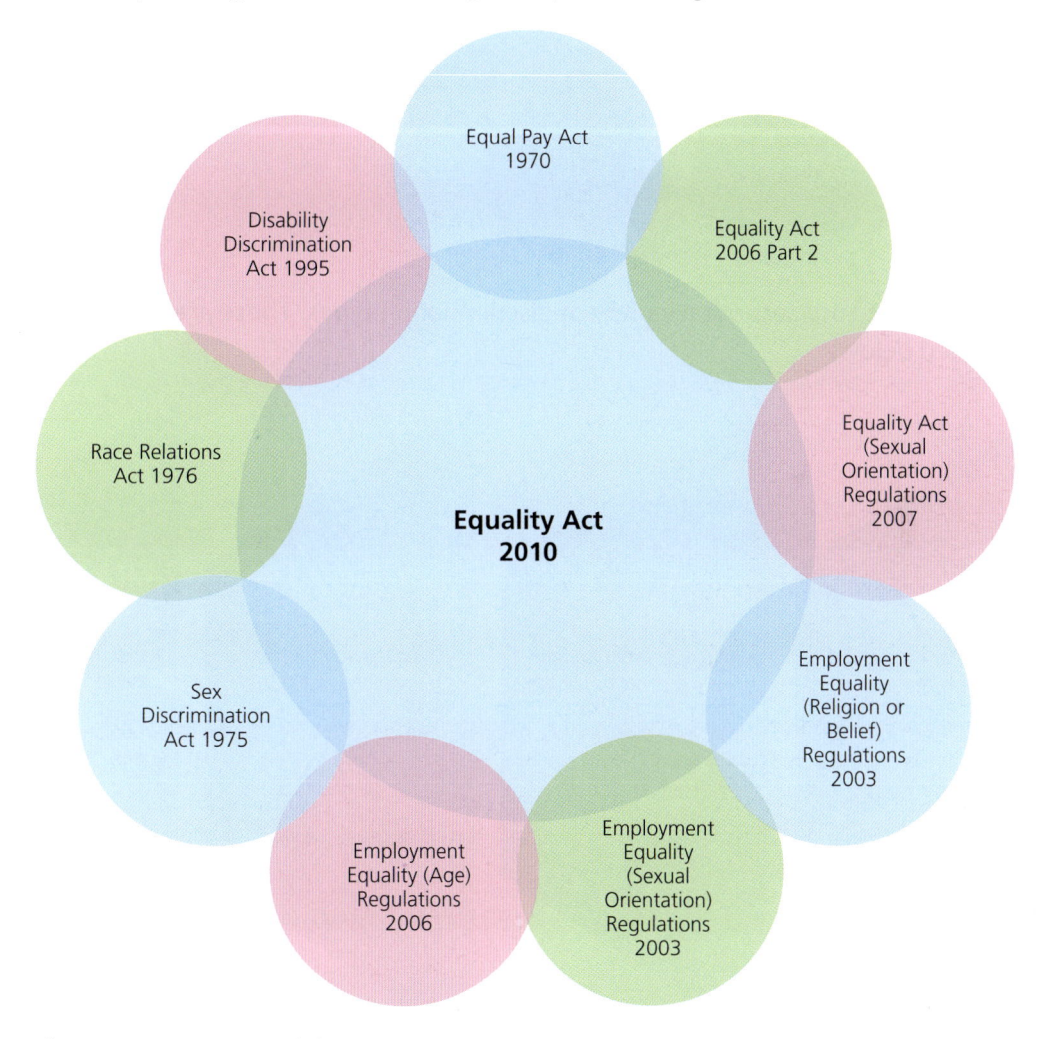

- Equal Pay Act 1970
- Equality Act 2006 Part 2
- Equality Act (Sexual Orientation) Regulations 2007
- Employment Equality (Religion or Belief) Regulations 2003
- Employment Equality (Sexual Orientation) Regulations 2003
- Employment Equality (Age) Regulations 2006
- Sex Discrimination Act 1975
- Race Relations Act 1976
- Disability Discrimination Act 1995

All feeding into the **Equality Act 2010**.

The main provision of the Equality Act 2010 is its identification of nine protected characteristics (PCs). These have been singled out in order to reduce inequalities in the working environment.

SECTION 4 MANAGEMENT OF PEOPLE

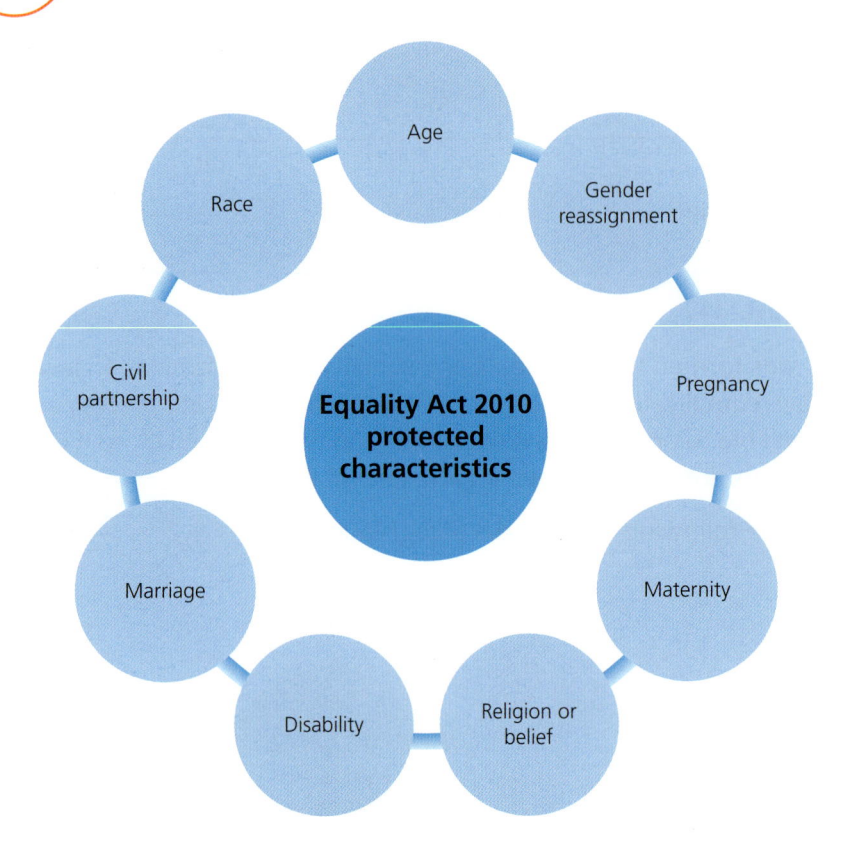

Equality Act 2010 protected characteristics:
- Age
- Gender reassignment
- Pregnancy
- Maternity
- Religion or belief
- Disability
- Marriage
- Civil partnership
- Race

The Equality Act 2010 sets out a variety of discrimination types. These are listed and exemplified below.

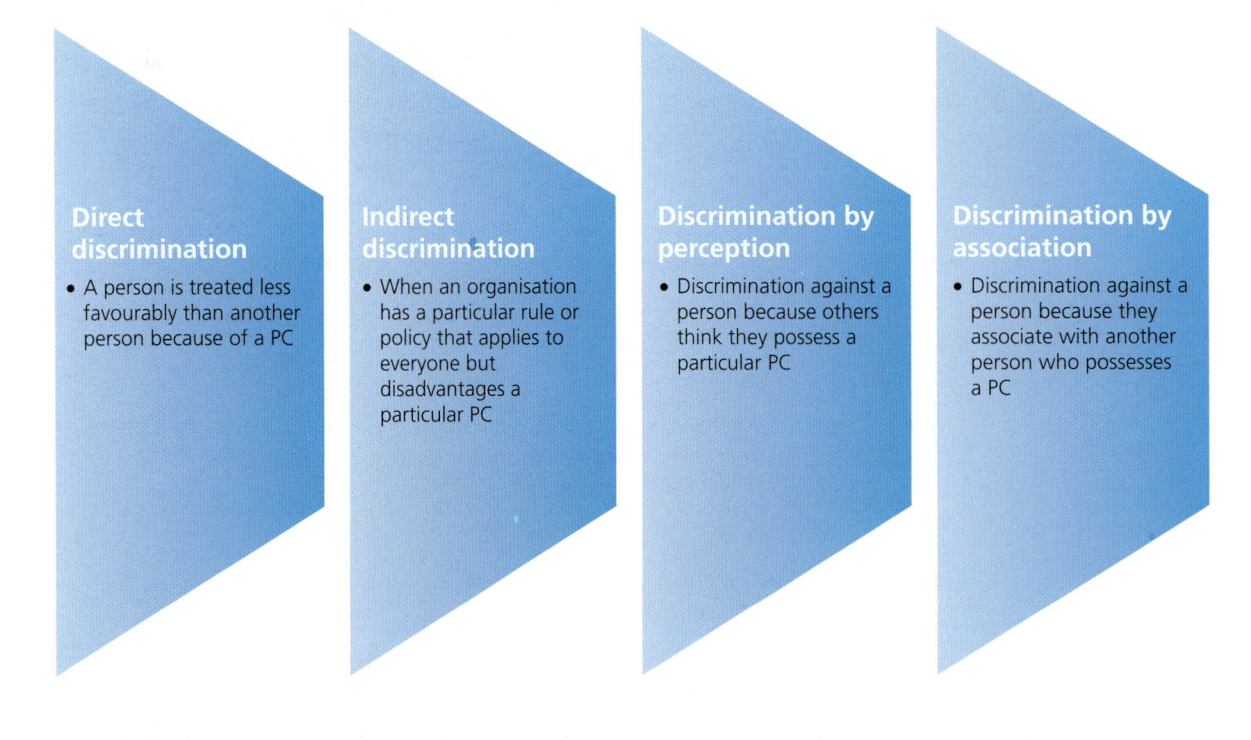

Direct discrimination
- A person is treated less favourably than another person because of a PC

Indirect discrimination
- When an organisation has a particular rule or policy that applies to everyone but disadvantages a particular PC

Discrimination by perception
- Discrimination against a person because others think they possess a particular PC

Discrimination by association
- Discrimination against a person because they associate with another person who possesses a PC

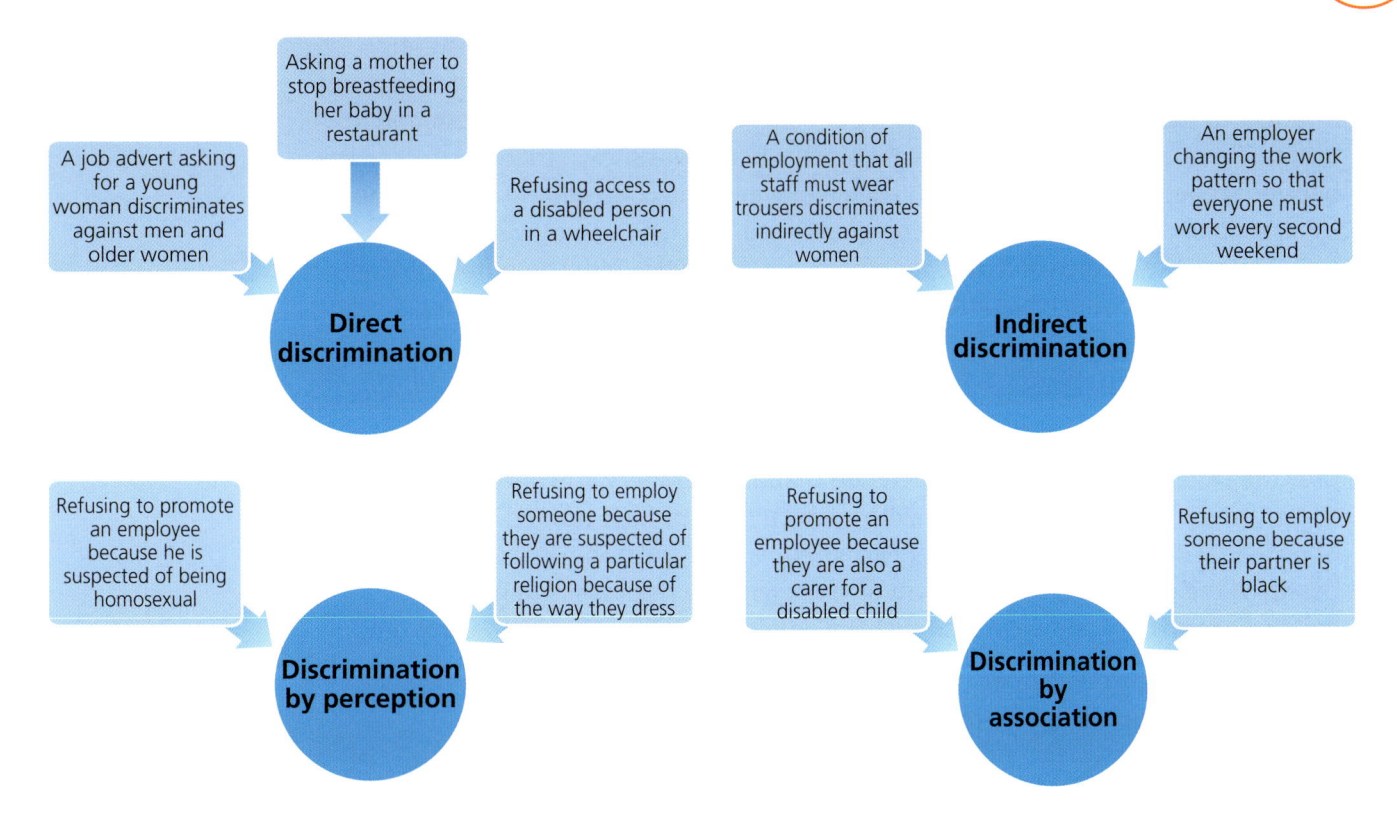

Direct discrimination
- A job advert asking for a young woman discriminates against men and older women
- Asking a mother to stop breastfeeding her baby in a restaurant
- Refusing access to a disabled person in a wheelchair

Indirect discrimination
- A condition of employment that all staff must wear trousers discriminates indirectly against women
- An employer changing the work pattern so that everyone must work every second weekend

Discrimination by perception
- Refusing to promote an employee because he is suspected of being homosexual
- Refusing to employ someone because they are suspected of following a particular religion because of the way they dress

Discrimination by association
- Refusing to promote an employee because they are also a carer for a disabled child
- Refusing to employ someone because their partner is black

The Equality Act 2010 gives employees the right to complain about behaviour towards them that they feel is discriminatory. Employees also have the right to complain about behaviour that they find offensive, even when it is not directed at them.

Due to the wide-ranging impact of the Equality Act 2010, it is necessary for all employers to have a clear understanding of its provisions and how they may impact on the organisation. All employers owe an overarching duty of care towards their employees and this Act serves to strengthen that position by extending legal rights to the protected characteristics of all employees.

Some other examples of discrimination at work include:

- Deliberate selection of someone for redundancy when they have a PC
- Failure to make reasonable adjustments for a person with a disability
- Harassing or firing someone because they are a member of a union
- Disciplining or firing someone because they have made an allegation of discrimination
- Failure to give proper consideration to a request for flexible working from a new parent

Health and Safety at Work Act 1974

The main aim of this piece of legislation is to raise the standard of health and safety in the workplace for all workers, and to protect the public whose safety may be put at risk by the actions of people at work.

What is covered by the Act and the associated duties of an employer is constantly being updated. For example, when research shows that there is a practice which poses a danger to the health of staff, then there is a duty on the employer to take action to ensure the safety of all staff. Such a case arose when it was shown that there was a link between repetitive strain injury (RSI) and employees who constantly undertook the same actions in a job, such as typing on a keyboard. This led to employers providing wrist rests for keyboards and mice for employees who work with computers. It is an example of how research has influenced and updated the provisions of the legislation.

Employers' duties

Under the Health and Safety at Work Act 1974, the employer must make sure that they take every reasonable step to ensure that all machinery is properly maintained, all hazardous substances are dealt with correctly, all staff are trained and informed of potential dangers and that the environment is safe and non-hazardous to the health of the employees. This may involve the use of a risk assessment of the building, machinery and each task that the employees are expected to carry out.

This may also mean that safety officers need to be appointed to carry out regular inspections of the workplace to assess the dangers involved in each job.

Where prosecutions are brought against employers under this Act, the resultant financial penalties and fines can be substantial, particularly where an employee has lost their life.

Employees' duties

Employees also have duties under the Act. This means that they are expected to behave in a reasonable manner at work and must take some responsibility for their own actions. They must co-operate with their employers in ensuring that all health and safety requirements are met, and must follow all instructions and accept training where appropriate.

Other relevant legislation

In addition to the Health and Safety at Work Act 1974, there are a number of other Acts and regulations that employers and employees must follow. This includes, but is not limited to:

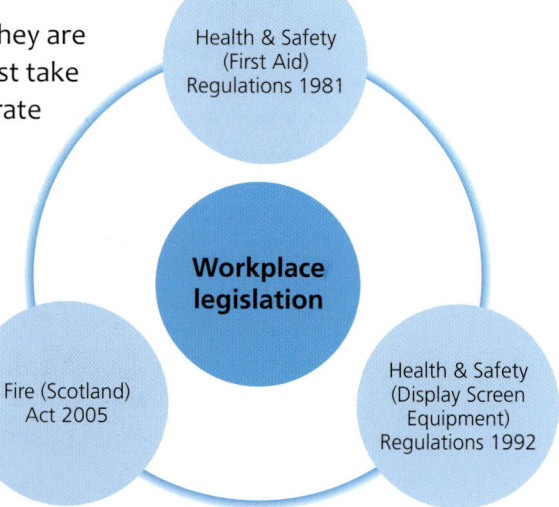

- Health & Safety (First Aid) Regulations 1981
- Fire (Scotland) Act 2005
- Health & Safety (Display Screen Equipment) Regulations 1992
- Workplace legislation

Research task

Research and summarise the provisions of the two pieces of workplace legislation that have just been covered and list the main impact of each on businesses.

National Minimum Wage Act 1998

This states the minimum wages that must be paid to employees. In recent years, this has been increasing. At the time of writing, the UK minimum wage is dependent on age.

There is often political discussion about the minimum wage rate compared to the living wage. The living wage is the minimum wage that it is calculated to enable people to live above the poverty line. It is argued that the minimum wage rate falls short of the level required to survive without being in poverty.

National Living Wage Regulations

The National Living Wage (NLW) is the minimum pay per hour most workers aged 25 and over are entitled to by law. The rate depends on a worker's age and if they are an apprentice.

The current rates for the minimum and the living wage are shown below:

Date of rate	25 and over	21–24	18–20	Under 18	Apprentice
From April 2018	£7.83	£7.38	£5.90	£4.20	£3.70
From April 2017 to March 2018	£7.50	£7.05	£5.60	£4.05	£3.50
From October 2016 to March 2017	£7.20	£6.95	£5.55	£4.00	£3.40
From April 2016 to September 2016	£7.20	£6.70	£5.30	£3.87	£3.30

As you can see, the rates change every April. Go to www.gov.uk/national-minimum-wage-rates to find out more.

Employment Rights Act 1996

This states the duties and rights of the employer and the employee, and includes:

- the employees' rights to maternity and paternity leave
- termination of employment
- the right to a written contract of employment within 60 days of starting work
- Sunday working
- the right to a written payslip.

Revision questions

1. Describe the main features of the Equality Act 2010.
2. Describe the impact of the Equality Act 2010 on an organisation.
3. Discuss the importance of the Health and Safety at Work Act 1974 on both employees and employers.
4. Describe the impact on businesses of the national minimum wage and the national living wage.

4.6 Technology

Technology has an increasing number of uses in human resource management. Here are some specific examples that relate to the people function:

Technology	How it is used in human resource management
Databases	Database technology can be used to store electronic records on every employee, tracking work history, performance, attendance, etc.
Video conferencing/Skype	This can be used to host virtual meetings or interviews, saving on time, travel and money.
Online application forms	The use of online (rather than paper) application forms means that organisations can more easily track and manage applications for vacancies. In some organisations this also ties into a fully electronic recruitment system.
Job advertising	Job adverts can be posted on the organisation's website, giving better control over when and where the adverts are made available.
E-diary	The use of an e-diary in human resources enables employees to manage their time efficiently and also be able to access the diaries of other employees in the organisation.
Presentation software	Presentation software can be used in the human resources department to present information and training to employees.
Virtual learning environment (VLE)	A virtual learning environment can be used to host training materials and courses for employees to update skills and deliver new skills.
Electronic testing	Electronic testing can be used on potential employees as part of the recruitment and selection process managed by the human resources department.
Payroll	Payroll functions can be completely controlled and linked into the finance function using software such as Sage. This is a preferred option nowadays for many organisations, as the linking of the HR and finance functions through the use of common software allows far greater control and monitoring.
Performance management/appraisal	Performance management and appraisal can be managed using bespoke software, enabling all aspects to be monitored by the human resources function.

Benefits of technology to support the people function
- Better monitoring and control is possible through the use of specific software.
- Training can be better supported in-house, making it easier to provide and administer.
- The recruitment and selection process can be fully controlled by HR, making more efficient use of time.

Costs of technology to support the people function
- There are financial costs associated with using technology in human resources. They include initial set-up as well as ongoing replacement of hardware and software.
- Even employees in the human resources department will need training and support when implementing the use of new technology.

Technology and the management of people

Technology can be used effectively by organisations to manage the people function of the business. Businesses typically use technology to make their management of people more efficient. A benefit of making the people-management function more efficient is that employees may be more motivated and happier in their work. It also makes it easier for the organisation to link parts of the business. For example, the calculation of wages and salaries by payroll can feed into finance.

Some examples are shown below.

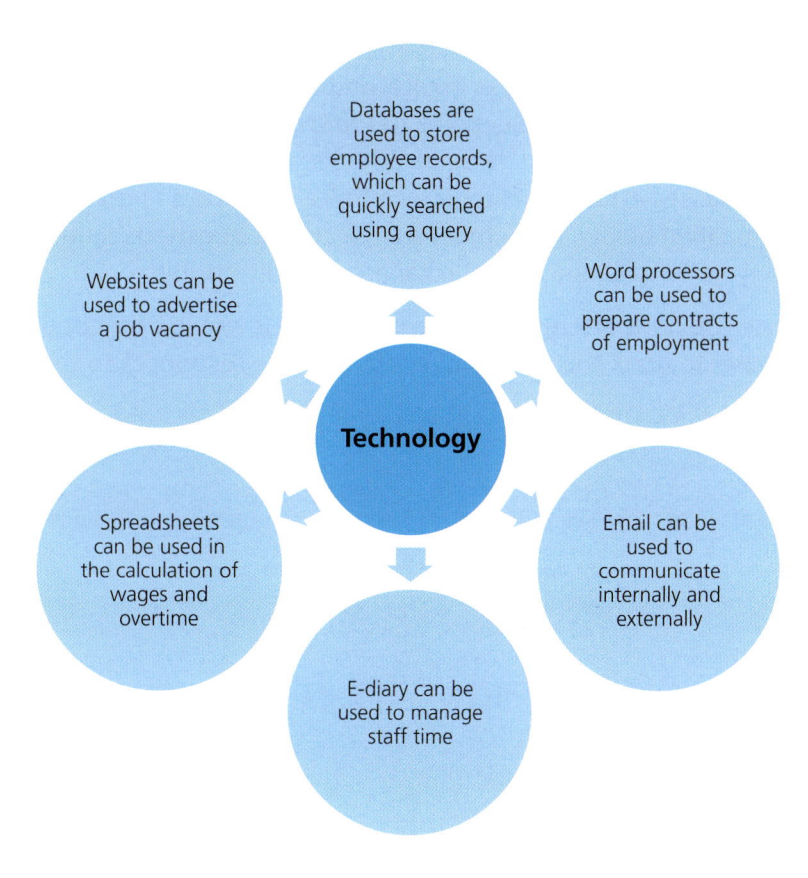

Technology
- Databases are used to store employee records, which can be quickly searched using a query
- Word processors can be used to prepare contracts of employment
- Email can be used to communicate internally and externally
- E-diary can be used to manage staff time
- Spreadsheets can be used in the calculation of wages and overtime
- Websites can be used to advertise a job vacancy

Revision questions

1. Describe the benefits of using technology to manage the human resources function of an organisation.
2. Describe the benefits to employees of having a technologically advanced human resources function.
3. Describe the benefits to managers of having access to appropriate technology when managing staff who are not office-based.
4. Discuss the use of a company intranet.

Report

Choose one use of technology in the management of people that is not already listed in the diagram on page 169, and write a short report on the impact for an organisation.

Section Assessment: Management of People

This segment aims to test your knowledge of the preceding section with exam-standard questions. It is recommended that you answer the questions based on the standard timing for the external examination, which allows around two minutes per mark. There is a selection of questions that you might expect to find in both Section 1 and Section 2 of the question paper.

Section 1 is worth 30 marks in total and the allocation of each question can range from 1–8 marks. Section 2 has four questions of 15 marks each, containing individual questions in the range of 1–8 marks. The difference with Section 2 is that it specialises in individual topics, so there could be a 15-mark question on People, as exemplified below. Remember that Section 2 questions tend to dig a little deeper into your knowledge of particular areas of the course.

Once you have attempted these questions, it would be a good idea to ask your teacher to mark them or go over appropriate responses to them.

Section 1 questions

		Marks
1	Describe the impact of current employment legislation on an organisation.	4
2	Compare the motivational theories of Maslow and Herzberg.	3
3	Describe the role of management in motivating employees.	4
4	Distinguish between autocratic and democratic leadership styles.	3
5	Discuss the steps that can be taken to improve poor employer–employee relations.	3
6	Explain the potential effect of continued absenteeism on an employee.	2
7	Describe potential reasons for disciplinary procedures being taken against an employee.	3
8	Describe the requirements of the Health and Safety at Work Act on organisations.	4
9	Describe the operation and benefits of appraisal.	6
10	Describe the benefits to an organisation of using technology to manage the recruitment of new employees.	5

Section 2 questions

			Marks
11	a	Describe the benefits to an organisation of offering apprenticeships.	4
	b	Describe the importance of induction training.	3
	c	Describe the role of works councils.	3
	d	Justify the following styles of leadership: • autocratic • laissez-faire.	5
12	a	Discuss the costs and benefits of different methods of recruitment.	5
	b	Explain why democratic leadership might not always result in positive results.	2
	c	Describe the role of ACAS in terms of employee relations.	3
	d	Describe the provisions and impact of the Health and Safety at Work Act.	5
13	a	Describe the impact of the Equality Act on an organisation.	4
	b	Explain why it is necessary for an organisation to have a grievance policy.	3
	c	Describe the benefits of using a VLE for staff training and development.	4
	d	Describe the purposes of carrying out a skills analysis of employees.	4

Section 5

Management of Finance

Once you complete this section you will be able to:

- ✓ analyse factors influencing financial management and suggest strategies for improved performance in these functional areas

- ✓ apply knowledge and understanding of key business theories and concepts relating to financial management in familiar and unfamiliar contexts

The Management of Finance section of this book looks at how businesses are managed in terms of how their finance is organised and managed in today's economy.

Finance is an important function of every organisation. Its importance in today's society can be viewed not only in terms of business success or failure, but increasingly, from the point of view of business ethics and public perception and accountability. It is therefore essential that in any organisation there is proper planning, monitoring and control in place to manage the finance function. While the main role of the finance function of any organisation is to provide information to managers and decision makers in the business, your understanding of finance will enable you to comment on and interpret financial statements and make sound business judgements.

Topic 5.1 Sources of finance	You should be aware of:
	
	• the suitability of different sources of finance for large organisations
	• internal and external sources, for example:
	  • retained profit
	  • sale of assets
	  • share issue
	  • mortgages
	  • debt factoring
	  • debentures
	• external long-term and short-term sources
	• determining factors for selecting sources of finance, for example:
	  • interest rates
	  • payback term
	  • short term or long term.

Topic 5.2 Cash budgeting	You should be aware of: • the purpose of budgeting as an aid to decision making • the interpretation of cash budgets as a means of solving cash-flow issues.
Topic 5.3 Financial statements	You should be aware of: • the purpose, main elements and interpretation of an income statement (trading and profit and loss account) • the purpose, main elements and interpretation of the statement of financial position (balance sheet) • users of financial information and what they use it for.
Topic 5.4 Ratios	You should be aware of: • the purpose of ratio analysis • the limitations of ratio analysis • the interpretation of profitability, liquidity and efficiency ratios to make evaluative comments on business performance.
Topic 5.5 Technology	You should be aware of: • the uses of technology in financial management and the costs and benefits of using it.

5.1 Sources of finance

All organisations need to borrow money at some point in their existence. This can be for a variety of reasons, such as to purchase new equipment, move premises or simply to expand. Since this course deals with larger types of business organisations, we will consider some sources of finance that are more appropriate to this size of business. For completeness, we will also consider other sources of finance that are used by other sizes of organisation as well.

Larger organisations may decide to obtain finance from the following sources:

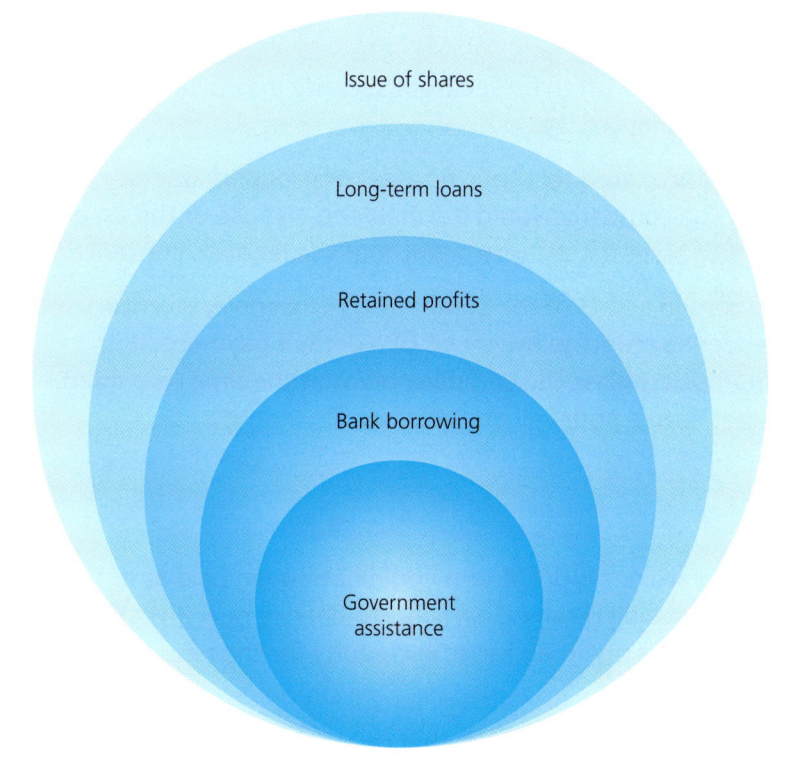

- Issue of shares
- Long-term loans
- Retained profits
- Bank borrowing
- Government assistance

Ordinary (equity) shares

Ordinary shares are issued to the owners of a company. They usually have a nominal or 'face' value of £1.

Ordinary shareholders put funds into their company:

- by paying for a new issue of shares
- through retained profits.

By retaining profits instead of paying them out in the form of dividends, the organisation has access to a low-cost source of finance. This may not be enough to finance whatever the organisation has planned, but it may provide a starting point before having to resort to other sources which would cost money.

Long-term loan

A long-term loan is a long-term debt raised by an organisation for which interest is paid at a fixed rate. Holders of long-term loans are therefore long-term creditors of the business.

Debentures are a form of long-term loan normally containing provisions about the payment of interest and the eventual repayment of capital.

Debentures with a floating rate of interest are debentures for which the rate of interest can be changed by the issuer, in accordance with changes in market rates of interest. They may be attractive to both lenders and borrowers when interest rates are fluctuating.

Security

Long-term loans and debentures will often be secured. Security may take the form of either a fixed charge or a floating charge.

Fixed charge is where security is related to a specific asset or group of assets, typically land and buildings. The company would be unable to dispose of the asset without providing a substitute asset for security or without the lender's consent.

Floating charge applies to certain assets of the company (for example, inventory and debtors) and is the lender's security in the event of a default payment. It is whatever assets of the appropriate class the company owns at the time (provided that another lender does not have a prior call on the assets).

Retained profits

Profit re-invested as retained earnings is profit that could have been paid as a dividend. The major reasons for using retained earnings to finance new investments rather than to pay higher dividends and then raise new equity for the new investments are as follows:

- The management of many companies believes that retained earnings are funds that do not cost anything because the company is not paying interest on borrowing.
- The use of retained profits as opposed to new shares or debentures avoids additional costs.
- The use of retained profits avoids the possibility of a change in control of the business resulting from an issue of new shares.

Bank borrowing

Borrowings from banks are an important source of finance to organisations. Bank lending is still mainly short term although medium-term and long-term lending is also common.

Short-term lending may be in the form of:

- an overdraft which a company should keep within a limit set by the bank. Interest is charged (at a variable rate) on the amount by which the company is overdrawn on a daily basis.
- a short-term loan for up to three years.

Medium-term loans are generally for a period of three to ten years. A loan may have a fixed rate of interest or a variable interest rate, so that the rate of interest charged will be adjusted every three, six, nine or twelve months in line with recent movements in the base lending rate, which is usually set against the rates determined by the Bank of England.

Longer-term bank loans will sometimes be available, usually for the purchase of property, where the loan takes the form of a mortgage. A mortgage is a special type of long-term loan that is secured on a piece of property such as an office block.

When asked by a business customer for a loan or overdraft facility, a banker will consider several factors known commonly by the mnemonic PARTS.

P	Purpose of the loan. A loan request will be refused if the purpose of the loan is not acceptable to the bank.
A	Amount of the loan. The customer must state exactly how much they want to borrow. The banker must verify, as far as s/he is able to do so, that the amount required to make the proposed investment has been estimated correctly.
R	Repayment. Will the customer be able to obtain sufficient income to make the necessary repayments?
T	Term of the loan. Traditionally, banks have offered short-term loans and overdrafts.
S	Security. If required, is the proposed security adequate?

Government assistance

The government may provide finance to companies in cash grants and other forms of direct assistance as part of its policy of helping to develop the national economy, especially in high-technology industries and in areas of high unemployment. Grants do not usually need to be repaid.

Sale of assets (asset stripping)

Sale of assets (or asset stripping) can occur in several different instances. Firstly, it may be a way for the organisation to raise funds through the sale of assets which are no longer of use. It is usually associated with the sale of fixed assets, e.g. vehicles or buildings that are no longer required for the continuing operation of the business.

In another example, this may occur after a hostile takeover or where the organisation has been in a vulnerable financial position and has found itself being bought over by another business. The incumbent business may then raise cash for itself by selling off the organisation's assets, hence the term 'asset stripping'.

Debt factoring

Debt factoring (also known as invoice or accounts receivable factoring) is used by organisations that wish to quickly improve cash flow. Rather than the business waiting for its customers to pay the invoices that it issues, the business 'sells' these customer invoices to a factor from whom they immediately receive the cash. The factor then chases the customer for payment of the invoice.

The immediate disadvantage of this type of arrangement is that the factor will charge a percentage of the value of the invoices it is taking over as payment for its services. As such, it may prove a relatively expensive way to improve cash flow in the short term, while also having the potential to damage relationships with your customers.

Venture capital

Venture capital is a type of funding that is best suited to a new or growing business. The funding itself usually comes from specialist venture-capital businesses. Venture capital is usually provided to the start-up business in exchange for an equity share in the business.

It is usually considered to be a high-risk activity, but the high rewards, when there is a positive outcome, mean that it is an active and attractive area for many businesses and individuals.

Debentures

A debenture is a medium- to long-term loan typically used by large organisations to borrow money which is then repaid with a fixed rate of interest. The legal term 'debenture' originally referred to a document that either creates a debt or acknowledges it. A debenture identifies that the business is liable to pay a specified amount with interest.

Debentures are generally freely transferable by the debenture holder. Debenture holders have no rights to vote in general meetings of shareholders. The interest paid on a debenture is shown as a charge against profit in the financial statements.

Crowdfunding

Crowdfunding is a way of raising money by asking a large number of people for a small amount of money each to contribute to a business or business idea. This is an approach which has recently become popular and is the opposite of traditional finance for new business, where only a few people or organisations (or even one) are asked to contribute/lend a large sum of money.

Most crowdfunding activity takes place online and there are many websites dedicated to this kind of activity. There are different types of crowdfunding:

1. Donation/reward crowdfunding is where people simply invest because they believe in the product or what is trying to be achieved by the business. Typically, the organisation will then offer some type of 'reward' for the funding provided. This could be something as simple as an acknowledgement or free tickets and the rewards associated with this are considered intangible. With this type of crowdfunding, the investors have no expectation of a return on their investment.
2. Debt crowdfunding operates on the basis that investors will receive their money back plus interest. This allows funding for projects/business ideas to progress without using traditional methods of finance such as banks.
3. Equity crowdfunding operates on the basis that investors will provide investment in exchange for equity or a share in the business.

Factors associated with the selection of sources of finance

All organisations will give consideration to the sources of finance that they decide to use. There are several factors which need to be considered and the particular circumstances of each individual organisation will need to be taken into account in making a decision. Some of the factors which may be considered include:

- finance costs, for example, interest rates and charges associated with the source of finance
- level of risk, for example, some organisations may only have a desire to select low-risk sources of finance while others may be more open to products that have a higher associated risk
- payback term, i.e. the length of time that it will take to pay off the money borrowed
- level of control – it is important for the business to consider how much control it will have over the source of finance, for example, if interest is chargeable, is this fixed or can it vary over the course of the term of borrowing?
- penalties – are there any penalties (financial or otherwise) that may come into effect if the finance is settled early?

Other types of finance

Leasing

A lease is an agreement between two parties, the 'lessor' and the 'lessee'. The lessor owns a capital asset but allows the lessee to use it. The lessee makes payments under the terms of the lease to the lessor for a specified period of time.

Leasing is a form of rental. Leased assets are usually plant and machinery, cars and commercial vehicles but might also be computers and office equipment or even furniture. There are two basic forms of lease: operating and finance.

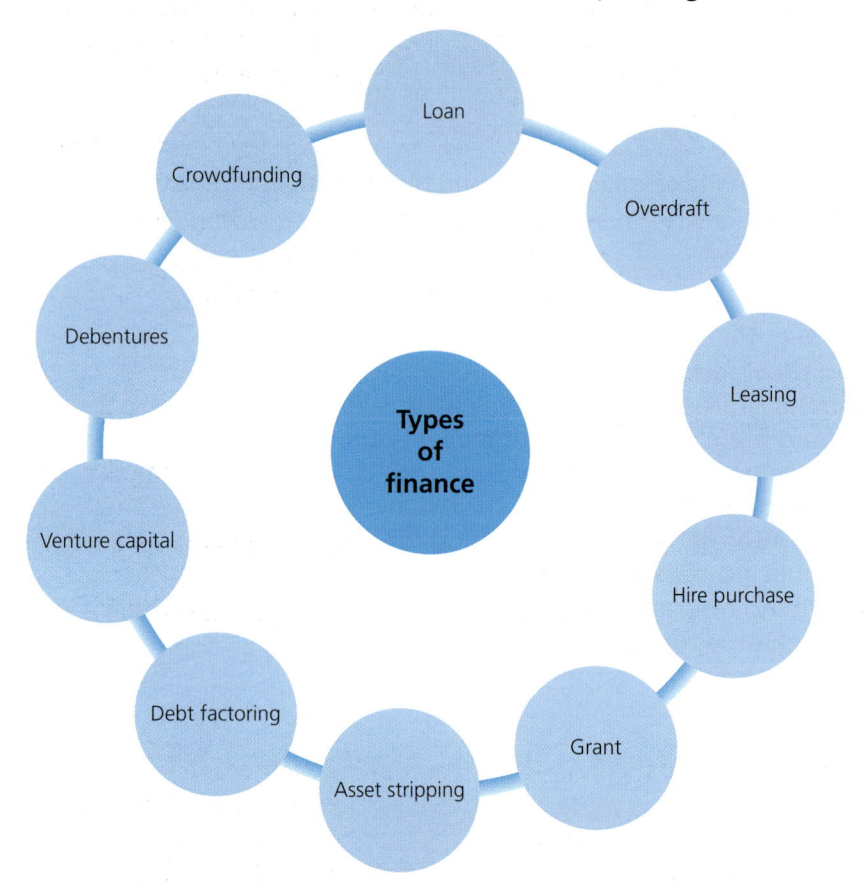

Types of finance: Loan, Overdraft, Leasing, Hire purchase, Grant, Asset stripping, Debt factoring, Venture capital, Debentures, Crowdfunding

Operating leases

Operating leases are rental agreements between the lessor and the lessee where the lessor supplies the equipment to the lessee and the lessor is responsible for servicing and maintaining the leased equipment. The period of the lease is usually short and less than the economic life of the asset, so that at the end of the lease agreement, the lessor can either lease the equipment to someone else and obtain a good rent for it or sell the equipment on.

Finance leases

Finance leases are lease agreements between the user of the leased asset (the lessee) and a provider of finance (the lessor) for most, or all, of the asset's expected useful life.

A company may decide to obtain a car and finance the purchase by means of a finance lease. A car dealer will supply the car. A finance provider will agree to act as lessor in a finance leasing arrangement and so will purchase the car from the dealer and lease it to the company. The company will take possession of the car from the car dealer and make regular payments to the finance house under the terms of the lease.

Important characteristics of a finance lease:

- The lessee is responsible for the upkeep, servicing and maintenance of the asset. The lessor has no legal responsibility for this.
- The lease has a primary period that covers all or most of the economic life of the asset. At the end of the lease, the lessor would not be able to lease the asset to someone else as the asset would be worn out. The lessor must ensure that the lease payments during the primary period pay for the full cost of the asset as well as providing the lessor with a suitable return on the investment.
- It is usual at the end of the primary lease period to allow the lessee to continue to lease the asset for an indefinite secondary period in return for a very low charge. Alternatively, the lessee might be allowed to sell the asset on the lessor's behalf (since the lessor is the owner) and to keep most of the sale proceeds, paying only a small percentage (perhaps ten per cent) to the lessor.

Why leasing is popular

The attractions of leasing are as follows:

- The supplier of the equipment is paid in full at the beginning and the supplier has no further financial concern about the asset.
- The lessor invests finance by purchasing assets from suppliers and makes a return out of the lease payments from the lessee.
- Finance leasing can be cheaper than a bank loan. The cost of payments under a loan might exceed the cost of a lease.

Operating leases have a further advantage:

- The equipment is leased for a shorter period than its expected useful life. In the case of high-technology equipment, if the equipment becomes out of date before the end of its expected life, the lessee does not have to keep using it and it is the lessor who must bear the risk of having to sell obsolete equipment second-hand.

Hire purchase

Hire-purchase (HP) is a form of credit where payments are made in instalments. Hire purchase is similar to leasing with the exception that legal ownership of the goods passes to the hire-purchase customer on payment of the final credit instalment, whereas a lessee never becomes the owner of the goods.

Hire-purchase agreements usually involve a finance provider. Typically, the supplier sells the goods to the finance provider and the supplier delivers the goods to the customer who will eventually purchase them. The hire-purchase arrangement then exists between the finance provider and the customer.

The finance provider will always insist that the hirer should pay a deposit towards the purchase price. The size of the deposit will depend on the finance provider's policy and its assessment of the hirer. This is in contrast to a finance lease where the lessee might not be required to make a large initial payment.

An industrial or commercial business can use hire purchase as a source of finance. With industrial hire purchase, a business customer obtains hire-purchase finance from a finance provider in order to purchase the fixed asset. Goods bought by businesses on hire purchase include company vehicles, plant and machinery, office equipment and specialist machinery.

Description of source of finance	Benefits
Investment from selling shares.	No interest to be paid back or repayments to be made.
Bank loan – agreed sum of finance paid back over time **with interest**.	Paid back in instalments, which assists with forecasting/budgeting.
Bank overdraft – a limit to which an account holder can borrow from the bank when no funds are available.	Easily arranged with the bank and useful to help with short-term cash-flow problems.
Grant – sum of finance (possibly from the government) **with attached conditions** such as to improve employment in an area.	Does not have to be paid back.
Retained profits from previous years.	Does not involve any repayments or interest. Does not dilute control as no need to sell equity/bring in a new partner.
Venture capital – investment in return for equity.	Often provided for strategies that the banks deem too high a lending risk.
Hire purchase – assets are paid for in instalments over an agreed time period and eventually become the property of the business.	Assets eventually belong to the business. Payment over time helps with cash flow and avoids heavy initial costs for expensive assets.
Asset stripping – selling off unnecessary assets, usually fixed assets such as vehicles, etc.	Internal source of finance without incurring debt. Assets can always be leased back to aid cash flow.

Stock markets

The 'stock market' is a term used to describe the combination of buyers and sellers of stocks (and shares) in companies that are traded using a stock exchange. The stock exchange is a place where this trading can take place. Perhaps the most famous stock exchange that you will have heard of is the London Stock Exchange. London, for many years, has been considered one of the main financial trading hubs in the world.

Trade in stock markets means the transfer for money of a stock or security from a seller to a buyer. This requires two parties to agree on a price. Stocks or shares confer an ownership interest in a particular company. Participants in the stock market range from small individual stock investors to larger investors who can be based anywhere in the world. Their orders to buy or sell may be managed on their behalf by a stock exchange trader.

The stock market is one of the most important ways for organisations to raise money. This allows organisations to be publicly traded and to raise additional financial equity for expansion by selling shares of ownership of the company in a public market.

Shares traded on the stock market can go up as well as down in value. The stock market itself is susceptible to outside influences and will react both positively and negatively to them. A stock market crash is often defined as a sharp dip in share prices of stocks listed on the stock exchanges. Panic and loss of confidence is one reason for a stock market crash. Stock market crashes often end lengthy periods of economic uncertainty.

Revision questions

1 Describe some of the sources of finance that are available to large organisations.
2 Justify the use of a loan by an organisation to fund the purchase of new company cars.
3 Explain why leasing is a popular way of financing assets.
4 Discuss the benefits of using hire purchase.
5 Discuss the use of a bank overdraft by a large organisation.
6 Compare two different sources of finance available to a large organisation.
7 Explain the use of crowdfunding as a source of finance.
8 Give a reason why venture capital may be considered 'risky'.
9 Explain why asset stripping may not be a desirable action for an organisation.
10 Describe the operation of debt factoring.
11 Describe three factors which might be considered when selecting a source of finance.

5.2 Cash budgeting

Cash and cash management are the most important aspects of business. Lack of cash flow is one of the single biggest reasons that businesses fail. Even apparently successful and profitable businesses can fail due to a lack of cash. This usually happens because the lack of cash starves the business of its ability to meet its short-term obligations and daily operations.

The role of cash in any business at any time (whether business is good or bad) cannot be underestimated. The cash-flow cycle demonstrates the role of cash in business. Consider the following diagram.

As the diagram suggests, the movement of cash (cash flow) in and out of the business is central to the success and efficient operation of the business. The concept of cash flow is centred around liquidity, which is the provision of or the ability to have access to cash or near cash assets to meet the everyday commitments of the business. Without access to liquid assets (or cash), the business will fail.

The terminology of cash flow is concerned with the movement of money in and out of the business. In this context, the following terms are used:

- 'Cash inflow' – a movement of cash into the business, for example, cash sales.
- 'Cash outflow' – a movement of cash out of the business, for example, cash purchases.

A cash-flow statement is produced as part of the year-end accounts of a limited company and also as a useful financial statement by many other organisations. It shows the movements of cash in and out of the business over the course of the financial year. The term 'cash' has a special meaning in the context of a cash-flow statement and can mean cash, money in the bank and other cash-equivalent assets (these are assets that can be converted to cash quickly if required).

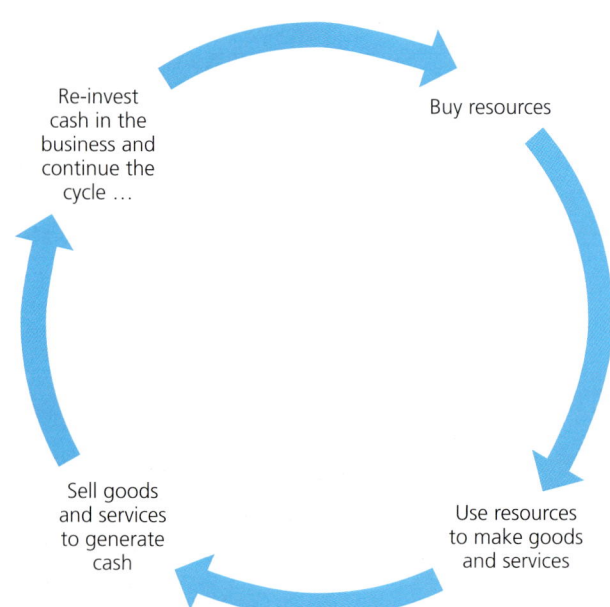

The cash-flow statement itself is constructed from the information contained in the statement of financial position and the income statement. When a cash-flow statement is produced at times other than the financial year end, the business will have to collate information from its accounting records in order to produce it.

A cash-flow statement can provide an easy means by which to track the movements of cash in the business.

Here are some common examples of cash inflows and cash outflows.

> The International Accounting Standards Board governs the accounting profession by setting and enforcing professional standards. It encourages all businesses to produce cash-flow statements on a regular basis.

Cash inflows
- decrease in trade receivables
- increase in trade payables
- loan received
- new capital invested
- profits
- sale of a fixed asset
- sale of inventory

Cash outflows
- decrease in trade payables
- dividend payment
- drawings
- increase in trade receivables
- loan repaid
- losses
- purchase of a fixed asset
- purchase of inventory

Cash budgets

A budget is simply a statement of anticipated future expenditure. It usually covers a specific time period such as one month or a year. Budgets are usually financial in nature in so far as they are expressed in terms of money, although they can be expressed in other units. The main uses of budgets are shown on the following page.

SECTION 5 MANAGEMENT OF FINANCE

Improved decision making	• Budgets allow managers to see how well the business is performing by comparing one time period to another.
Monitoring and control	• Setting a budget and then comparing it to actual performance means that comparisons can be made on a regular basis and changes made quickly to solve problems.
To set targets	• This gives managers and employees targets to reach.
To delegate authority	• The use of budgets means that managers can give additional responsibility to employees.
To plan ahead	• They are useful to highlight areas of strength or plan for areas of estimated deficit.

A cash budget is a common type of budget that is used by most businesses to monitor, control, obtain and present information.

Budgets can be used to monitor the cash position of a particular department, section, project or the business as a whole. They can also be used as a management decision-making tool to assess the validity of a particular project or scenario. A cash projection may be used as part of a submission to a lender to secure finance for a project or the expansion of the business.

Budgets are often produced using accounting software or a spreadsheet package. This means that changes can be made to the budget very easily and the effects of the changes will be automatically updated in the rest of the budget. An example of a cash budget is shown below.

Airwave Ltd
Budgets for the 6-month period – April to September

Cash Receipts Budget:

	Apr £	May £	Jun £	Jul £	Aug £	Sep £	Total £
Trade receivables	5,000	5,000	6,000	7,000	4,000	6,000	33,000
Total Cash Inflows	5,000	5,000	6,000	7,000	4,000	6,000	33,000

Cash Payments Budget:

	Apr £	May £	Jun £	Jul £	Aug £	Sep £	Total £
Trade payables (inventory)	2,000	3,000	4,000	4,000	3,000	2,000	18,000
Direct labour	2,000	2,000	2,500	2,500	1,100	1,100	11,200
Variable overheads	300	400	300	200	400	500	2,100
Maintenance contracts	100	200	300	400	400	400	1,800
Total Cash Outflows	4,400	5,600	7,100	7,100	4,900	4,000	33,100

Cash Budget:

	Apr £	May £	Jun £	Jul £	Aug £	Sep £	Total £
Opening Cash/Bank Balance	1,000	1,600	1,000	(100)	(200)	(1,100)	1,000
Cash Inflows	5,000	5,000	6,000	7,000	4,000	6,000	33,000
Cash Outflows	4,400	5,600	7,100	7,100	4,900	4000	33,100
Closing Cash/Bank Balance	1,600	1,000	(100)	(200)	(1,100)	900	900

A cash budget is just one type of budget. It is normal for other budgets to 'feed into' the cash budget. These other types of budgets are usually referred to as functional budgets. An example of a functional budget is shown below.

The Shennan Company Ltd

Budgets for the 3-month period – April to June

Raw Materials Usage Budget (units):

	kg Per Unit	Apr (kg)	May (kg)	Jun (kg)	Total (kg)
Opening Inventory		15,000	21,290	25,085	**15,000**
Purchases		5,000	2,500	3,000	**10,500**
Materials available for production		20,000	23,790	28,085	**71,875**
Used for Budgeted Production	5.00	(1,290)	(1,295)	(1,290)	**(3,875)**
Closing Inventory		21,290	25,085	29,375	**29,375**

The main benefits to management of using cash budgets are shown below.

Planning
- Look ahead to set aims and strategies.
- Allows problem solving to be planned rather than having to react to situations.

Organisation
- Allows the right resources to be in the right place and at the right time.

Command
- When management are able to make informed decisions, this enables them to instruct their subordinates.
- Management will have access to all the budgets for each department which will be fed into the master budget.

Co-ordinate
- Management can give instructions to those in charge of departmental budgets and keep a clear overview of the business as a whole.

Control
- The evaluation and review of budgets allows management to exert control over the budgets and keep a clear overview of the business as a whole.

Delegation
- Management should make subordinates responsible for a suitable range of tasks and give them the authority to carry them out.

Motivation
- Management have a responsibility to motivate their staff. This can be done through setting realistic targets in the budgets and introducing concepts and practices such as teamwork, empowerment and incentives for meeting targets or operating within budget.

Research task

Prepare a simple cash budget of your own. Detail your income and expenditure over the course of a four-week period. Do you have enough money to do all the things you want to do?

Solutions to temporary cash-flow problems

From time to time, all organisations experience issues with their cash flow. It is important to plan ahead for potential cash shortages so that action can be taken in advance of it becoming a major problem. Many businesses fail today and go bankrupt because they run out of cash to keep operating on a day-to-day basis. There can be many reasons for a lack of cash in the business as shown below.

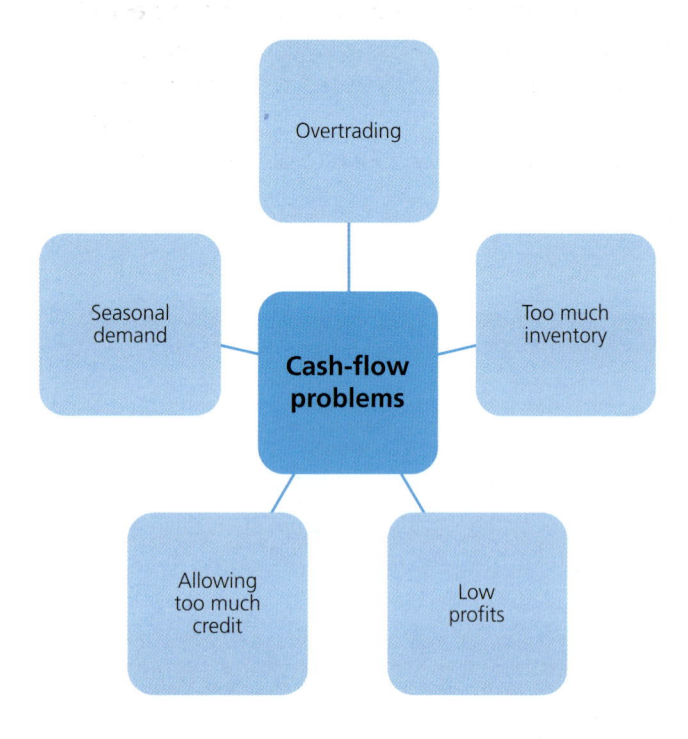

- Overtrading
- Too much inventory
- Low profits
- Allowing too much credit
- Seasonal demand

Cash-flow problems

Overtrading	• Overtrading occurs when a business expands rapidly and there is too much pressure put on short-term finance.
Too much inventory	• Holding too much inventory means that cash is tied up in that inventory until it is sold. There is also a risk that inventory held for a long period could become obsolete.
Low profits	• There is a direct link between low profits and cash-flow problems.
Allowing too much credit	• If too much credit is allowed to customers or too many customers are offered credit, it increases the risk that late or slow payments can have a negative impact on cash flow.
Seasonal demand	• Predictable changes in seasonal demand can be planned for to some extent but unpredictable changes can cause cash-flow problems.

Cash-flow problems	Potential solutions
• Too much money tied up in inventory • Allowing customers too much credit • Borrowing too much money at a high interest rate • Owners taking too much in drawings • Low sales	• Sell unnecessary fixed assets • Arrange a bank overdraft • Improve credit control by chasing trade receivables • Offer promotions to encourage sales and shift inventory • Arrange credit with suppliers • Reduce owners' drawings • Find a cheaper supplier • Buy assets on hire purchase

There is a variety of options available to organisations that encounter cash-flow problems. The key to surviving them is to plan ahead and work around expected problems. This means keeping accurate accounting records, following good business practices and using budgets to forecast and identify future cash-flow problems. An action plan can then be put in place to take account of the cash-flow issue in advance of it happening. This means that the business can continue to operate 'business as usual'.

Solutions to cash-flow problems
- Better planning
- Produce accurate budgets
- Constantly revise and compare budgets
- Have an overdraft facility or other short-term finance set up in advance

Revision questions

1. Describe the term 'cash budget'.
2. Describe the benefits to management of using a cash budget.
3. Describe the cash-flow problems that may be faced by an organisation.
4. Describe the solutions to cash-flow problems that may be used by an organisation.
5. Explain why holding too much inventory could affect cash flow in an organisation.
6. Explain the impact of overtrading on cash flow.
7. Describe the use of a cash budget as a planning tool.
8. Justify the use of a bank overdraft as an ongoing solution to managing cash flow.

5.3 Financial statements

Financial information may be presented by a business in different formats. For example, the business will have different formats for information that is used internally and for information that is presented externally. Large organisations such as multinational businesses must present their externally published accounts in formats controlled by International Accounting Standards.

There are three main financial statements that all businesses use:

- income statement
- statement of financial position
- cash-flow statement.

In addition to these statements, which will usually be produced for both internal and external use, most businesses will also find it useful to calculate accounting ratios based on their financial records. The three main financial statements are normally used as the basis for the calculation of the accounting ratios.

Income statement

The income statement is used by businesses as a statement for both internal and external reporting. The form that it takes will differ according to its use but nonetheless it will still provide the same basic information. For example, the income statement used for internal reporting may be produced on a monthly basis and go into great detail whereas the income statement that is produced as a statutory requirement at the end of the financial year will take a much reduced form and will contain much less detail in the information that it provides.

The income statement details the business income and expenditure over the course of the financial year. The business expenditure is matched to the business income and where the business income is greater than the expenditure, a profit is recorded. Conversely, where the business expenditure is greater than the income, a loss is recorded.

It is an important feature of the income statement, and a requirement of accounting conventions, that the business properly matches its income and expenditure for the period for which the income statement is drawn up. This ensures that the profit (or loss) for the year calculated is not over-stated and that a true reflection of the business's trading activities is shown.

Income statement terminology	
Trading account	Provides a summary of the business's trading activity during the financial year.
Sales	Monies that the business has received from selling goods and/or services.
Revenue	The value of the business's sales less the value of any returns.
Cost of sales	The cost of the sales to the business, i.e. before a sales or profit margin is added.
Opening inventory	The value of the inventory of goods at the start of the financial period.
Purchases	The cost of goods that the business has bought for resale to its customers.
Carriage inwards	The cost of transporting or delivering goods purchased by the business for resale.
Purchase returns	The value of goods purchased but returned to the supplier, e.g. wrong colour, faulty.
Closing inventory	The value of unsold inventory at the end of the financial period.
Gross profit/loss	The profit (or loss) recorded as the difference between the business's sales and purchases.
Expenses	Any expenses incurred by the business in the course of its normal operation.
Profit for the year/Loss for the year	The profit (or loss) recorded after all business expenses have been deducted.
Corporation tax	A tax on business profits payable to the government.
Dividend	Proportion of the business profit paid to shareholders and dependent on the number of shares that they own.
Unappropriated profit	Profit retained in the business, i.e. not distributed to either owners or shareholders.

The income statement is a continuation of the business's trading account. The trading account records the difference between how much money the business generates from selling and how much the goods (or services) it is selling actually cost, i.e. cost of sales.

The trading account then shows the gross profit of the business. The gross profit is the profit before any of the business's expenses are taken into account; it gives an indication of the business's general trading performance. It is a crude measurement of profit.

A simple trading account might look something like this:

Scott's Trading Company
Trading Account for the year ending 31 March

	£	£
Net sales		150,000
Cost of sales		
Opening inventory of goods	20,000	
Purchases	75,000	
	95,000	
Less closing inventory of goods	(25,000)	70,000
Gross profit		80,000

The income statement follows on from the trading account and a simple version would look something like this:

Scott's Trading Company
Income Statement for the year ending 31 March

	£	£
Gross profit		80,000
Other operating income		
Rent received	9,000	
Interest received	1,000	10,000
		90,000
Expenses		
Rent and rates	25,000	
Heating and lighting	8,000	
Telephone	900	
Advertising	250	
Postage	400	
Wages and salaries	45,000	
Insurance	2,000	81,550
PROFIT FOR THE YEAR		8,450

A more complicated format of the income statement is used for larger companies. Multinational companies fall under the jurisdiction of the Companies Act and must produce their year-end accounts in accordance with the formats prescribed by the law. All other types of business will produce a similar type of income statement but it will usually be less detailed than that required of a multinational company.

You can look online at a huge variety of company reports. Visit the company website of your choice to look at their published accounts or use a website such as www.annualreports.co.uk where you can choose which accounts you would like to view.

Statement of financial position

The income statement records a history of the business activity throughout the financial year, but the statement of financial position shows a snapshot at a particular date in time, usually the last day of the financial year.

Whereas the income statement details trading activity, the statement of financial position records the financial worth and the financial position of the business at a particular point in time. For this reason alone, the statement of financial position of any company is out of date by the time it is published. It forms part of the historic accounting records of the business.

Historic accounting is so called because it uses information from the past to compile statements and reports that are of use to other businesses and individuals.

The statement of financial position shows three different things:

- assets
- liabilities
- equity.

We can combine each of these three categories of items in the accounting equation:

$$\text{Equity} = \text{Assets} - \text{Liabilities}$$

Statement of financial position terminology	
Non-current asset	Something the business owns and depends on to operate on a daily basis. Usually has a degree of permanence.
Current asset	Assets that are likely to be changed into cash in the short term. They frequently change in value.
Current liability	Something that the business owes money for in the short term, i.e. a debt. They must usually be paid within one year.
Non-current liability	Debts of the business that are not due to be repaid for more than twelve months.
Equity	A special kind of liability. The money invested by the owner(s) of the business to set it up. This money is owed back to the owner(s) by the business.
Net assets employed	This is the difference in value between the total assets and the total current liabilities. The total of the assets should be more than the total of the current liabilities.
Reserves	Money and profits that are retained in the business, perhaps to buy new assets or to safeguard against future losses.
Net assets	The financial value or worth of the business.

The statement of financial position is presented in two parts: the top half and the bottom half (when displayed in the usual vertical format). The top half displays the assets and liabilities of the business. Assets are things that the business owns and these are categorised as either non-current or current. Liabilities are the opposite of assets and are things that the business owes money for. They too can be either current or non-current.

Non-current assets are the productive assets of the business. Without these assets, the business would not be able to function on a day-to-day basis. These are things like buildings, machinery and other equipment. They are normally listed in descending order of permanence, i.e. the one that is expected to last the longest will be listed first.

Current assets are assets that change on a daily basis and can be turned easily into cash. They are listed in descending order of liquidity, i.e. how easily they can be turned into cash. The most illiquid (or most difficult to turn into cash) is usually listed first. Examples of current assets are money in the bank, inventories of goods and debtors.

Current liabilities are also listed on the top half of the statement and are shown as a deduction from current assets. This is because the business will (eventually) turn all of its current assets into cash and subsequently use this cash to pay its current liabilities. These liabilities are known as current because they will normally have to be repaid within a period of twelve months. The most common example of a current liability is trade payables, i.e. people or other businesses to whom the business owes money for goods or services supplied on credit.

The difference between the total assets and the total current liabilities is highlighted on the statement of financial position. This is known as net assets employed. Where the total current liabilities is greater than the total current assets of the business, this shows that the company is in potential financial difficulty as it may be unable to meet its most immediately payable debts. In extreme cases, where the company does not have sufficient current assets to pay its short-term debts, it may have to resort to selling off some of its non-current assets to survive. This is, however, a dangerous practice as without its non-current (productive) assets, the company will not be able to function properly and may ultimately fail.

Non-current liabilities are listed on the top half of the statement. These represent liabilities that the business must repay after more than one year. Examples include debentures and other longer-term loans which may or may not be secured on assets belonging to the business.

The total fixed assets plus the net current assets minus long-term liabilities is known as the business's net assets. This means the 'value' of the business in monetary terms on the particular date specified on the statement of financial position. The relative usefulness of the statement is, however, limited as it only provides a snapshot of the business and, like other accounting records, is based on transactions from the business history.

The bottom half of the statement of financial position represents the 'equity' side of the accounting equation. Depending on the type of business, this half of the statement may comprise owners' funds (equity) or share capital contributed by the shareholders of the company.

As the statement of financial position comprises two halves that represent the accounting equation, the total of the top half of the statement must equal the total of the bottom half of the statement, i.e. the accounting equation must be satisfied.

A statement of financial position would look something like this:

Mitchell Media Productions Ltd
Statement of Financial Position as at 30 April

	£000	£000	£000
Non-current assets			
Premises			1,500
Computer equipment			800
Motor vehicles			200
			2,500
Current assets			
Inventory	600		
Trade receivables	400		
Cash at bank	200	1,200	
Current liabilities			
Trade payables	500		
Taxation	150		
Dividends	100	750	
Working equity		450	
Net assets employed			2,950
Non-current liabilities			
Bank loan	200		
Debenture loan		1,000	1,200
Net assets			1,750

	£000	£000	£000
Equity and reserves			
Ordinary share capital			1,000
Retained profits			750
			1,750

Cash-flow statement

The cash-flow statement is produced by organisations to show the movement of cash in the business across the year. It details all of the cash inflows and cash outflows. It is a legal requirement for limited companies and most large organisations, and forms part of the annual accounts along with the income statement and statement of financial position.

> Remember that this is different from a cash budget.
> The differences between a cash-flow statement and cash-flow forecast (budget) are shown below.

A cash-flow statement is produced for external use by an organisation as part of its final accounts for the year. It shows movements of cash (inflows and outflows) over the past year.

A cash-flow forecast (cash budget) is produced for internal management use to predict the receipts and payments of cash and plan ahead for shortfalls.

Examples of cash-flow statements
Marks and Spencer plc

Consolidated cash-flow statement

	Notes	52 weeks ended 31 March 2018 £m	52 weeks ended 1 Apr 2017 £m
Cash flows from operating activities			
Cash generated from operations	26	944.1	1,165.7
Income tax paid		(94.3)	(98.0)
Net cash inflow from operating activities		**849.8**	**1,067.7**
Cash flows from investing activities			
Proceeds on property disposals		3.2	27.0
Purchase of property, plant and equipment		(274.9)	(309.1)
Proceeds on disposal of Hong Kong business		22.9	–
Purchase of intangible assets		(74.3)	(101.1)
Reduction of current financial assets		0.8	4.6
Interest received		6.0	6.6
Net cash used in investing activities		**(316.3)**	**(372.0)**
Cash flows from financing activities			
Interest paid[1]		(112.2)	(111.2)
Cash inflow/(outflow) from borrowings		43.8	(32.7)
Repayment of syndicated loan		–	(215.3)
Decrease in obligations under finance leases		(2.6)	(2.0)
Payment of liability to the Marks & Spencer UK Pension Sheme		(59.6)	(57.9)
Equity dividends paid		(303.4)	(377.5)
Shares issued on exercise of employee share options		0.1	5.5
Purchase of own shares by employee trust		(3.1)	–
(Redemption)/issuance of medium-term notes		(328.2)	300.0
Net cash used in financing activities		**(765.2)**	**(491.1)**
Net cash (outflow)/inflow from activities		**(231.7)**	**204.6**
Effects of exchange rate changes		(3.5)	5.6
Opening net cash		406.2	196.0
Closing net cash	27	**171.0**	**406.2**

1. Includes interest on the partnership liability to the Marks & Spencer UK Pension Scheme.

	Notes	52 weeks ended 31 March 2018 £m	52 weeks ended 1 April 2017 £m
Reconciliation of net cash flow to movement in net debt			
Opening net debt		**(1,934.7)**	**(2,138.3)**
Net cash (outflow)/inflow from activities		(231.7)	204.6
Decrease in current financial assets		(0.8)	(4.6)
Decrease in debt financing		346.6	7.9
Exchange and other non cash movements		(6.9)	(4.3)
Movement in net debt		**107.2**	**203.6**
Closing net debt	27	**(1,827.5)**	**(1,934.7)**

Tesco plc

Group cash-flow statement

	Notes	52 weeks 2017 £m	52 weeks 2016 £m
Cash flows generated from/(used in) operating activities			
Operating profit/(loss) of continuing operations		1,017	1,072
Operating profit/(loss) of discontinued operations		(117)	102
Depreciation and amortisation		1,304	1,334
(Profit)/loss arising on sale of property, plant and equipment and intangible assets		(78)	164
(Profit)/loss arising on sale of subsidiaries and other investments		3	–
(Profit)/loss arising on sale joint ventures and associates		(5)	(1)
Impairment loss on goodwill		46	18
Net impairment loss/(reversal) on other investments		(12)	(7)
Net impairment loss/(reversal) on loans/investments in joint ventures and associates		–	1
Net impairment loss/(reversal) on property, plant and equipment, software and other intangible assets and investment property		(5)	182
Adjustment for non-cash element of pensions charge	27	7	(395)
Additional contribution into pension schemes	27	(248)	(223)
Share-based payments		15	283
Tesco Bank fair value movements included in operating profit		98	72
Retail (increase)/decrease in inventories		124	251
Retail (increase)/decrease in development stock		16	99
Retail (increase)/decrease in trade and other receivables		(74)	20
Retail increase/(decrease) in trade and other payables		510	260
Retail increase/(decrease) in provisions		11	(280)
Tesco Bank (increase)/decrease in loans and advances to customers		(1,529)	(868)
Tesco Bank (increase)/decrease in trade and other receivables		(24)	(78)
Tesco Bank increase/(decrease) in customer and bank deposits, trade and other payables		1,474	463
Tesco Bank increase/(decrease) in provisions		25	(35)
(Increase)/decrease in working capital		533	(168)
Cash generated from/(used in) operations		2,558	2,434
Interest received/(paid)		(522)	(426)
Corporation tax received/(paid)		(47)	118
Net cash generated from/(used in) operating activities		1,989	2,126
Cash flows generated from/(used in) investing activities			
Purchase of property, plant and equipment, investment property and non-current assets classified as held for sale		(1,205)	(871)
Purchase of intangible assets		(169)	(167)
Disposal of subsidiaries, net of cash disposed	31	205	3,237
Acquisition of subsidiaries, net of cash acquired	31	(25)	(325)
Proceeds from sale of joint ventures and associates		–	192
Proceeds from sale of property, plant and equipment, investment property, intangible assets and non-current assets classified as held for sale		512	350
Net (increase)/decrease in loans to joint ventures and associates		15	(1)
Investments in joint ventures and associates		–	(77)
Net (investments in)/proceeds from sale of short-term investments		736	(2,894)
Net (investments in)/proceeds from sale of other investments		141	(103)
Dividends received from joint ventures and associates		28	41
Interest received/(paid)		41	3
Net cash generated from/(used in) investing activities		279	(615)
Cash flows generated from/(used in) financing activities			
Proceeds from issue of ordinary share capital	28	1	1
Increase in borrowings		185	586
Repayment of borrowings		(2,036)	(1,328)
Net cash flows from derivative financial instruments		475	154
Repayment of obligations under finance leases		(12)	(17)
Dividends paid to equity owners	8	–	–
Net cash generated from/(used in) financing activities		(1,387)	(604)
Net increase/(decrease) in cash and cash equivalents		881	907
Cash and cash equivalents at beginning of the year		3,082	2,174
Effect of foreign exchange rate changes		(131)	1
Cash and cash equivalents including cash held in disposal group at the end of the year		3,832	3,082
Cash held in disposal group	7	(11)	–
Cash and cash equivalents at the end of the year	18	3,821	3,082

Revision questions

1. Explain the importance to an organisation of producing financial statements.
2. Describe the purpose of producing an income statement.
3. Describe the purpose of producing a statement of financial position.
4. Describe the purpose of producing a cash-flow statement.
5. Give reasons for competitor interest in an organisation's financial statements.
6. Describe the differences between a cash-flow statement and a cash-flow forecast.
7. Explain why different financial statements are produced for internal and external use.
8. Explain why profit and cash are not the same thing.

5.4 Ratios

Accounting ratios

Accounting ratios are used as a tool in the decision-making process and as an aid to financial interpretation and planning. They may be used by managers within the business as well as outsiders who are interested in the performance of the business or who have an interest in the business.

Ratios can be categorised according to the function that they perform as shown below.

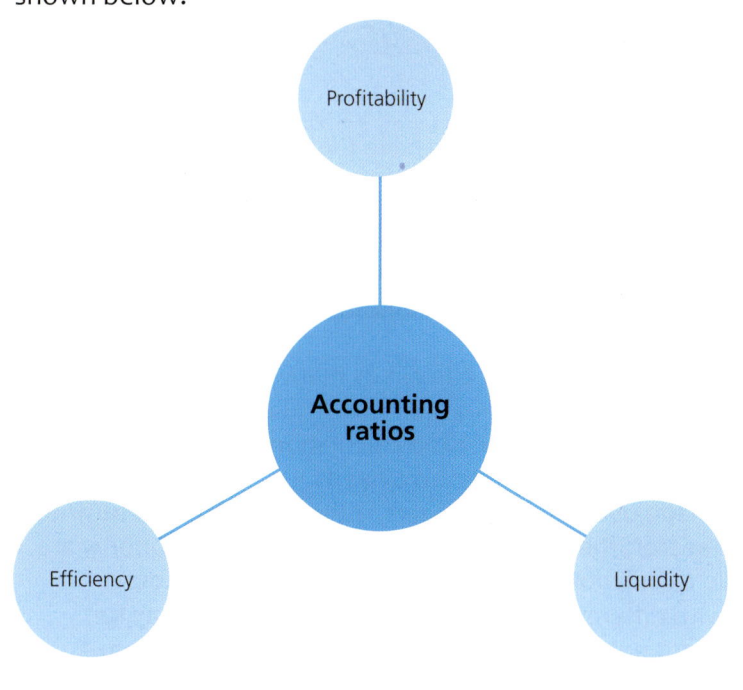

Several different ratios can be calculated under each of the headings. This can then allow comparisons between different years for the same business, comparisons with other businesses in the same sector or comparisons with averages for a particular business sector. This process is often referred to as ratio analysis.

Ratio analysis may also be used for more sinister purposes, for example, by another business or individual planning a takeover. It may also prove to be a useful tool in the forecasting or budgeting process.

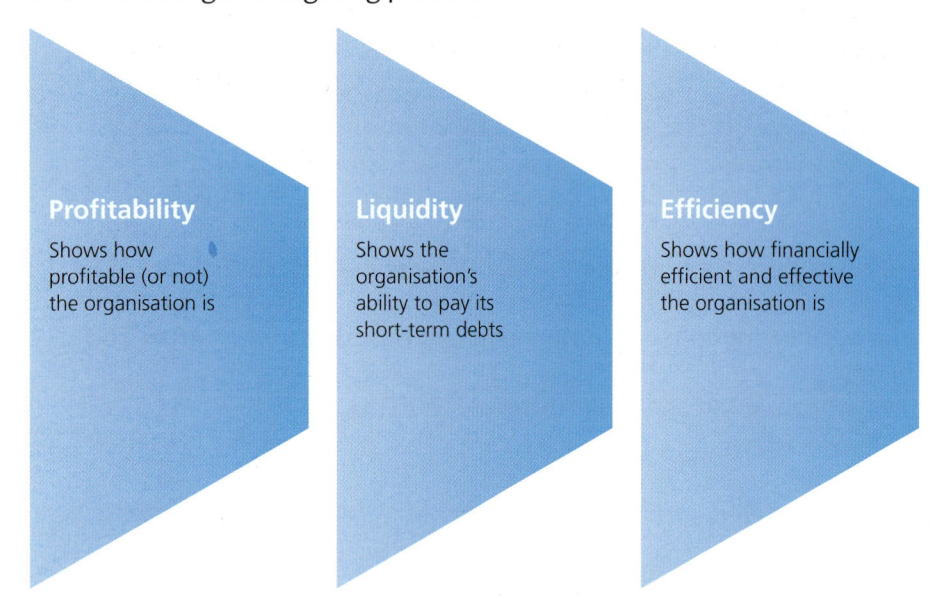

Profitability
Shows how profitable (or not) the organisation is

Liquidity
Shows the organisation's ability to pay its short-term debts

Efficiency
Shows how financially efficient and effective the organisation is

Some of the uses of accounting ratios are shown below.

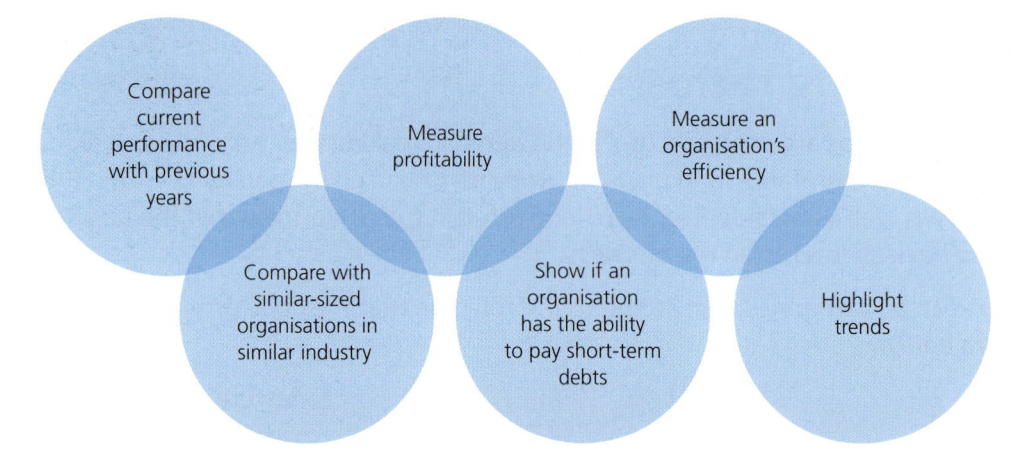

- Compare current performance with previous years
- Measure profitability
- Measure an organisation's efficiency
- Compare with similar-sized organisations in similar industry
- Show if an organisation has the ability to pay short-term debts
- Highlight trends

It is worth noting, however, that accounting ratios have their limitations:

- The accounting information used to calculate the ratios is historic, i.e. it is based on information that is out of date.
- When comparisons are made with other businesses, the comparison is only valid where the business is of the same type and size and the same information is available to calculate the same ratios.
- Comparisons with other businesses can be difficult as many businesses publish only very limited financial information.
- Comparisons must be made using the same ratio calculations – many businesses 'tweak' the ratio formulas to better suit their own needs.
- When comparisons are made over a series of years, either for the same business or in the same business sector, the external effects of the general economy are not reflected in the ratio calculations and this must be taken into account.
- Comparisons of ratios with different businesses in the same sector may be meaningless if the ratios are not calculated on the same basis, i.e. using the same formulae.

- Ratios are of little use on their own. They must be used as an aid to interpretation and in the context of the business sector to which they apply. It is, therefore, essential that the user is also able to understand both how the particular business operates and how it reports its financial results.
- Other sources of information should also be utilised when interpreting the accounts, such as the directors' report, auditors' report, notes to the accounts and accounting policies of the business.
- The users of financial ratios must beware of 'window dressing'. This is where a company temporarily improves its working capital (net current assets) in order to improve its ratios. This effect can be achieved through increasing inventory levels or taking out a short-term loan.

The users of financial information can include stakeholders in the business, investors, creditors, customers and employees. They will want to know the answers to questions such as:

- Is the business profitable?
- Can the business pay its debts on time?
- How is the business financed?
- What percentage of the full business's worth is financed?
- How does this year's performance compare with last year's?
- How does the performance of the business compare to other businesses in the same sector?

Ratio analysis can provide easy answers to all of these questions without the need to study pages and pages of accounts. If you have had the opportunity to access company accounts online at www.annualreports.co.uk or been able to look at a set of published company accounts, then you will appreciate that it can be difficult to interpret the huge amount of information provided.

Profitability ratios

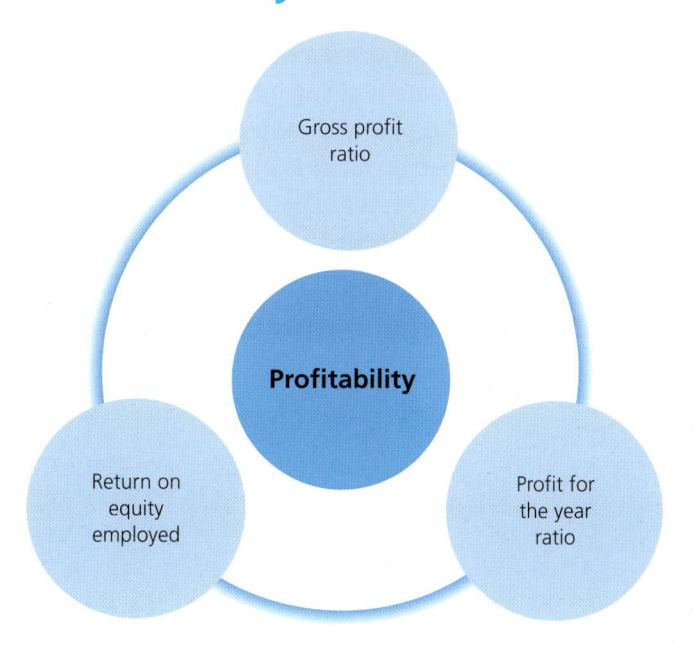

Gross profit ratio

Profitability

Return on equity employed

Profit for the year ratio

Gross profit ratio or gross profit as a percentage of sales revenue

This ratio is used to calculate the gross profit as a percentage of sales revenue. Where the percentage is high, it may indicate that the business has a prudent buying policy. Changes in the ratio can be caused by an increase or a decrease in the selling price (usually a deliberate company policy) or an increase or a decrease in the cost of goods sold (usually outside the company's control).

The formula used to calculate gross profit is:

$$\left(\frac{\text{gross profit}}{\text{sales revenue}}\right) \times 100\%$$

Profit for the year ratio or profit for the year as a percentage of sales revenue

This ratio is used to calculate the return on sales when compared to the total costs of the business. Where a low figure is calculated, this shows that the company's expenses may be high and should be further investigated. This ratio is often used to highlight efficiency and control of costs.

The formula used to calculate profit for the year is:

$$\left(\frac{\text{profit for the year}}{\text{sales revenue}}\right) \times 100\%$$

Return on equity employed

This ratio measures how well, or how badly, a business has utilised the equity that has been invested in it. This gives a more useful interpretation of performance than merely looking at the profit figure.

For example, imagine Company X reports a profit of £1m and Company Y reports a profit of £500,000. Company X would appear to be the more successful company based on the information provided, but a quick calculation taking into account the equity invested in these companies shows that Company X earned £1m profit from equity invested of £10m while Company Y earned profit of £500,000 from just £4m equity invested. Company Y has made better use of its equity as Company X used more than twice the amount of equity to produce just double the profit of Company Y.

The formula used to calculate return on equity employed is:

$$\left(\frac{\text{profit for the year}}{\text{capital equity}}\right) \times 100\%$$

Liquidity ratios

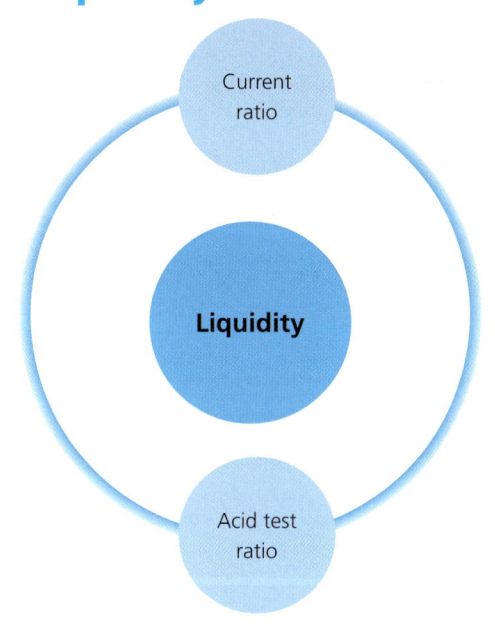

Current ratio

The current ratio is used to indicate the business's ability to meet its short-term debts without having to borrow money. There is no ideal figure for this ratio although it should normally fall within the region of 1:1 and 3:1. Where the ratio is very low, this indicates that the business may have problems in meeting its short-term debts. Conversely, while a high ratio indicates that there is more than enough money to cover short-term business debts, it can also indicate that there is too much cash in the business not being utilised to best advantage. Spare cash can be invested, even in the short term, and earn additional income for the business.

The formula used to calculate current ratio is:

current assets : current liabilities

The answer should be expressed as a ratio, for example 1.35 : 1.

Acid test ratio

The acid test ratio is similar to the current ratio, although it takes into account the fact that inventories of raw materials and goods for resale may take some time to be turned into cash. The business's ability to pay its short-term debts is therefore assessed without the inclusion of the value of inventories. The average figure of 1:1 should be used as a guideline, although anything less than this would indicate that the business would not be able to meet its short-term debts without selling inventory or borrowing money. It is worth noting that some businesses can operate with an acid test ratio of less than 1:1 and the typical ratio will depend on the type of business.

The formula used to calculate acid test ratio is:

current assets – inventory : current liabilities

The answer should be expressed as a ratio, for example 1.15 : 1.

Efficiency ratios

Rate of inventory turnover

This ratio measures the number of times that the inventory held by the company is turned over. If the figures are taken from the end of year accounts then the calculation will tell us the number of times that the inventory has turned over in the year.

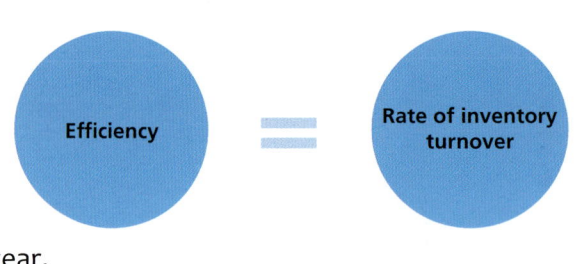

Efficiency = Rate of inventory turnover

There is no correct figure for this as it depends on the type of inventory that the company holds. For example, businesses that deal in perishable goods will have a high rate of inventory turnover compared to businesses that deal in high-value luxury goods.

The formula used to calculate rate of inventory turnover is:

$$\frac{\text{cost of sales}}{\text{average inventory}}$$

The answer is expressed as a number of times.

Reasons for changes in the accounting ratios

Part of the reason for calculating accounting ratios is to calculate the ratios for two or more different time periods (or years) so that a comparison can be made. There are a number of different reasons why the ratios can change. Some of these are listed below. When analysing changes in accounting ratios, you should also use some common sense and take into account the type of business that you are analysing.

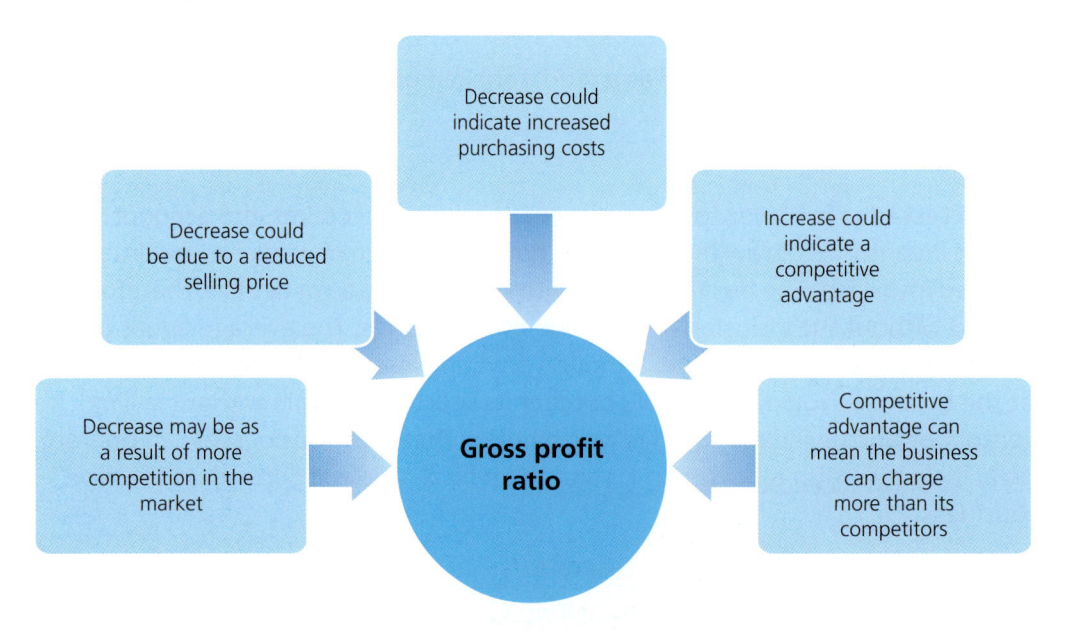

Gross profit ratio

- Decrease could indicate increased purchasing costs
- Decrease could be due to a reduced selling price
- Increase could indicate a competitive advantage
- Decrease may be as a result of more competition in the market
- Competitive advantage can mean the business can charge more than its competitors

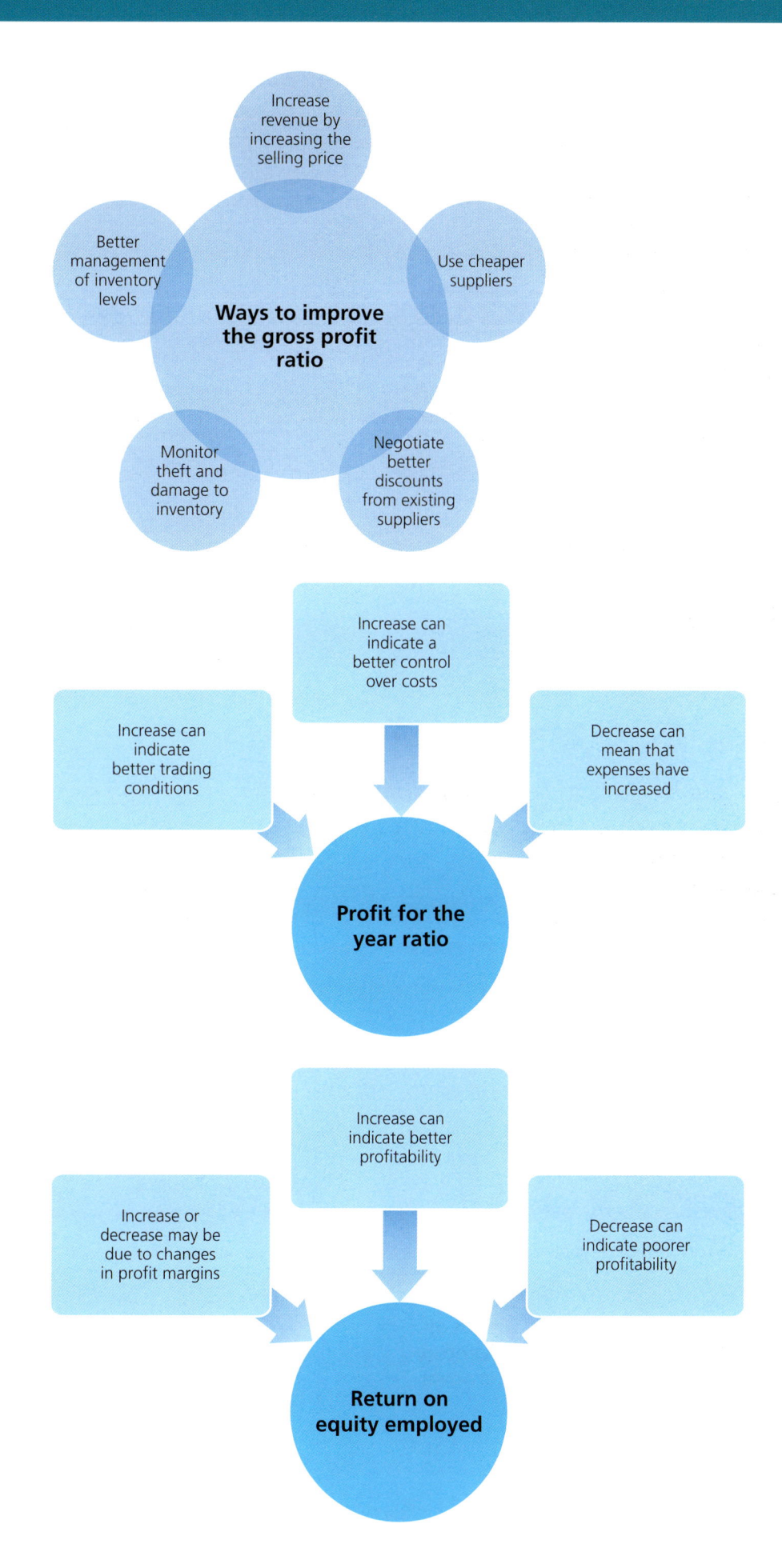

5.4 RATIOS

Ways to improve the gross profit ratio

- Increase revenue by increasing the selling price
- Use cheaper suppliers
- Negotiate better discounts from existing suppliers
- Monitor theft and damage to inventory
- Better management of inventory levels

Profit for the year ratio

- Increase can indicate a better control over costs
- Increase can indicate better trading conditions
- Decrease can mean that expenses have increased

Return on equity employed

- Increase can indicate better profitability
- Increase or decrease may be due to changes in profit margins
- Decrease can indicate poorer profitability

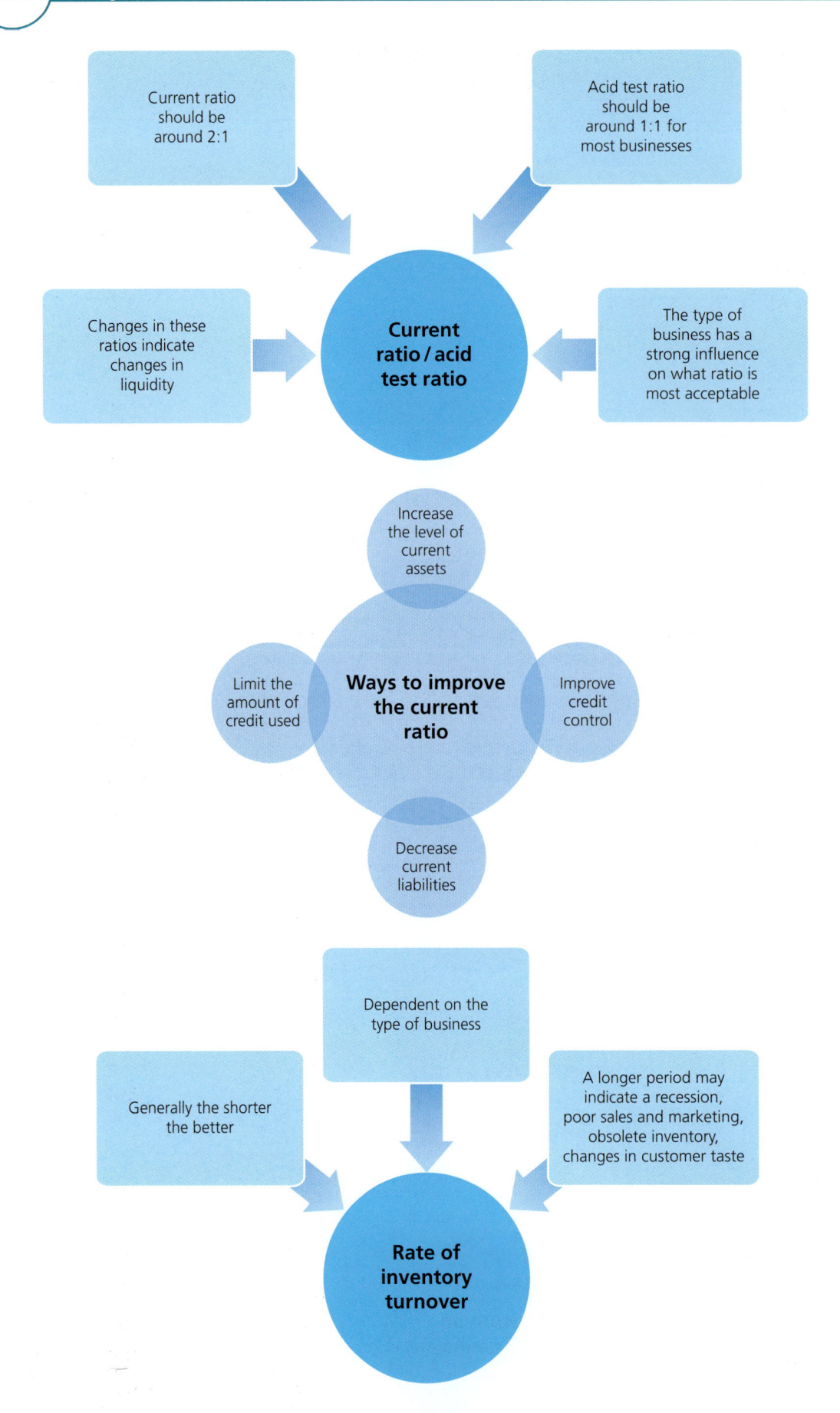

Current ratio / acid test ratio

- Current ratio should be around 2:1
- Acid test ratio should be around 1:1 for most businesses
- Changes in these ratios indicate changes in liquidity
- The type of business has a strong influence on what ratio is most acceptable

Ways to improve the current ratio

- Increase the level of current assets
- Limit the amount of credit used
- Improve credit control
- Decrease current liabilities

Rate of inventory turnover

- Dependent on the type of business
- Generally the shorter the better
- A longer period may indicate a recession, poor sales and marketing, obsolete inventory, changes in customer taste

5.4 RATIOS

The table below shows the ratios for Scott's International Gym Equipment Ltd. Check that you are able to apply the formulae to give the correct results as shown in the table that follows.

Income statements for the years ending 30 June

	Year 1 £000s	Year 2 £000s
Sales revenue	850	900
Gross profit	90	110
Interest payable	(15)	(15)
Taxation	(50)	(60)
Profit for the year	25	35
Dividends	(15)	(20)
Retained profits	10	15
Note to the accounts:		
Cost of goods sold	600	700
Credit purchases	350	400

Statements of financial position as at 30 June

	Year 1 £000s	Year 2 £000s
Non-current assets	600	700
Current assets:		
Inventory	300	350
Trade receivables	200	100
Cash	50	250
	550	700
Less current liabilities (trade payables)	(250)	(350)
Working equity	300	350
Net assets	**900**	**1050**
Financed by:		
Shareholders' funds:		
Ordinary shares	760	935
Retained profits	20	15
	780	950
15% debentures	120	100
	900	1050

Scott's International Gym Equipment Ltd – Financial ratios	Year 1	Year 2
Gross profit ratio	10.6%	12.2%
Profit for the year ratio	2.9%	3.9%
Return on equity employed	3.3%	3.7%
Current ratio	2.2:1	2.0:1
Acid test ratio	1:1	1:1
Rate of inventory turnover	0.86 times	0.88 times

Report

Write a short report to give reasons for the change in each of the ratios for Scott's International Gym Equipment Ltd from Year 1 to Year 2.

The following companies (X and Y) operate as electronic goods retailers in many European countries. They are direct competitors. Consider their accounting ratios, which have been calculated for you. Are their accounting ratios similar? Give reasons for those that are similar and those that are not. What may cause the similarities and differences?

Ratios	Company X	Company Y
Gross profit ratio	8.5%	5.2%
Profit for the year ratio	7.5%	3.9%
Return on equity employed ratio	10.9%	2.9%
Current ratio	2.3:1	0.77:1
Acid test ratio	1.8:1	0.43:1
Rate of inventory turnover	15 times	12 times

Research task

Use the internet to locate a set of company accounts for a large company of your choice – preferably a multinational. Use the figures from two years to calculate a set of ratios (you may wish to lay them out as in the table in the previous example). Write a report on a comparison of the ratios calculated for the two years.

Revision questions

1. Describe the uses of accounting ratios.
2. Describe the use of each of the following ratios:
    a) Gross profit ratio
    b) Profit for the year ratio
    c) Return on equity employed ratio
    d) Current ratio
    e) Acid test ratio
    f) Rate of inventory turnover
3. Using each of the ratios in question 2, describe the actions that an organisation could take to improve them.
4. Explain why an organisation might be interested in the accounting ratios of a competitor.
5. Identify a ratio that would be of interest to potential investors.
6. Explain why it is dangerous for an organisation to have a current ratio of less than 2:1.

5.5 Technology

Technology and the management of finance

Technology can be used effectively by organisations to manage the finance function of the business. It is normal for most organisations to use electronic recording for accounting and taxation purposes. This means that it is easier to maintain and store financial records and there is the added benefit that management-accounting information is easy to produce.

Some other examples are shown in the diagram on the next page.

SECTION 5 MANAGEMENT OF FINANCE

Technology (central concept) with surrounding uses:
- Spreadsheets can be used to prepare accounting layouts and create graphs for financial analysis
- Email can be used to issue invoices quickly
- Online banking can be used to manage accounts remotely or to set up an overdraft without travelling to the branch
- Word processors can be used for preparing financial reports to shareholders
- The internet can be used to compare lenders for the best deal
- Taxation can be paid online using the government website

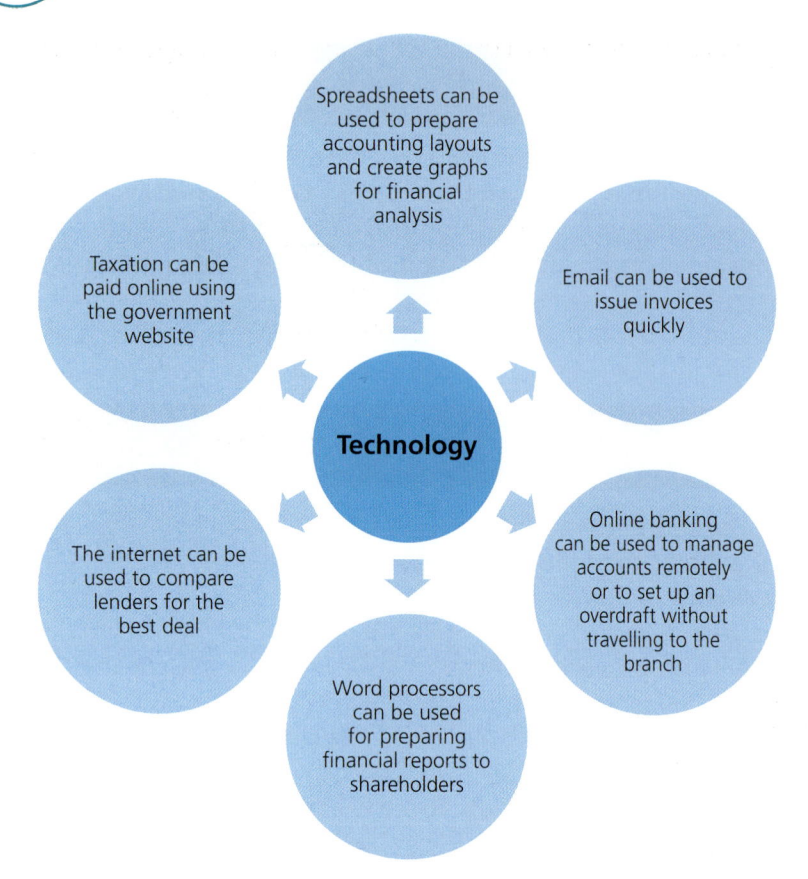

Technology has an increasing number of uses in terms of financial management. Here are some specific examples that relate to the finance function:

Technology	How it is used to manage finance
Spreadsheets	Spreadsheet software is very powerful and can be used to set up templates and layouts, draw up budgets and forecasts, prepare and manipulate management information, produce graphs and charts.
Internet banking	This allows management of banking functions by the business without having to physically visit the bank. Most banks have their own system, but they all allow the normal banking functions to be carried out easily and remotely. It can be accessed by desktop computer, laptop, tablet and smartphone.
BACS payments	BACS stands for 'bank automated clearing system' and it is the means by which banks make automatic payments on behalf of businesses and individuals. BACS payments can be made using internet banking.
Sage software	Sage is a brand of accounting software which is preferred by many businesses, accountants and auditors. It makes the tracking, monitoring and reporting of business transactions much simpler and allows the automatic production of reports, accounting and tax returns. This makes it easier for the business to monitor its transactions.
EFTPOS	EFTPOS stands for 'electronic funds transfer at point of sale'. If you have ever used a debit or credit card to make a purchase in a shop or for an online transaction then you have used EFTPOS. It basically means that when you pay for something, the payment to the retailer is more or less instant. It applies to debit and credit card transactions, contactless payments, Apple Pay and Android Pay.

There are costs and benefits associated with using technology to manage finance:

Benefits
- better control over finance and recording of data
- better security with up-to-date systems in place
- better-trained staff in the use of helpful technology to manage the finance function.

Costs
- financial costs associated with purchasing and introducing new technology, including training costs for staff
- increased risk that the business will become dependent on technology and have increased future costs of maintaining it
- increased potential security risks.

Report
Choose one use of technology in the management of finance that is not already listed in the diagram on page 210, and write a short report on the impact for an organisation.

Revision questions

1. Describe the benefits of using technology to manage the finance function of an organisation.
2. Describe the impact on employees of introducing new technology to the finance function of an organisation.
3. Describe the reasons for management using a technology system to store financial information.
4. Describe the benefits to an organisation of using internet banking.
5. Explain why an organisation may prefer to use accounting software to manage the finance function.
6. Describe the costs associated with introducing new technologies to manage the finance function in an organisation.

Section Assessment: Management of Finance

This segment aims to test your knowledge of the preceding section with exam-standard questions. It is recommended that you answer the questions based on the standard timing for the external examination, which allows around two minutes per mark. There is a selection of questions that you might expect to find in both Section 1 and Section 2 of the question paper.

Section 1 is worth 30 marks in total and the allocation of each question can range from 1–8 marks. Section 2 has four questions of 15 marks each, containing individual questions in the range of 1–8 marks. The difference with Section 2 is that it specialises in individual topics, so there could be a 15-mark question on Finance, as exemplified below. Remember that Section 2 questions tend to dig a little deeper into your knowledge of particular areas of the course.

Once you have attempted these questions, it would be a good idea to ask your teacher to mark them or go over appropriate responses to them.

Section 1 questions

		Marks
1	Describe the benefits of using the following sources of finance: • sale of assets • grants • crowdfunding.	3
2	Describe the operation of debt factoring.	3
3	Explain the use of a cash budget as a planning tool.	3
4	Describe three limitations of ratio analysis.	3
5	Justify the use of the current ratio as a measure of liquidity.	2
6	Justify the use of internet banking for a business.	3
7	Describe the benefits of using accounting software such as Sage.	4
8	Explain why a long-term overdraft may be a cheaper finance option than taking out a fixed-term loan.	3

Section 2 questions

			Marks
9	a	Explain why a profitable business may still suffer from cash-flow problems.	3
	b	Describe the use of crowdfunding.	4
	c	Describe the main elements and purpose of an income statement.	6
	d	Justify the use of EFTPOS by an organisation.	2
10	a	Discuss the costs and benefits of introducing new technologies to the finance department.	5
	b	Shennan Shareholdings Ltd has the following ratios for 2017 and 2018 trading: Profit for the year percentage 2017 – 33% 2018 – 29% Describe the actions that Shennan Shareholdings Ltd could take to improve its profit for the year percentage for 2019.	3
	c	Describe the external uses of financial information.	3
	d	Describe the impact of liquidity problems on an organisation.	4
11	a	Compare two different sources of finance that are available to a large organisation.	3
	b	Explain the use of venture capital.	3
	c	Explain the difference between gross profit and profit for the year.	2
	d	Describe the purpose of a statement of financial position.	3
	e	Describe the costs and benefits associated with: • short-term debt • long-term debt.	4

Index

A

ACAS (Advisory, Conciliation and Arbitration Service) 151–2, 155
accounting ratios 174, 199–209
    efficiency ratios 204
    liquidity ratios 203
    profitability ratios 201–2
    ratio analysis 199–1
    reasons for changes in 204–6
acid test ratio 203, 206
advertising 75–6, 84
after-sales service 91
air transport 108
Apple 93–4
appraisal systems 142–3
apprenticeships 141
aptitude tests 134
Asda 108
assets
    asset stripping 20, 178
    statement of financial position 193, 194, 195
association, discrimination by 164, 165
autocratic leadership 148
automation/mechanisation 110–11, 124

B

banks
    borrowings from 177, 182
    online banking 210
    as stakeholders 14, 34, 35
benchmarking 118
Boston Matrix 78–9
BT 18
budgets *see* cash budgeting
buy-ins 20
buyouts 20

C

CAM/CAD (Computer Aided Manufacture/Design) 110, 124
capital-intensive production 109–10, 112
cash budgeting 184–189
    cash-flow cycle 184–85
    cash-flow problems 188–89

cash cows 78
cash-flow statements 184–85, 196, 197, 198
CE marking 116
celebrity endorsements 89
centralised structures 41
chain stores 85
charities 6, 12
clubs 6, 12
coaching 139
collective bargaining 151, 154, 155–6
communities as stakeholders 14, 34–5
competency-based interview techniques 133
Competition and Markets Authority 23
competitive factors in business 22, 29
consumer audits 66, 68
continual improvement 115
corporate culture 30–1
corporate social responsibility 13, 120
corporation tax 8, 9, 25, 191
current ratio 203, 206
customers 60, 62–3
    consumer behaviour 63–5
    customer grouping 48
    customer satisfaction 90–3, 111, 113
    and distribution channels 82–3
    market-led and product-led approaches to 62–3
    and quality management 115
    social classifications of 65
    as stakeholders 34, 35, 36
CV (curriculum vitae) 132, 133

D

databases 95, 124, 168, 169
de-integration 20
de-layering organisations 43
de-mergers/divestment 19
debentures 176, 178–79, 180, 194
decentralised structures 42
decision making 3, 51–6
    operational decisions 52

    quality decisions 52–3
    strategic decisions 51
    SWOT analysis 54–5
    tactical decisions 51–2
democratic leadership 148–50
demographics of consumer behaviour 63–5
department stores 85
desk research methods 66, 71
direct discrimination 164, 165
direct mail 84
direct selling 82–4
discipline procedures 159–61
discrimination 163, 164–5
distribution channels 82–3
diversification 18
dividends 176, 191
dogs (products) 78
downsizing 45

E

economic boom/recession 24–5
economic factors in business 22, 24–5
economic sectors 5–6
efficiency ratios 204
electronic inventory management 103
email 95, 96, 97, 124, 169, 210
employee relations 128, 150–162
    ACAS 151–2
    arbitration 151–2, 155
    collective bargaining 151, 154, 155–6
    consultation 155
    employer actions 158–62
    employers' associations 152
    industrial action 154, 156–7
    management of 157–158
    negotiation 154–5
    see also trade unions
employees
    and organisation structure 37, 38, 39
    as stakeholders 34, 35, 36
    see also people management
employers' associations 152
employment change
    and industry sectors 5

Employment Rights Act (1996) 167
entrepreneurial structures 39
environmental issues
see ethical and environmental issues
EPOS (Electronic Point of Sale) systems 95, 103, 123, 124
Equality Act (2010) 163–5
equity
 return on equity employed 201–2, 205
 shares 175–6, 182–3
 statement of financial position 193, 194, 195
ethical and environmental issues 22, 26–7, 120–3
 fair trade 121–2
 marketing 13, 89
 problems and solutions 122–3
 waste management/control 120–1
exchange rates 24–5
extended marketing mix 90–3
external business growth 16–21
external factors
 impact on organisations 22–30
external recruitment 131

F

fair trade 121–2
finance leases 180–1
financial management 175–209
 availability of finance 32
 cash budgeting 184–190
 cash-flow statements 184–85, 196, 197, 198
 financial statements 190–198
 ratios 199–9
 role of technology in 209–11
 sources of finance 175–183
flat structures 37
flexible working 136, 165
franchising 10–11
functional grouping 46

G

governments
 financial assistance from 175, 178, 182
 impact on business success 23–4
 organisations 7–8
 services 5–6
 as stakeholder 34, 35, 36
 statistics 66, 71
graduate training schemes 141

grievance procedures 159
groupings 46–50
growth
 organisations 14, 16–18
 product life cycle 76

H

hall tests 66, 68
Health and Safety at Work Act (1974) 165–6
Herzberg, Frederick 145
hierarchical (tall) structures 38
high-street shopping 86, 87
hire purchase 181–2
horizontal integration 17, 18
human resources see people management
hygiene factors in motivation 145

I

income statements 190–193, 207,
 ratios 207
independent retailers 85
indirect discrimination 164, 165
induction training 139
industrial action 154, 156–7
industry sectors 4–5
inflation 24
information technology see technology
interest rates 24
internal business growth 16
internal factors
 impact on organisations 2, 30–4
internal recruitment 131
International Accounting Standards 185, 190
international trade 24
internet
 advertising 95
 and market research
 banking 210
 searches 71
 surveys 69
 online retailing 87
 recruitment 131
 selling 83
interviews
 market research 67
 staff recruitment 133–4
inventory management 101–8
 benefits of technology 124
 centralised 104
 de-centralised 105
 electronic 103
 logistics 107–8
 purpose of inventory control systems 101–2

 warehousing 105–6
ISO 9000 award 117

J

JIT (just-in-time) systems 103–4
job analysis 64

K

kitemark symbol 116
knowledge-based economy 4

L

labour-intensive production 111, 112
laissez-faire leadership 149
leadership
 managers and leaders 148
 and quality management 115
 styles 148–50
leasing 180–1
legislation 23, 162–7
 Employment Rights Act (1996) 167
 Equality Act (2010) 163–5
 Health and Safety at Work Act (1974) 165–6
 National Minimum Wage Act (1998) 167
liabilities
 statement of financial position 193, 194, 195
limited companies 8–10
liquidity ratios 203
loans
 bank borrowing 177, 182
 debentures 176, 178–179, 180, 194
 long-term 176
local government services 5–6, 7
local stores 85
logistics 107–8
London Stock Exchange 182
long leets 132
loyalty cards 70, 91

M

McDonald's 93–4
magazines
 market research 65, 66, 71
 selling through specialist magazines 84
mail order 83
managerial objectives 14
managers
 decision making role of 55–6

leadership styles 148–9
and organisation structure 37, 38, 39
span of control 37, 38, 43, 44
as stakeholders 34, 35
training 139–140
market research 62, 63, 66–73
desk methods 66, 71
field methods 66, 67–71
sampling 72–3
use of 71
market saturation 76
market-led approaches 62
marketing mix 73–94
extended/service 90–3
Physical evidence 92–3
place 82–7
People 90–1
price 79–81
Process 91–2
product 74–9
promotion 88–9
Marks & Spencer 87, 197
Maslow's hierarchy of needs 144–5
matrix structures 40
medical tests 135
mission statements 15, 31
mobile shops 86
mortgages 25, 177
motivation theories 144–6
Herzberg 145
Maslow 144–5
motivators 146
multinational companies 11–12
financial statements 190, 192
mystery shoppers 71, 94, 119

N

National Minimum Wage Act (1998) 167
net assets employed 193–4
newspapers
market research 65, 66, 71
NHS (National Health Service) 5, 7
graduate training scheme 141

O

Oak Furniture Land 87
objectives of organisations 13–15
corporate social responsibility 13, 120
growth 16–21
managerial objectives 14
mission statements 15
outsourcing 20–1
profit maximisation 14
satisficing 14

observation of consumers 69
off-the-job training 139–40
on-the-job training 139
operating leases 180
operational decisions 52
organic/internal business growth 16
organisations
types of 7–12
see also structures
outsourcing 20–1
owners as stakeholders 34, 35, 36

P

packaging 13, 27, 121
participative leadership 148–9
PCs (protected characteristics) 163–4, 165
people management
employee relations 150–162
flexible working 136
and technology 168–69
legislation 162–167
motivation and leadership 144–147, 148–49
recruitment and selection 130–132
training and development 137–142
see also employees
people and the marketing mix 90–91, 92, 93
perception, discrimination by 164, 165
personal selling 84
personality tests 135
PESTEC factors in business 22–9
and desk research 71
physical evidence
and customer service 92, 93
place 82–7
channels of distribution 82–7
grouping 49
and the marketing mix 73, 82–7
political factors in business 22, 23–4
pollution 28, 29, 120
postal surveys 66, 67
price 73, 79–81
primary industries 4
private limited companies (Ltd) 8–9
private sector 5–6, 8–12
problem children products 78
processes
and customer service 91–92, 93, 94

and quality management 115
producers
and distribution channels 82–3
product development 63
product endorsement 88, 89
product-led approaches 62–3
product/service grouping 47
production methods 109–12
automation/mechanisation 110–11, 124
capital-intensive production 109–10, 112
labour-intensive 111, 112
labour-intensive v. capital-intensive 112
and technology 124
products 45, 47, 50, 62–3, 64, 74–9
extension strategies 76–7
market saturation 76
and the marketing mix 74–9
portfolios 77–8
product life cycle 74, 76, 78
and distribution 82–3
profit maximisation 14
profitability ratios 201–2
profits
financial statements 190–2, 193–198
gross profit ratio 202, 204, 205
profit for the year ratio 202, 205
retained 175, 176, 182
promotions 61, 88–9, 90
and ethical marketing 13, 89
into the pipeline 88
and the marketing mix 88–9
out of the pipeline 88
public relations (PR) 89
psychometric tests 134
public limited companies (plc) 8–9, 10
public relations (PR) 89
public sector 5–6, 7–8

Q

quality 100, 113–119
decisions 52–3
mystery shoppers 71, 94, 114, 119
quality assurance 114
benchmarking 118
quality circles 114, 118
quality control 113–14
quality management 114–16
standards and symbols 114, 116–118

quaternary industries 4, 5
question marks 78
questionnaires 67, 69
quota sampling 73

R

rail transport 107
random sampling 72
rate of inventory turnover 204, 206
ratios *see* accounting ratios
recruitment and selection 130–2
    flexible working 136
    internal versus external recruitment 131
    recruitment process 130
    selection methods 131–2, 133, 134–5
    workforce planning 129–130
redundancy 111, 159, 161–2
references 135
retailers 82, 85–6, 87
retained profits 175, 176, 182
road transport 107
robotics 110, 124

S

sampling 72–3
satisficing 14
Scotland 7
Scottish Enterprise 7–8
sea transport 107, 108
secondary industries 4, 5
sectors
    of the economy 5–6
    of industry 4–5
selection *see* recruitment and selection
service marketing mix 90–3
shareholders 34, 35, 36
    and limited companies 8, 9, 10
shares (equity) 175–6, 182–3
shopping
    changing shopping habits 26
    mystery shoppers 71, 94, 119
    online or in-store 87
short leets 132
skills
    upgrading 138
    use of skilled workers 110, 111, 112
social enterprises 12

social factors in business 20, 26
social media and marketing 27, 70, 88
society, role of business in 3–6
span of control 37, 38, 43, 44
spreadsheets 53, 169, 186, 210
staff appraisal 142–3
staff development 137–38
staff training 137, 138–140, 141
staffing 30, 32–3
stakeholders 34–6
    conflicts of interest 35–6
    differing objectives of 2
    interdependence of 36
stars 78
statements of financial position 193–195
stock markets 182–3
strategic decisions 51
stratified sampling 72
street surveys 67
strikes 156–7
structures 3, 37–50
    centralised 41
    de-layering 43
    decentralised 42
    downsizing 45
    entrepreneurial 39
    factors affecting structure 45
    flat 37
    groupings 46–50
    hierarchical (tall) 38
    matrix 40
    span of control 44
style theory of leadership 147–49
suppliers
    and quality management 115
    as stakeholders 34, 35, 36
surveys 66, 67–8
    sampling 72–3
SWOT analysis 54–5
    and desk research 71
systems approach to quality management 115

T

tactical decisions 51–2
takeovers 17
taxation
    corporation tax 8, 9, 25, 191
    multinational companies 12
    online payments 210
technology 22, 26, 33, 209–11
    costs of using 125, 169, 211

    and financial management 209–10, 211
    grouping by 50
    inventory management 124
    managing marketing 96–7
    managing operations 123–4
    people management 169
    use in training and development 140
telephone surveys 66, 68
tertiary industries 4
Tesco 26, 81, 198
test marketing 66, 69
third sector organisations 6, 12
trade journals 66, 71
trade logos 117
Trade Union Congress (TUC) 152–3
trade unions 151, 153–4
trading accounts 191, 192
training and development 137–142
    staff appraisal 142–3
    staff development 137–38
    staff training 139
    technology use in 140
    training schemes 141
    work-based qualifications 142
transportation 107–8

U

unemployment 25

V

venture capital 178, 180, 182
vertical integration 16–17
Virgin 18, 47
VLE (Virtual Learning Environment) 140, 168
voluntary groups 6

W

wages
    minimum wage and living wage 167
    skilled workers 110, 111, 112
warehousing 105–6
waste management/control 120–1
websites 66, 71, 91, 95, 96, 169
wholesalers 82, 86, 88
word processors 169, 210
work-based qualifications 142
workforce planning 129–136
works councils 157–58